The Origins of Self

The Origins of Self

An Anthropological Perspective

Martin P.J. Edwardes

UCL PRESS

First published in 2019 by
UCL Press
University College London
Gower Street
London WC1E 6BT

Available to download free: www.uclpress.co.uk

A CIP catalogue record for this book is available from The British Library.

ISBN: 978-1-78735-632-0 (Hbk)
ISBN: 978-1-78735-631-3 (Pbk)
ISBN: 978-1-78735-630-6 (PDF)
ISBN: 978-1-78735-633-7 (epub)
ISBN: 978-1-78735-634-4 (mobi)
ISBN: 978-1-78735-635-1 (html)
DOI: https://doi.org/10.14324/111.9781787356306

For Philip, my strongest critic still, my fiercest defender always.
And for Matthew, without whom I would be in a very different place today.

Contents

List of figures and tables

Acknowledgements

I would like to thank all the people who have helped to make this book possible: my students and colleagues, who have inspired me in ways they were probably unaware of; and my friends, who have tolerated my habit of thinking out loud and hijacking conversations, and who have helped me through my weirder moments.

I thank the following readers of early drafts of this book: Guy Cook, Tore Janson, Adriano Reis E. Lameira, Philip Rescorla, Jim Toller and two anonymous publisher's reviewers. Your comments have improved clarity, readability and structure, and have added scholarship that I missed or was unaware of. Philip, in particular, provided me with an informed layperson's view, and he has mitigated – no, toned down – my habit of reaching for little-known specialist terms when simpler words are available. I must also thank Sören Stauffer-Kruse for his help with the subtleties of German.

Finally, I would like to thank those great minds that created this cognitive playground of selfhood research. Many of you have been mentioned or discussed in this book (but not all, and not enough). Without your thought and imagination I would have had no base on which to build my own ideas – and no book to write.

Prologue: Down the Rabbit-hole

> So she was considering in her own mind (as well as she could, for the hot day made her feel very sleepy and stupid), whether the pleasure of making a daisy-chain would be worth the trouble of getting up and picking the daisies, when suddenly a White Rabbit with pink eyes ran close by her.
>
> There was nothing so *very* remarkable in that; nor did Alice think it so *very* much out of the way to hear the Rabbit say to itself, 'Oh dear! Oh dear! I shall be late!' (when she thought it over afterwards, it occurred to her that she ought to have wondered at this, but at the time it all seemed quite natural); but when the Rabbit actually *took a watch out of its waistcoat-pocket*, and looked at it, and then hurried on, Alice started to her feet, for it flashed across her mind that she had never before seen a rabbit with either a waistcoat-pocket, or a watch to take out of it, and burning with curiosity, she ran across the field after it, and fortunately was just in time to see it pop down a large rabbit-hole under the hedge.
>
> In another moment down went Alice after it, never once considering how in the world she was to get out again.
>
> (Lewis Carroll 1865, Chapter 1: 'Down the Rabbit-Hole')

I am me and you are you: a banal statement that is hardly worth writing a book about. Yet, in the paraphrased form of *I have me-ness and you have you-ness*, it suddenly begins to raise interesting questions. What is the nature of the *me* that *I* can appreciate as being me? How does the *me* relate to the *I* that is recognising the *me*? Are me-ness and you-ness the same thing looked at from different angles, or is there an important difference between the two? How does the *you* relate to the *I* that is recognising the *you?* And what is the nature of the *you* that I identify as being you; is it the same as the *me* you identify as being *you*? All of the questions raised here are from the first-person perspective because, in the end, it is the only perspective each of us has; but is it the only perspective we use? And, if not, how do I incorporate the perspectives of others into my view of the Universe?

In fact, having a self of which I am aware is perhaps one of the most astounding and unexpected outcomes of being human. Current scientific evidence seems to indicate that it is unusual in nature for an organism to be able to recognise itself (although the number of species able to pass the mirror test of self-recognition is growing constantly – see Chapter 2); and we have no evidence that any individual of any species – apart from humans – is able to imagine how others might see them. Our personal relationship with our selves may even be the 'holy grail' that has been sought for centuries: the thing that makes us different from other animals. If such a difference really exists, selfhood would seem to be a good candidate.

We know our species is different from others in important ways: every species is a particular outcome of a series of challenges to its individuals, such that individuals with strategies to meet the challenges do better than those without such strategies. After enough time, the species consists of only those individuals with useful strategies; and it is those useful strategies that define the nature of the species. Charles Darwin (1859 [2001]) formalised this understanding in his theory of descent with modification by means of natural selection, and Herbert Spencer (1864) summarised it, somewhat controversially, with the phrase *survival of the fittest*. You can identify the challenges that a species has met by looking at what its members are good at: for instance, the challenge of surviving predation has, in different species, resulted in climbing or running or hiding or fighting skills. Monkeys climb, antelope run, stick insects hide (in plain sight) and porcupines fight – or, at least, they are equipped with an effective active defence mechanism with which to discourage predators. So what are humans good at? And how does having self-awareness help us to be good at it?

First, humans are clearly very good at cooperating; perhaps not as effectively as the eusocial insects (ants, wasps, bees and termites) but certainly more effectively than any other primate. Second, we have language – a communication system that may itself be unique in nature, and which seems to be both an outcome of cooperation and a cause of even greater cooperation. Third, compared to other primates, we are abnormally willing to work together in joint enterprises that require specialisation and role-taking. Fourth, and most mysterious of all, we seem to be happy to subordinate our own needs to those of others, often to the point of self-sacrifice: we are willing to die to keep others living. Eusocial insects also sacrifice themselves; but that is because they only get their genes into the future by keeping their reproductive parents and siblings alive. When a non-reproductive eusocial insect sacrifices itself, it does not disadvantage itself reproductively, and often it advantages itself by protecting its fertile relatives: the self-sacrifice of the non-reproductive individual does not contradict their evolutionary self-interest. In contrast, when humans sacrifice themselves, they forego future reproductive opportunities. This could be viewed in some circumstances as somehow advantaging their offspring, but humans often self-sacrifice before they have even had the chance to reproduce – which looks, in evolutionary terms, completely nonsensical. Could the capacity to imagine ourselves as having a self somehow be behind this willingness to self-sacrifice? If this is the case, it only leaves us with a different evolutionary conundrum: if having a self is implicated in such an evolutionarily unfit activity as self-sacrifice, how has the peculiarity of human self-awareness survived the inevitable evolutionary extinction that self-sacrifice entails?

About this book

This book looks at human selfness as the outcome of evolutionary selection: what, in our evolutionary history, made having a self a fit strategy? Humans have selves, and we consider having a self to be mostly a *Good Thing* (as Sellar and Yeatman 1930, would say); but having those selves can often make us unselfish and willing to subordinate our self-interest to that of others – which, in evolutionary terms, is a *Bad Thing*. We cannot convert our Darwinian self-interest into self-disinterest unless we become aware that we have a self that has an interest in its own survival; but how were we able to maintain our awareness of our selfness when doing so made us less likely to survive than our selfish neighbours? There is clearly an evolutionary tale to be told here.

This book also looks at the role self plays in language. We can self-reference – a capacity not unknown outside of our species, but rare. We can also model ourselves into a range of circumstances – not just in the factual present, but into the future, the past, the might-have-been and the maybe-will-be. We can even model ourselves in the never-has-been and the never-will-be – once again, a capacity that seems evolutionarily pointless. We can also, through language, share our knowledge of our self with others; and we seem more than happy to do so, even though it further reduces our relative fitness by giving away information that others can use against us. Language could be, like many other communication systems, either non-volitional or strictly about external facts; but it is actually, compared to the communication systems of other species, highly volitional and often about inner cognition, especially what we know about our own and others' selves. Strangest of all, the fact that we are able to choose to share own-self and other-self knowledge seems to be all the reason we need to do so.

Finally, the book will look at the models of self we hold in our heads. What are we modelling when we model a self? Is there a difference between our models of our own self and our models of other selves? And how did this capacity to model our selves survive and thrive in humans, when it seems not to play a significant or useful role in the lives of other animals? Does the capacity to model our selves mean that the only self of which we can be aware is actually a model, or is there something more basic, substantial and actual on which we build our models?

This book proposes a new hypothesis about selfhood, which I call the Seven-Selves Modelling Hypothesis (SSMH). The argument for the hypothesis is given across eight chapters, the first of which looks at some of the existing theories of selfhood. The chapter discusses religious viewpoints and the approaches of various key philosophers, what leading psychologists think, what neurologists have found about selfhood as a cognitive phenomenon and what anthropologists have observed about selfhood in human individuals and groups. By sampling the wide range of ideas about selfhood available in the literature, the chapter shows that the question 'What is a self?' still has no single answer from any single discipline. Perhaps a new, cross-disciplinary approach will prove more productive.

Chapter 2 approaches the question of selfhood from a different direction: where did it come from? It tells a story about the evolutionary development of selfhood from single-celled animals to modern humans, showing that it can be seen as the outcome of a series of developments in sensing and cognition about self and other individuals. Conscious awareness is a key event in the evolutionary process leading to selfhood, creating new ways for individuals to interact and new tools, such as Theory of Mind (ToM) and language, to facilitate the interaction. The chapter looks at the capacities for self-awareness in other animals and considers how human self-awareness may be different.

Chapter 3 concentrates on more recent evolutionary events to show how modern *Homo sapiens* evolved to be able to model a personal self. It shows that a necessary precursor is the capacity to make models of other individuals and the relationships between them – something that requires a special rule-driven system. Here I use Derek Bickerton's (2002) term, social calculus, to label this system. The chapter explores how this social calculus could have arisen, how it became shareable through language and how the grammatical complexity of language corresponds to the systemic complexity of social calculus. It also considers some of the particular features of language that closely reflect those of social calculus, and how the sharing of social modelling requires a communication system that is mainly used not for the sharing of truths and facts but for the sharing of opinions – a mode of communication for which language is especially suited.

Chapter 4 looks at how humans develop self-awareness in childhood: we are not born with it, but rather it is something that develops progressively through our childhood. The chapter considers developmental and social features that mould human children in a species-specific way, in particular our extended childhood and the extended caring network that supports it. A range of current theories of childhood are examined in relation to cognitive capacities such as delayed gratification, deception and self-expression.

In Chapter 5, the genetic and cognitive origins of social calculus are examined in greater detail. If self-awareness relies on the sharing of social calculus, then the origins of social calculus are a significant aspect of selfhood. The chapter looks for signs of social arithmetic and social calculus among a range of non-primate social species – parrots, corvids, naked mole rats, meerkats and bottlenose dolphins – before examining the development of social calculus in our own evolutionary clade. The path to the sharing of social calculus is traced, from the social arithmetic in the Machiavellian intelligence of chimpanzees, through various forms of altruistic behaviour (kin selection, reciprocal altruism, indirect reciprocity, costly signalling, altruistic punishment, vigilant sharing and reverse dominance) and on to the outcomes of shared social calculus, such as our capacity for self-sacrifice.

Chapter 6 looks at the role of self in language, and the role of language in sharing modelled selves. The linguistic and socialising roles of pronouns and pronominalisation are explored in relation to a selection of the world's languages, and the use of names as personal labels is discussed as a route into pronominalisation. The origins of the three linguistic persons, *they*, *you* and *me*, are also considered – as markers of selfness, possession and reflexivity. The extended self, indicated by possessive pronominalisation, and the recursive self, indicated by reflexivity, are also analysed. Finally, the chapter considers how selfhood and language synthesise to increase communicative complexity.

Chapter 7 examines the importance of metaphor within language, looking at five key conceptual metaphors of selfhood and self-modelling. The first of these, THE MODEL IS THE ACTUAL, shows that we treat our social modelling as if it were a calculus of actual relationships between members of our group, even though it is just a representation of a set of opinions. The second metaphor, THE GROUP IS AN ENTITY, lets us treat a group as if it had the same motives and purpose as an individual; and the third, SELF IS OTHER, treats both my self and your self as third-person constructs, slightly more privileged than *they*, but essentially the same as *they*. The fourth metaphor, I AM ME, equates the objective self (*me*) with the active and interactive self (*I*): acting and being acted-on do not create different self-models, they are functions of a single self-model. The fifth metaphor is a little different from the others: ONE AMONG EQUALS reduces the status of my self as represented to myself, making it no more important than other selves as represented to myself; we self-police our own humility and obedience to the group.

Chapter 8 sets out the seven selves of the SSMH, showing how they work together to create our sense of selfhood. First, there is the unknowable Actual self, the genetic but subliminal recognition of the importance of the self to the self. Next, there is the Social self, the self others believe me to be; this is a self of which I am consciously aware, and it is generated from the social models of me that others have shared with me. The third self is the self-model, the self I believe me to be; it is my own conscious model of me generated from other people's models of me. Fourth is the Episodic self, my self as modelled in my individual memories; and fifth is the Narrative self, my self as a continuous entity through time, the story that links the individual Episodic selves. The Cultural self is the sixth self, the self I *should* be; it is the model of the perfect citizen offered by others in the group, the best me I can be. This leaves the final self, the Projected self, the self I want others to believe me to be – which may only vaguely resemble my own self-model. The chapter also explores how these selves operate together to define our selves to ourselves and to our group.

In this book, we follow the white rabbit of selfness down the rabbit-hole of self. We are entering a strange universe where nothing is quite as it seems (and even *nothing* is not quite as it seems); and, once we have entered, we will not leave unchanged. Sometimes our self will seem very large and complicated, at other times it will seem to shrink and may even disappear. One moment we will be running as fast as we can just to stand still, the next we will find things changing around us without apparent logic or reason. I hope that you will find this journey informative or, at least, enjoyable – it is, after all, about you. And I hope you will come to realise, by the end of this book, that there is considerably more down the rabbit-hole than white rabbits:

> If any one of them can explain it,' said Alice, (she had grown so large in the last few minutes that she wasn't a bit afraid of interrupting him,) 'I'll give him sixpence. *I* don't believe there's an atom of meaning in it.
>
> (Lewis Carroll 1865, Chapter 12: 'Alice's Evidence')

1
What Is a Self?

> The Caterpillar and Alice looked at each other for some time in silence: at last the Caterpillar took the hookah out of its mouth, and addressed her in a languid, sleepy voice.
>
> 'Who are *you*?' said the Caterpillar.
>
> This was not an encouraging opening for a conversation. Alice replied, rather shyly, 'I – I hardly know, Sir, just at present – at least I know who I *was* when I got up this morning, but I think I must have been changed several times since then.'
>
> (Lewis Carroll 1865, Chapter 5: 'Advice from a Caterpillar')

Alice's disorientation is not merely a young girl's response to a particularly confusing afternoon. It raises perhaps the most fundamental question of human existence: *who am I?* It is a question that has exercised human minds throughout most of our species' existence, and it was probably first asked when we were still hunter-gatherers living in Africa – or, possibly, even earlier, before *Homo sapiens* had even evolved. Yet the fact that a self can ask questions about its own nature is an unexpected and inexplicable capacity. The interests of any living organism are necessarily directed outward: survival and replication, the two drivers of Darwinian evolution, are both matters of expropriation of external resources – and the better the expropriation, the fitter the organism. Where is the evolutionary fitness for an organism in being able to introspect?

As humans, we have access to many different types of knowledge, not just in terms of what we know but in terms of *how* we know. One particular distinction is between things we know even if we are not consciously aware that we know them, and things that we know we know. This is often referred to as the difference between implicit and explicit knowledge (Dienes and Perner 1999). Other terms are available – especially for implicit knowledge, which is also known as tacit, inherent, inarticulate, unaware, subconscious or subliminal knowledge. However, whichever term is used, it is not the same as innate knowledge, which is knowledge we have because we are genetically human – it is written into our genes. Innate knowledge is a subset of implicit knowledge, which means that, while all innate knowledge is implicit, not all implicit knowledge is innate.

Knowing something implicitly means that I may not know intellectually that something is the case, but my body behaves as if it were the case. For instance, my lack of understanding of how my digestion works does not interfere with its working – my body can do the job without my head even being aware that the job is being done. Driving a car is a different kind of implicit knowledge, because it involves learning followed by sublimation. I did not start out with an inbuilt ability to drive – I had to learn a complex multi-tasking activity involving steering, changing the gears, listening to the engine, spatial awareness, judging distances and so on. However, one sunny June day, many years ago, I realised that I was no longer consciously aware of the individual driving tasks I was performing; my conscious driving now involved strategic activities, while the tactical activities had sublimated into implicit knowledge.

Because implicit knowledge seems to be distributed through the body, even though the brain may be acting as a control node for the process, it is often referred to as body knowledge. In contrast, explicit knowledge involves conscious awareness of 'facts' about the universe (the facts do not need to be ontologically true, just culturally – or even personally – plausible). And, as it is explicit knowledge, we need to be able to explain it to ourselves and to others – both the facts themselves and the how and why of our knowing. This type of knowledge is essentially cognitive, so it is also known as *head knowledge*. Explicit knowledge can also involve explanations of implicit knowledge, a process known as explication; our explanation may not actually be correct, but the fact we can express it to others makes it explicit. Figure 1.1 shows how these different types of knowledge work together.

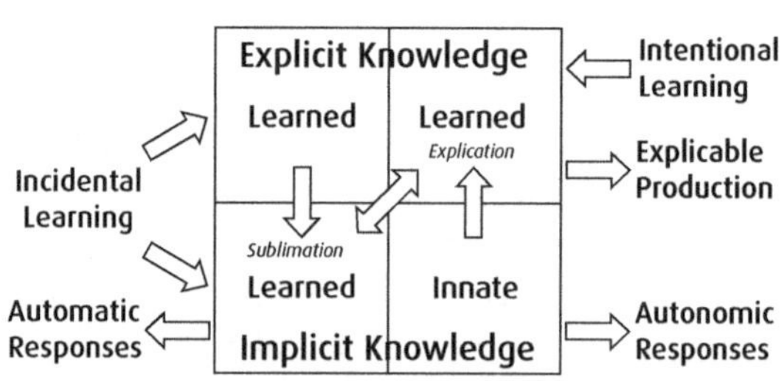

Fig 1.1 Types of knowledge, ways of learning, ways of responding

For most animals on this planet, selfhood is implicit, or body knowledge. As a non-human animal, I do not need an internal cognitive model of myself, I can just let my body do what it has to do. My body is dedicated to preserving and promoting itself, and it does not need cognitive self-knowledge to do its job. It has skills honed through millions of generations of hundreds of species by a simple rule of fitness: bodies that try to self-preserve get their genes into the future more frequently than those that do not. Head knowledge is not needed here – and, indeed, in our own species, it sometimes seems to get in the way: head knowledge has overlaid our instinctive self-preservation with a range of self-destructive mechanisms (suicide, self-sacrifice, martyrdom) that are difficult to explain in simple evolutionary terms.

As Charles Whitehead (2001) shows, these self-destructive mechanisms seem to be linked to our capacity to model ourselves; and this, in turn, seems to be linked to the information-sharing we are able to do with language. The basic question behind self-awareness, 'Who am I?', is therefore unlikely to have been given 'headroom' until the invention of language; and this book will argue that it is a question that exists only because of language, a necessary internal response to the externally asked question 'Who are you?' The question 'Who am I?', therefore, may not have been the first question to be asked, but the fact that we are able to ask it may be fundamental to the definition of our species.

While it was language itself that allowed us to pose the question 'Who am I?', it was the invention of writing that allowed some of the many answers to be recorded, debated and refined over the generations. Indeed, we can still explore some of the earlier answers given, because of their existence in the written record. This provides us with a rich and ongoing debate across the generations, and it shows that the question of selfhood has been an active topic and a continuing human conundrum for at least millennia. Different intellectual and scientific disciplines have, as our knowledge has grown over the centuries, taken their turns in offering an answer – or, more often, answers – to the 'Who am I?' question. The range of possible responses has become quite bewildering and contradictory, as new ideas are constantly being put forward and the literature continues to grow. Some of the solutions offered so far are discussed here – more in an attempt to map the territory than to identify a winner.

The priest's turn

Religion has long had a view on self, and its nature has always been central to belief structures. Animists believe that all natural things (such as plants, animals, rocks and thunder) have spirits and can influence human events; and they have personified natural phenomena as self-aware entities for tens, probably hundreds, of millennia, projecting self as a universal characteristic throughout nature. For animists, everything has a self on some level, or is caused by a self (Moor and Luks 2015). A little more recently, belief in the survival of selves after death has extended self beyond the natural, physical bounds of birth and death – although the evidence for such survival is belief-based rather than artefact-based (Olson 2015). Even more recently, the invention (or, for some people, the discovery) of the soul by the modern Abrahamic religions (Judaism, Christianity and Islam) created a whole new type of selfness: a non-physical entity that seems to have little or no control over the physical self, but which is nonetheless held responsible for the actions of that physical self (Durkheim 1912). The ongoing intellectual debate over the different interpretations of self-realisation that are espoused by scions of these religions is, currently and all too frequently, being approached with bombs and bullets rather than thoughtfully nuanced argument.

Despite the many brutal battles over what self-realisation involves and means, actually defining what a self is has never been high on the agenda for most religions: it has always been enough that there *is* a self (or aspect of the self) that is more persistent than the body, which must take responsibility for the physical actions of its body and which can be punished or rewarded regardless of the physical status of the body. For most religions, humans are metaphysical selves with physical annexes; and the annex is a temporary adjunct to the eternal metaphysical self. The Abrahamic religions have even gone so far as to say that the physical self is the least important aspect of selfhood, and everything that is valuable about *me* is contained in my metaphysical self, or soul. However, as the soul remains immeasurable, the metaphysical viewpoint does not lend itself readily to a scientific, evidential approach.

The religious approach to selfhood has usually required a constantly intervening deity (or group of deities) to keep existence trotting along, following the arbitrary rules set out historically in scripture or currently by the religious gatekeepers – the priests, rabbis and imams. Some modern religious interpretations have accepted that the universe actually needs no such supernatural micro-management, although they do seem to maintain the proviso that management is needed at some level or other. This approach, however, brings its own problems: the reduced need for micro-management by God or gods has distanced the deities from our everyday existence, and this distancing has limited their role as interveners in our personal lives. As the gods have receded, the unchallenged, everyday religious concept of the eternal self has been steadily losing ground: ever since Nicolaus Copernicus (1543) first cast doubt on humanity's physically central position in the universe, the proposed eternal self has become increasingly compromised as the arbitrary, interventionist universe of gods is replaced by the rule-driven universe of science. Science has both reduced our role in the universe and increased our role in, and responsibility for, our local environment. It is hard for the priests to insist that we should continue to trust in God when the solutions to today's problems are completely in our own hands, and there is absolutely no evidence of help from outside.

Indeed, the major contribution to modern society of some of the Abrahamic sects seems to be an increasingly ostrich-like tendency to ignore the needs of the physical world, because it is soon to be destroyed or remade. The social and scientific problems in today's human society are seen as evidence of an inevitable forthcoming apocalypse; they are not viewed as vital challenges that we need to address urgently. The metaphysical-annex approach to the self lends itself all too easily to denial of the physical – a choice that, in the current world, may prove to be self-fulfilling: if you spend your time trying to sever your link with the physical world then, sooner rather than later, you are likely to find a rather terminal way to do so.

I suppose I should declare an interest when discussing the religious interpretation of the self, but that interest is probably self-evident by now. And, despite my personal opinions, the religious answers to the question 'Who am I?' should not be underestimated: they have survived for thousands of years – and in the case of animism, maybe hundreds of thousands of years. A religious view of self was the only answer we needed for a long time; and, although there must frequently have been dissenting opinions in the pre-literate past, the different religious solutions are the only ideas to have come down to us from those pre-literate times. They therefore provide the backdrop against which other theories of selfhood need to be viewed.

The philosopher's turn

With the advent of writing, the belief-driven solutions of the priests began to give way to the logic-based explanations of the first scientists, the philosophers. The attempts of the philosophers to answer the question 'Who am I?' initially came directly out of the religious approach. Indeed, pre-Enlightenment philosophers seem to have considered the metaphysical self to be a sufficient explanation. Plato (~370 BCE [1871]), for example, saw the self as an eternal soul trapped for a while in a physical body. That is, the metaphysical has more truth, and therefore more reality, than the physical. For Aristotle (350 BCE [1908]), the self was the essence of the activity of the person. An object has a pre-ordained nature and function, and its essence is in the completion of that function. Just as the essence of a knife is cutting, the essence of a human is what that human does – and, for Aristotle, what every human does is think rationally. His explanation for the self is, therefore, essentially metaphysical. However, unlike Plato, Aristotle sees no need for an external power source, or gods, to maintain the form of the soul: the soul is the capacity to act.

Aristotle profoundly influenced Abrahamic religious thinking up to the European Enlightenment of the seventeenth and eighteenth centuries, when new approaches to selfhood became popular. René Descartes (1641 [1998]) was one of the first Enlightenment philosophers to adopt a new approach to selfhood, when he took the view that answering the question 'Who am I?' does not just prove our essential humanity, it proves reality itself. His *Dubito ergo cogito, cogito ergo sum* ('I doubt, therefore I think; I think, therefore I am') became one of the founding principles of modern Western Philosophy. In his effort to find something irrefutably real in the universe, Descartes felt able to dismiss all external presentations to his senses as possible deceptions by a particularly malevolent demon. Everything I receive from outside my own self is an interpretation of reality, not reality itself; so it cannot prove reality, only indicate that there is something to be interpreted. That thing, however, need not be outside myself, it could be inside: a subliminal thought about an object or event becomes consciously interpreted as a subjective experience, without the actual world intervening. This is not just an intellectual exercise in metaphysics. This kind of hallucination happens frequently under the influence of drugs, when hypnotised, or when suffering certain psychoses: whether the object or event comes from inside or outside my head does not matter in terms of my interpretation of reality, for my experience is the same for both. These states of altered reality are all conditions in which others' judgement is a surer indicator of reality than my own.

Descartes' demon is a philosophical dilemma, indeed; but does *cogito, ergo sum* release us from the dilemma? Ambrose Bierce (1911 [1999]) thought not, when he rephrased the expression as *Cogito cogito, ergo cogito sum* – 'I think that I think, therefore I think that I am'. My thoughts do not prove my existence absolutely, only relatively. If

I imagine a self, then I can imagine that self thinking; and one of those thoughts could be 'I (the imagined I) think, therefore I (the imagined I) am'. Does this mean that the imagined *I* is real? Clearly not, because the imagined *I* is … well, imaginary. So all we can really say is, 'for a given characterisation of *I*, if that characterisation can believe itself to doubt, then, doubt being a form of thought, that characterisation can believe itself to think; which means that the given characterisation can be seen to believe itself to be'. The malevolent demon is even more malevolent than Descartes thought.

The Moody Blues (1969), a rock group in the 1960s and 1970s, provided another way of looking at the problem, on their album *On the Threshold of a Dream*:

> [First man] I think … I think I am … therefore I am … I think.
> [Establishment] Of course you are my bright little star, I've miles and miles of files, pretty files of your forefather's fruit; and now to suit our great computer, you're magnetic ink.
>
> (Moody Blues, Graeme Edge 1969)

This post-modern exchange between a human voice and a mechanical voice provides an unexpected solution to Descartes' demon: if I wish to prove I exist, I need objective evidence of my existence; and that objective evidence can only come from outside myself, from someone (or something) else. So the fact that I need you to exist if I am to have evidence that I exist means that, for me, you have to exist – and, therefore, that I can believe in your belief that I exist. In Cartesian terms, if Descartes is being deceived by a demon, then the demon must exist; and the demon must believe that Descartes exists to expend effort deceiving him. *Cogitant ut sum, ergo sum*: 'they think I am, therefore I am'. To put it more simply, we get validation of our existence from other people. It is a view that Aristotle (330 BCE? [1915]) took when he said: 'If, then, it is pleasant to know oneself, and it is not possible to know this without having some one else for a friend, the self-sufficing man will require friendship in order to know himself'.

David Hume (1739 [1896]) spotted another problem with Descartes' *Dubito ergo cogito, cogito ergo sum*: before thinking – and before doubting – comes sensation. There must be a sensing-relationship between the self and the actual world before there is anything to doubt; and there must be thought about that sensing-relationship before there can be doubt about it. The order should be *Cogito ergo dubito*; but then *cogito ergo sum* is unprovable, because there is no prime cause for thought itself; and *dubito ergo sum* is meaningless. Instead, Hume proposed that our self is actually a series of individual ideas and impressions that we treat as if they formed a continuous experience; the self is an object constructed after the event of sensing, useful both to tie together the different sensations into a logical whole and to see them as having a common location. Directly regarding selfhood, Hume said that:

> … all the nice and subtile [sic] questions concerning personal identity can never possibly be decided, and are to be regarded rather as grammatical than as philosophical difficulties. Identity depends on the relations of ideas; and these relations produce identity, by means of that easy transition they occasion. But as the relations, and the easiness of the transition may diminish by insensible degrees, we have no just standard, by which we can decide any dispute concerning the time, when they acquire or lose a title to the name of identity.
>
> (Hume 1739: Part IV *Of the Sceptical and Other Systems of Philosophy*, Section VI *Of personal identity*, para.21).

For Immanuel Kant (1798 [1974]), this tricky problem of selfhood could be sidestepped: the world works in a particular way, and our minds are designed to appreciate and understand how the world works; but this physical understanding requires no self-knowledge. Instead, self-knowledge is a transcendent quality, existing alongside the physical world in a metaphysical space. This overcomes any need to explain the self: it is not physical, so it is not subject to physical laws and cannot be studied with physical laws.

This approach does, however, lead back to another problem that Descartes also encountered: how do the physical and metaphysical worlds interact? There has to be a link between them. Descartes settled, somewhat arbitrarily, on the pineal gland in the brain as the link; he saw it as a physical organ that also connects to the metaphysical world of the soul. Kant overcame the problem by viewing space and time as impositions by the metaphysical self on our appreciation of physical reality. Things in the real world have existence independent of our minds; but the detail of when and where physical things exist is established by the mind, which itself exists in the metaphysical realm. This imposes a heavy burden on Kantian reality: it has to exist in an unchanging actual state while accommodating mind-established qualities such as change, creation, destruction and multiple viewpoints. It was a problem that Kant was never able to fully rationalise.

While Kant took the view that self-knowledge was not the concern of philosophy, and that we could never really know ourselves, Friedrich Nietzsche (1899 [1909]) found this lack of self-knowledge interesting in and of itself. Influenced by Herbert Spencer's (1864) interpretation of Darwinian evolutionary calculus as *survival of the fittest*, Nietzsche proposed levels of self-awareness in the human species. Most of us are kept unaware of our true selves by the cultural conventions of our socialisation – the primary convention being, for Nietzsche, religion. Religion directs our self-knowledge away from our actual existence and toward a metaphysical entity, which therefore means that we allow our Actual selves to be manipulated toward goals that are not self-directed. If we were able to transcend the bounds put upon us by society, then we could also transcend the limits to our selfhood and become *Übermenschen* (supermen); or, rather, we could revert to the superman state that humans were in before civilisation limited us.

At this point, Nietzsche becomes somewhat vague, leaving many questions hanging. What is the enhanced state of self-awareness that supermen achieve? The self-awareness that Nietzsche attributes to his superman seems to be a misplaced sense of confidence, rather than an enhanced self-awareness. Have some of us already become supermen? Nietzsche's one given example, Richard Wagner, became a born-again Christian and rather blotted his superman copybook. Can everyone become supermen, or just a select few? And if just a few, how many? One answer to this was given by Adolf Hitler (you have to be Aryan, whatever that may be), and the practical application of Hitler's solution would have appalled Nietzsche. Two of the most telling questions highlight significant flaws in Nietzsche's thinking. The first is, what is so super about supermen? If getting rid of supermen was a *Good Thing* for civilisation and socialisation, why would society want them back now? And second, perhaps the biggest question of all, what about the women? What about the women, indeed …

Nietzsche's philosophy of the undiscovered self seems to raise more questions than it answers, and the fact it is interpretable in so many ways has distracted other philosophers into taking some strange and dark paths. For instance, the less said about Martin Heidegger's (1933 [1993]) interpretation of the superman model, the better. Heidegger's interpretation made him Hitler's favourite philosopher, but history has indicated that this was probably not a *Good Thing*. Nietzsche attempted to show the essential contradiction between existential philosophy and metaphysicality, an attempt that existentialist philosophers through the ages would have supported; but he became enslaved by his own metaphors, confusing his idealised superman selfhood with actual selfhood. He remains a much-studied philosopher, but he is regarded by many as a cautionary tale rather than a valuable contributor to modern knowledge about selfhood.

While these ideas of selfhood could be seen as 'false starts', they nevertheless emphasise the importance of the contribution of philosophy to scientific method, even when it seems unscientific: where philosophy does not directly support scientific method, it complements it, because philosophy celebrates lateral thinking, which the scientific method disfavours. Where science is supposed to move linearly from hypothesis to evidence to theory to new hypothesis, philosophy relies much more on the possible than the probable. Philosophers can 'jump the tracks' and take us into unexplored territory – and recently, in the study of selfhood, Daniel Dennett and Galen Strawson have done just that.

For Daniel Dennett (1991), the self is not a real, physical entity that can be identified and measured; it is, instead, more like a story we tell ourselves. One of the key features of being human is our willingness to tell, and listen to, stories that we know are not directly true. Instead of demanding truth in what is actually said, we identify worth in the telling of the tale rather than the tale itself. As part of the tale-telling, we are able to place models of others – and ourselves – into our stories; and as part of tale-listening, we are able to identify models of others and ourselves in the stories we hear. My belief in my selfhood, my selfness, is therefore determined by the tales I hear and tell about myself: my selfness is not physically real, but it has a cultural and psychological reality in that it affects my own behaviour and that of others toward me. Dennett's approach does not fully explain the simultaneous feelings of continuity and discontinuity of selfhood – the fact that I can see my historical self as both me and not me – but he does answer many questions about the arbitrariness of self-definition. And his explanation, that a self is neither an existent fixed entity nor a non-existent delusion, allows us to study selfhood scientifically as both a cultural and a personal concept.

Galen Strawson's (2009) approach is a little different. He, like Dennett, accepts the essential non-materiality of the self, and he rejects the unprovable metaphysical self. However, he also rejects the narrative nature of the self that Dennett (and Bruner – see *The psychologist's turn*) views as so important. Strawson contends that there are two ways of relating to the world: seeing yourself as a diachronic entity with continuity through time; or seeing yourself as an episodic entity, a series of selves existing at particular points in time. While the first lends itself to a narrative view of the self, establishing a single self that can have a continuous story, the second view has no single self and no continuity. For Strawson, being episodic is a viable alternative to being diachronic: you do not need a sense of being a continuous Narrative self to live a fulfilled human existence, and to insist that you do is to ignore some famous episodic figures from history, such as the twentieth-century novelist Jack Kerouac and the sixteenth-century essayist Michel de Montaigne.

The fact that people without a grounded Narrative self can, and do, exist supports Strawson's position over Dennett's; but that may not automatically mean that Dennett is wrong. The two extremes may represent a range of capacities rather than a binary choice, and most people probably live their lives between the extremes, able to adopt either position. In my own case, when I think about events in my childhood, they seem to have involved a different person who has no logical connection to my present self; but when I think about my thoughts in childhood, the relationship is close and personal: the child that had those thoughts is, intimately, the person I am today.

One final philosophical approach to selfhood that I would like to mention is that proposed by Thomas Metzinger (2003). For Metzinger, the key question is not about the nature of the self, but its very existence. He takes the view that nobody has an actual, core self; all we have are so-called phenomenal selves, created by our awareness as explanations after the fact for our actions. What we call a self is actually just a way of explaining the fact that I experience and remember my actions in a different way to my experience and memory of your actions. Phenomenal selves are not real, and they do not act as anchors for a psychologically real self, whether that self is Narrative or Episodic; they are just ways of explaining my actions – and, by extension, your actions – to myself. They are internal representations of how the human brain works; but the representations are false, both in what they represent and how they represent it. Metzinger's view of the self could be dismissed as nihilistic, telling us nothing useful; but it is nonetheless philosophically coherent, and it has its supporters in other disciplines.

The list of philosophers presented here gives only a flavour of the many views on selfhood offered over the centuries since writing was invented. The intention in this discussion was not to provide a comprehensive history, but to show that the philosopher's turn at defining selfhood is the most carefully argued effort and, after the priest's turn, that with the longest pedigree. Philosophers were working on the problem before two of the three Abrahamic religions even became established, and they are still providing new ways of looking at the problem. Despite centuries of introspection, however, philosophy still has not provided conclusive proof of selfhood. It remains, as the twentieth-century comedian Spike Milligan commented, 'all rather confusing, really'.

The psychologist's turn

While psychology is one of the youngest disciplines discussed here, it is nevertheless a distinct discipline from all the others, and it asks different questions. For instance, where anthropology (as we shall see) asks the question 'What does it mean to be human?', psychology asks a deceptively similar question: 'What does it mean to be *a* human?' However, that indefinite article sets psychology on a different trajectory to anthropology. Where anthropology is interested in the individual as a social creature, psychology is interested in the internal cognition of the creature. This means that psychology is intimately involved with questions about selfhood: what can make an effective self, a happy self, a fulfilled self, a useful self? How does the self know itself? What cognitive activities are involved in forming the self? ... and so on.

Psychology's intimate view of the individual should mean that it has a lot to tell us about the nature of selfhood, but this is not necessarily the case. Some psychological approaches see the individual as a mechanism – and a mechanism is not, by itself, motivated. Just as a bicycle is merely a pile of metal without the social conventions that allow it to be used as a bicycle, so a person is just a pile of cells without the motivating force of other people to provide meaningful purpose. This mechanistic approach would seem inadequate as a way to describe human beings: a bicycle, to extend the metaphor, has no internal motivation or meaning, whereas a human being does. The mechanistic approach is, however, considered by behavioural psychologists to be a valid starting point. As behavioural psychologists do not concern themselves with the vagaries of selfhood, however, their approach will not be explored further here.

Sigmund Freud (1923 [2010]) is perhaps the best-known psychologist to look at internal motivation as a feature in itself. He saw the cognitive processes of the typical human as a melding of three types of self: the ego, which represents the everyday thinking we perform; the id, which is emotional, primal and largely subliminal; and the super-ego, which is the internalisation of externally enforced cultural rules. He referred to this triad of cognitive elements as the psyche.

Freud believed there was a continuing battle between the id (what the physical person wants) and the super-ego (what the intellectual person believes is best), with the ego acting as a referee and arbiter between them. He saw many of the neuroses that were generated by this battle as sexual in nature, and thought that sexuality was the main driving force throughout our lives. This sexual approach was strongly influenced by Darwinian evolutionary theory, in which the two main markers of the fitness of an organism are survival and reproduction.

For Freud, the self was like an iceberg, with the ego and the super-ego conscious and visible, and the large and powerful id unconscious and hidden. Neuroses were manifestations of the unconscious self, and they could only be resolved by bringing them into conscious awareness – and this was something only the self itself could do. Freudian therapy is, therefore, mostly a matter of getting the client to recognise their unconscious desires and then helping them to integrate those desires into their conscious cognition. The conscious self resists recognising the unconscious desires as part of the same psyche, and only time and continuous exposure can reconcile the conscious self to the unconscious desires. Freudian psychotherapy is therefore not a 'quick fix'.

Freud's approach generated several theoretical variants among his adherents. Carl Jung (1958 [2014]) saw the unconscious as having two halves: the personal subconscious, which is individual and develops throughout an individual's lifetime; and the collective unconscious, which is inherited and invariant in all individuals. It is a division that reflected the growing concern over the dichotomy of nurture and nature: some aspects of our personality are determined by our experience, and some by our genetic make-up. Nowadays we recognise that the picture is more complicated; most of the aspects of our personality are established by the genes we inherit, but they are governed by our experience and cognition throughout our lives. However, as a first approximation, Jung's view challenged Freud's discrete trinity of selves within the psyche, and it raised the possibility that the psyche did not need to be a single integrated system.

For Alfred Adler (1927), Erich Fromm (1964) and others, traditional Freudian analysis did not place the individual adequately within their social environment. For the neo-Freudians, as they came to be known, the healing of the self did not need to involve an essentially intimate exploration of the unconscious; instead, the therapist could establish a dialogue with the client, working with them to identify and address their issues. In this therapeutic model, part of the therapist's job was to represent the voice of society and social convention for the client. The neo-Freudians weakened the unity of the psyche in a different way from Jung, showing that the individual needs to be able to present different 'faces' to different social groupings, and the psyche may need to resolve contradictions between those different faces.

More recently, Jerome Bruner (1986) took a quite different psychological approach to selfhood. He saw the self as a product of a continuing narrative, an autobiography that we generate through a lifetime of experiences (and it was this approach to which Strawson took exception – see *The philosopher's turn*). For Bruner, there was no single, transcendent ego, but nor was there any multiplicity of selves. We are all extremely aware of our own personhood at a practical level, but the person of which we are aware is changeable, and constantly being incremented by the process of living. The *me* now is not the *me* of yesterday, and it will not be the *me* of tomorrow; but there is a continuity of memory between those selves that gives them a single wholeness, or *me-ness*.

Bruner's approach is based on a common-sense approach to selfhood. There is no value in pursuing a concept of fractured selfhood if the commonly accepted view is that each person is a single self. The single, continuous self is the basis of many different human social systems, and the generally agreed measure of social acceptability for a self is its continuity and unity. Bruner believes, therefore, that psychology should be in the business of protecting the Narrative self and promoting it as responsible for itself. The aim should be to create self-acceptance, rather than Freud's truce between the id and the super-ego, or Jung's communication with the subconscious. Bruner's approach has been widely applied, and he himself used it extensively in his work dealing with educational and linguistic development among children. It provided a timely reminder that the self is a social construct as well as a personal one, and that it needs to be addressed as such.

The final psychological approach to selfhood to be included here is that of Daniel Wegner (2002). His view is in the same tradition as Metzinger, and that tradition has provided inspiration for other psychologists, such as Tor Nørretranders (1991) and Bruce Hood (2012). For Wegner, the self is an attribution of intention, which happens not before but after an act. It seems completely counterintuitive that intention is caused by action and not the cause of it; but, as we will see in the next section, there is neurological evidence supporting Wegner's position.

Wegner says that attribution of intention requires three things. First is priority: the feeling of intention must occur very soon after the act has happened, so that the brain can switch the order of the act and the intention. If the actor does not identify an intention quickly enough, then intention feels like what it really is: a justification after the event.

The second requirement is consistency: the conscious thinking at the time of the action should be related to the action, although the action is not a product of the conscious thought. If the actor is not deliberately aware of the action then there is no need to attribute intention. Third is exclusivity: there should be no intimation that the action is caused by an external agency. The actor must feel that they could be the cause of the action. These three requirements mean that selfhood is only detectable in consciously aware acts; it plays no part in subliminal or autonomic acts.

The attribution of intention creates a false feeling that the cognitive self controls the actions of the physical self, and it leads to what Wegner calls the illusion of control: my physical self is a machine under the control of my brain, and my brain is under the conscious control of my cognitive self. The range of physical effects (breathing, digestion, waste-processing, blood transportation and so on) that maintain the body, yet which clearly need no conscious attention, belie this assumption of control; but it remains a powerful rationalisation. For Wegner, the self is just a cognitive reaction to the body's activity; it may not even exist in any actual sense – but nobody has been able to convince the self of that fact.

The different theories of selfhood presented here point to an important distinction between the psychological approach and other approaches to selfhood: the psychological approach is concerned with both the study of selfhood and with its application to the cognitive wellness of the self. This second role is not just investigative, it is authoritative: the theoretical approach to the nature of the self determines the appropriate therapeutic treatment to give. This means that different views of the self are not just a matter for discussion between psychological practitioners, but they also affect the wellness of the clients being treated by those practitioners. It may be that there is one approach that works better than any other, but we currently do not have enough evidence to say which it is. Fortunately, the main way that clinical psychology seems to work is to allow the client to identify themselves as 'under repair', and to give them the space and time in which to redefine themselves. It seems that the client's definition of self is more important to successful treatment than the psychologist's view of selfhood – something that psychologists readily recognise.

The neurologist's turn

For millennia, the physical nature of the self remained a matter for deduction and speculation; there was no way to see the cognitive self working inside the physical self. This changed in the 1990s, when Functional

Magnetic Resonance Imaging (fMRI) first appeared. This process uses the magnetic properties of red blood cells to show where blood is being concentrated in the brain. Active areas of the brain need more oxygen than inactive areas, and oxygen-rich blood has a different magnetic signature from oxygen-poor blood; so, during a particular cognitive task, the parts of the brain where oxygen-rich blood is being converted into oxygen-poor blood are likely to be the areas performing that task. It is a reasonable assumption to make, based on what we know of the role of blood and the functioning of living tissue; but it remains a theoretical rather than a proven assumption.

Before fMRI, electroencephalography (EEG) and Near-Infrared Spectroscopy (NIRS) had provided rough maps of brain activity. However, both these methods are quite limited in what they can show: neither is able to reliably penetrate more than a few millimetres into the brain. Another technique, Positron Emission Tomography, when combined with X-ray Computer Tomography (PET-CT) is able to penetrate more deeply, but its main use is to show structure, not activity; and it uses X-rays, so each subject can be studied for only short periods. So, while not dismissing earlier work conducted using less sophisticated techniques, we can say with some certainty that the neurologist's turn at defining selfhood began in earnest in 1992, when the first volunteer was slid into the first fMRI machine.

What have all the different ways of imaging the brain been able to tell us about the self? Currently, we do not have enough evidence to say for certain that the self resides in a particular part of the brain, or even that it is distributed across the brain. The nineteenth-century case of Phineas Gage is still quoted as evidence that the frontal cortex is the seat of the self, but that evidence is far from unequivocal. Gage was a railway engineer who suffered a terrible accident when a metal bar was driven through the front of his brain. Reports of a drastic change in his character (from honest and hard-working to feckless and lazy) seem to have been exaggerated, and he lived a productive and active life for another 12 years after the accident. While there did seem to be some effects on his definition of his self, it cannot reliably be shown whether those changes were caused by the brain damage or the stress of the accident – people often change their character after near-death experiences not involving brain damage. What is reliably evident in Phineas Gage's case is that the injury changed, but did not wipe out, his sense of selfhood (Kotowicz 2007).

To investigate the location of the self in the brain, Todd Feinberg and Julian Keenan (2005) reviewed the evidence from scans of healthy individuals, individuals displaying Delusional Misidentification Syndrome (a failure to reliably identify self and others) and individuals undergoing hemispheric anaesthesia (a medical procedure that suspends awareness in half of the brain). They took the view that selfhood comes in a range of types; and that the different types of selfhood are not separate phenomena, but actually form a functionally nested hierarchy. The lower (semi-aware) levels are not cognitively separate from the upper (fully aware) levels; instead, the upper levels incorporate the lower. By looking at how the subjects' brains reacted when presented with a series of self-identification tests, such as face recognition, self-voices and other self-related stimuli, Feinberg and Keenan were able to show that the right hemisphere seems to play a greater role in self-cognition than the left, and the frontal cortex plays a greater role than other areas. They did not claim that the right frontal cortex is where the self resides, but it does seem to be important in self-cognition. They also concluded that, while the unified self does seem to behave like a nested hierarchy, this does not mean that the neural system supporting it is similarly configured.

Alain Morin (2005) took a different approach. He looked at the role of inner speech (talking to ourselves inside our heads) as a determiner of selfness. He took the view that inner speech gave us both a mechanism to rationalise the actions of others and a method for scrutinising our self. By looking at the brain areas active during autobiographical recollection, Morin identified the left frontal cortex as implicated in selfhood. This fits well with his view that inner speech is associated with selfhood, because the left hemisphere is also the traditional locus for language (although it must be remembered that 1 in 20 normally functioning human brains do not match this model). However, Morin's theory contains its own confounding factor: because selfness involves inner speech, and inner speech involves speech, it is hard to separate out the parts of the brain involved in speech from the parts involved in selfness – they should both be active during autobiographical recollection. Whether Morin's model really indicates that the neurological self is located in the same hemisphere as language remains debateable.

Bernard Baars et al. (2003) looked at the problem from a different angle. By revisiting studies of individuals in a conscious resting state and in four different types of unconsciousness (deep sleep, general anaesthesia, vegetative state and epileptic loss of consciousness), they were able to determine the areas of the brain that were inactive in unconscious states. They identified two key areas: in the parietal cortex (traditionally associated with the integration of sensory information) and in the frontal cortex. They also found that there was no noticeable processing difference between the two hemispheres (they looked roughly like mirror-images of each other). Based on these findings, Baars et al. proposed two brain areas as components of a particular form of self-awareness, which they labelled the observing self: first is the parietal component, which is involved in placing the self within a sensory context; and second is the frontal component, which is involved in placing the self in a socio-cultural context and in self-evaluation. Together, these areas allow us to see ourselves as if we were observers outside our selves.

Benjamin Libet (2004) threw a spanner into the works regarding the 'awareness of selfness' debate, when he showed that many of the events where we appear to show awareness actually happen in the wrong order. We think that we perceive an event, become aware of it and then react to it; but it turns out that we perceive an event, react to it and *then* become aware of it. If a child walks out in front of a car we are driving, we are able to begin braking about 2/10 of a second after the child appears, but we become aware of the child at 5/10 of a second. Our awareness of the event is not the trigger for our reaction – it is, as Wegner surmises (see *The psychologist's turn*), a justification of our reaction after the event.

In a series of experiments, Libet showed that to become aware of an event takes a full half-second; the event itself can be considerably shorter, as little as 1/10 of a second in duration, but awareness of the event will not happen before the half-second has elapsed. He also showed that, where a short event was followed by a second short event within the half-second window, the subject did not become consciously aware of the first event. Another timing anomaly that Libet identified is the creation of simultaneity: although our awareness happens a half-second after an event begins, we believe the event and the awareness of it are simultaneous. Our brain is adjusting our awareness to match our expectations rather than our reality.

What does this cognitive chicanery tell us about the relationship between our physical self and our aware self? Our aware self is, by definition, a product of aware cognitive processes; it cannot be reduced to a set of subliminal reactions, because it can view itself reflexively – we can be aware of being aware of ourselves. If, however, all of our aware cognition is just an explanation after the fact of our subliminal cognition, then the aware self is not actually in charge of our physical self, it is just along for the ride. The aware self becomes a useful fiction we can employ in our interactions with the world, but it does not, itself, interact with the world. To put it another way, the physical electrochemistry of the brain can be measured while we are being aware of our self, but the self itself is not a substance or entity that can be scientifically measured.

Joseph LeDoux (2002) has attempted to explain the emergence of selfhood as a product of basic electrochemical events in the brain. He is interested in the structural features of the brain, what they do and how they work together to generate a sense of continuity of selfhood. He proposes seven principles to explain how brains work. First, the different subsystems of the brain all deal simultaneously with the same actual world, and they can use that common fact to work together. Second, the parallel synchrony between different subsystems means they do not need to be completely separated; they can work together when needed. LeDoux calls this functional plasticity. Third, the plasticity of parallel synchrony is coordinated by electrochemical modulators. Fourth, there are information-convergence zones in the brain, some of which are task-specific (such as the hippocampus) and some of which are the product of functional plasticity; and the human brain is particularly rich in these convergence zones. Fifth, the brain uses both a bottom-up process, building basic units of cognition into more complex units, and a top-down process, reducing complexity to components; and it is this continuous two-way process that coordinates cognitive change. Sixth, emotional cognition dominates the brain, and influences all other cognition, including self-definition. Seventh, the self consists of both implicit and explicit aspects, which overlap to produce the sense of a continuous self, but which are not coexistent.

LeDoux provides a persuasive model of the brain as a computational entity, but he remains somewhat vague about how it computes a self, or the nature of the self that is being computed. He defines the self as 'the totality of what an organism is physically, biologically, psychologically, socially, and culturally' (LeDoux 2002, 31); but is this a definition of the selfhood of the individual, or a more general definition of the boundaries of the individual? Is the self an emergent phenomenon, not directly related to the general computation role of the brain? Or is it a selected product of evolution, an inevitable component of cognition? How does having the human version of the self make our sense of self different to that of other animals? And is that difference qualitative or just quantitative? LeDoux is correct in his assumption that we need to understand the detailed working of the brain, but this may not be the correct level of study to show us how cognitive processes like selfhood work: understanding the *Haynes Manual* for our car does not teach us how to drive it.

Antonio Damasio (2010) approaches the subject of consciousness from the direction of selfhood, which reverses the normal method of using selfhood to study consciousness. In doing so, he relies less on brain-measuring techniques and more on accepted brain architecture. He sees the self as a series of interrelated modules that build upon, but do not necessarily nest within, each other. First, there is the protoself, the basic and irrefutable physical self. Then there is the core self, which is about the relationship between the protoself and the outside world; this is a two-way relationship, allowing the world to affect the self as well as allowing the self to affect the world. Next there is the autobiographical self, which involves the collection and ownership of past experiences and future plans; this self generates the story of our lives and gives us the feeling of integrated continuity through space, time and context. The core self and autobiographical self are, between them, able to generate a meta-knowledge about the self's knowledge, creating a self-as-knower; and they are also able to generate a meta-knowledge about the self's knowledge of itself, creating a self-as-object. However, while the protoself, core self and autobiographical self are permanent effects (although not always conscious effects), the self-as-knower and self-as-object are cognitive constructs, and only exist while they are being thought about.

Damasio concludes that these different instantiations of the self represent a long evolutionary journey for cognition. However, in a surprise move for a neurologist, he sees the appearance of the final version of human selfhood as 'a recent development, on the order of thousands of years'. With his knowledge of genetics, he must realise that this poses a big problem: how did the final version of selfhood propagate around the world, reaching even populations in Australia, which were otherwise isolated from the rest of humanity for over 60,000 years (Clarkson et al. 2017)? Yet it seems that the alternative to Damasio's timescale, involving a more ancient appearance of the currently final version of selfhood, is also problematic: if full human selfhood is so important in defining human capacities, then it should be accompanied by a sudden efflorescence of those capacities. Yet there seems to be no reliable sign of this cognitive blooming in the archaeological record before 100,000 years ago (Henshilwood and Dubreuil 2011), when humans were already widespread in Africa and the Near East (Lahr and Foley 2016). This timing dilemma is a problem not just for Damasio; it has influenced our understanding of human cognitive origins for nearly two centuries. In Chapter 6, we will see further examples of this dilemma.

Michael Graziano, like Libet, has asked questions about the role of attention and consciousness in our definition of selfhood (Graziano 2013). He looks at the theory of the cortical 'homunculus', originally developed by Penfield and Boldrey (1937), and takes issue with its view that our motor cortex and somatosensory cortex act as a physical representation of the body inside the brain. The motor and somatosensory cortices are two strips of cells lying laterally across the middle of the outer surface of the brain, approximately from ear to ear. The cortical homunculus theory says that the two cortices reflect our awareness of our bodies in terms of both activity and sensation: the larger the area of motor cortex dedicated to a particular part of the body, the more voluntary control we have over that body part; and the larger the area of somatosensory cortex, the more aware we are of sensations in that body part. Graziano et al. (2002) investigated the two cortical areas in monkeys, finding that they are more about attention to the movements made than about awareness of the body part making the movement; the motor and somatosensory cortices seem to be monitoring the process of movement, as opposed to controlling the movements themselves. Graziano described this awareness of body activity as a *body schema* rather than a homunculus.

Graziano (2016) went on to look at attention and consciousness in relation to subjective awareness, or awareness of self. Here, he showed that paying attention to something is not turning the spotlight of awareness onto the external object, it is a process of incorporating the something into the individual's model of reality. Our internal model does not just represent the world, it also allows new things that have come under conscious scrutiny to be incorporated into the model itself – what Graziano refers to as the *attention schema*. This attention schema maps attention in the same way that the body schema maps movement: it is not about controlling attention, it is about recognising attention. He describes his attention schema theory as:

> ... a theory of how information is constructed in the brain and used to model the world and guide decisions, conclusions, speech, and behaviour. It is a theory of how the human machine claims to have consciousness and assigns a high degree of certainty to that conclusion.
>
> (Graziano 2016, 11)

Graziano's attention schema theory turns much traditional neurology on its head. Humans are not cognitively exceptional in having novel tools of cognition; they just have a little bit more of what other animals have. Cognition is not about controlling the physically active (enactive) self, it is about supporting and justifying the physically active self. Information is not received from the world and stored in the cognitive self, it is constructed from data noticed in the world; and data is not information. The world is not understood by the brain, it is modelled by the brain; and the model need not be accurate. Consciousness is not a state of attention, it is an explanation after the fact of attention; it is not something we have, it is something we make. Awareness is not consciousness or attention, it is '... declarative. It is an informational representation that depicts, usefully if not entirely accurately, the process of attention' (Graziano and Kastner 2011, 113). Graziano's ideas about cognition form an important backdrop to the hypothesis discussed in this book, that self-awareness is attention to a model of the world, not true reflexive attention to the self.

Neurological theories of selfhood are usually supported with extensive evidential research, so the neurological approach is the most data-rich investigation of selfhood that we have. However, that is both its strength and its weakness: data is always more persuasive than theory, but it raises its own questions. What does the data represent? How should it be interpreted? What level of detail is needed to explain a cognitive phenomenon like selfhood? As we have seen in this section, having data is not the same as having answers, and the assumptions made in gathering and interpreting the data can affect the meanings extracted from it. Theory cannot be supported or disproved without data, but the data-gathering and analysis processes are not without bias.

The anthropologist's turn

Anthropology is a relative newcomer to the debate on selfhood. It emerged as a subject from the imperial ambitions of European states during the eighteenth and nineteenth centuries, and was initially an effort to identify the weaknesses and failings of other cultures so that they could be exploited and subjugated. It was only in the late-nineteenth and early-twentieth centuries that anthropology threw off its intimate links with the national and religious organisations it had been serving, and began to ask the big question that has informed its research ever since: 'What does it mean to be human?'

For Karl Marx (1844 [1959]), who opposed the imperial version of anthropology when it was at its strongest, the problem was socio-political. At some point in the past, humans had adopted a stratified social system in which individuals became specialised not only in their productive roles but also in their social roles. The individual became a puppet of society, required to act in certain ways to avoid sanction. Capitalism meant that some individuals became rulers and owners (the bourgeoisie), while the rest became the proletariat, workers without the freedom to choose in any useful way. The workers were alienated from their work – they had no control over what they did – and alienated from their own selves, from their innate potential as individuals. The solution proposed by Marx was communism, in which the workers would once again take control over their work. The illusion of selfish but powerless individual selfhood, fostered by capitalism, would be replaced by a communally aware selfhood in which the individual is fulfilled by their work for the collective.

The twentieth century was marked by a series of revolutions intended to introduce worker control over production and consumption (Russia 1917, Germany 1918, China 1946, Vietnam 1954, Cuba 1958 and Venezuela 1999, for instance). However, they all encountered opposition to worker control, both internally and externally, and they all succumbed quite quickly to *big man* rule (Sahlins 1963). It remains untested whether this was because of a failure of communist ideology, the lack of a sufficiently informed proletariat willing and able to police the revolution, external pressure to fail or a basic misunderstanding of the nature of being human (Lorimer 1997). From the viewpoint of the SSMH, however, the attempt to direct the consensus of social modelling away from individuals and toward collective institutions may have been an attempt to plug altruism into the wrong socket. Effacing the individual's model of their own selfhood seems, on the current evidence we have, to lead not to altruism but to apathy.

Émile Durkheim (1895), like Marx, saw modern society as a form of alienation of the individual; but for Durkheim the alienation was caused by an enhanced sense of personal identity, and it was not a *Bad Thing*. Traditional societies have collective awareness and weak self-identity, while modern Western societies have individual awareness and strong self-identity; traditional societies enforce conformity by dealing with deviant behaviour, while modern Western societies deal with the deviant individual; and, while conformity in traditional societies means adoption of a standard role, modern Western conformity is a matter of finding a specialist role in a complex and highly differentiated society. For Durkheim, the enhanced selfhood in modern societies is a necessary outcome of social complexity: social complexity generates new and varied ways of being human, so the individual has more choice in their way of being human.

Claude Lévi-Strauss (1962) thought that the individual was almost entirely the product of their social environment, and any selfhood was therefore imposed on the individual by the local culture. Like Durkheim, he saw the collectively defined self as the natural state in traditional societies, while modern humans were in a state of enhanced individuality. However, unlike Durkheim (and more like Marx), he believed the traditional state was preferable to the modern. Modern individuality leads to the celebration of individual creativity, which cannot actually exist. Everything created is continuous with what has gone before; which means that attempting to consciously add newness usually adds imperfection – it is not creation, it is destruction. Individuality works against the natural human state, and this led Lévi-Strauss (1955 [1963]), to assert Blaise Pascal's aphorism, '*Le moi est haissable*' ('The me is hateful').

Lévi-Strauss incorporated his idea of selfhood throughout his anthropology; he took the view that humans are not designed for individual fulfilment, and we can only reach personal fulfilment by abandoning our individuality. His work on mythology was concerned with the essentially impersonal nature of story-telling: mythology is not about a story being told, it is about a story being heard, and it is understood through the culture in which it is heard. It is not important that the story is told well, it is important that it is heard as the same story by everyone every time. The shaman's or bard's or skald's role is to convey the message behind the story, and it should therefore be possible to trace the same message through the stories told in any area of continuous culture. Lévi-Strauss traced one message, the *Birdnester* myth, through the stories told from the Antarctic to the Arctic of the Americas; and Chris Knight (1991) has since shown that the same *Birdnester* myth appears in different cultures dispersed across the globe. Lévi-Strauss' theories on individuality have also inspired writers such as Michel Foucault (Martin et al. 1988), Jacques Derrida (1998) and Pierre Bourdieu (2008) in their discussions of selfhood within society.

Joseph Campbell (1949), another anthropologist with an interest in myth, took a very different view of selfhood in traditional societies. He looked at the myths as hero-myths, descriptions of the growth and emancipation of the individual protagonist in the story – who is usually male, and usually forced to undertake a series of ego-enhancing tasks. However, like Lévi-Strauss, Campbell saw all myth as carrying one single message, which he called the monomyth. This myth has four functions: to explain nature; to reconcile the conscious experience of life to the subliminal experience; to establish the constraints that society must place on the individual to ensure group survival; and to provide a template by which individuals should live to ensure personal survival. Campbell was, therefore, interested in individuals and individuality as building blocks of society, and not as threats to it.

For Campbell, the monomyth was not a call to abandon individuality, but an explanation of the interface between the personal individual and the social individual, the 'selfish' self and the cooperative self. It explained how the selfish self can move from the safety of the known through the unsafe unknown, and emerge once again into the known, but with a new social awareness. Campbell acknowledged the similarity between his ascending hero and Nietzsche's superman when he said:

> Nietzsche was the one who did the job for me. At a certain moment in his life, the idea came to him of what he called "the love of your fate". Whatever your fate is, whatever the hell happens, you say, "This is what I need". It may look like a wreck, but go at it as though it were an opportunity, a challenge. If you bring love to that moment – not discouragement – you will find the strength is there. Any disaster you can survive is an improvement in your character, your stature, and your life.
>
> (Campbell, in Osbon 1991)

Lévi-Strauss and Campbell approached selfhood from two very different directions, and their research into myth led them to very different conclusions. There are striking similarities between their positions (relating to the existence of a single mythic story, and the difference between selfhood in modern and traditional societies, for instance), but they also illustrate the fact that, in anthropology, our own context is vital. The stories we tell about being human are the stories of our own humanity; the evidence we rely on is our own experience of being human; and when we hear stories, we understand them through the filter of our own experience.

Dorinne Kondo (1986) raised an important issue for selfhood in anthropology. Her experience while conducting fieldwork in Japan made her realise that her own selfhood had intruded onto her research in an unexpected and disturbing way: in her effort to understand the 'Japaneseness' of her subjects, she had increasingly identified with, and adopted, the attitudes and views of her subjects. The transformation did not happen in her objective knowledge of being Japanese but in her subjective knowledge. Yet it was only through her subjective knowledge that she was able to objectively identify the cultural differences between being Japanese and being American. Kondo was simultaneously two selves, and it was only the maintenance of both selves that allowed her ethnographic work to proceed. Her Japanese self was neither subsumed into, nor properly differentiated from, the local culture; instead, it was in a constant negotiation with her American self and the context in which it found itself.

Thomas Csordas (1990) took a somewhat different direction on selfhood, when he proposed that any anthropological study of the self needs to recognise the physical body. The existence of a body is the cause of the existence of the self, and the existence of groups of bodies is the cause of culture – both the physical culture evident in many non-humans and the symbolic culture evident in humans. The human self is both a subjective thing experienced in a physical culture and an objective thing experienced in a symbolic culture; but the subjective and objective selves are not different things, they are different sides of the same thing. Only by acknowledging the embodiment of the self can we hope to reconcile our subjective and objective experiences. For Csordas, the self is an enduring thing, defining culture by its very existence.

More recently, Deacon et al. (2011) presented another anthropological view of the self, as an emergent feature of cognition. Having a self is nothing unusual in nature – it can be viewed as an inevitable outcome of motivated matter: as soon as you have cellular life, you have, on some level, selfhood. Human selfhood has both subjectivity (we are aware of our selfness) and interiority (we can think about our selves); while we share subjectivity with other animals, interiority is an extra level of selfhood – which may, or may not, be exclusive to *Homo sapiens*, but is certainly not common in nature. Subjectivity and interiority are, in turn, products of the cognitive complexity permitted by our brains, they are not by-products of an inexplicable human nature. If we are to understand selfhood as a social or cultural phenomenon, we must first understand it as a cognitive phenomenon.

This short section has illustrated some of the views on the individual that anthropology has inspired, but it is only a representative sample. Modern analysis of selfhood in anthropology is usually extensively informed by scientific knowledge from a range of disciplines. Nowadays, anthropologists can look at other species to identify which aspects of our nature predate our species; they can identify genetic reasons for some of the aspects of our nature; and they can study human brains in action to see how some of the aspects of our nature are represented in our cognition. Anthropology is no longer a fully autonomous academic field; it is now, in large part, a nexus of zoology, neurology, psychology and genetics. It has become the study of the human as animal, as well as the human as phenomenon.

However, anthropology does express a unique view on the issue of selfhood: the anthropological approach both starts and finishes with the group. The self needs to be seen as a socially defined phenomenon, created by both the impression of the group upon the individual and the expression of the individual upon the group. Humans have a unique relationship with other members of their species, both communicatively and socially. Our capacity for group living and group institutions exceeds that of every other animal on the planet; as we saw in the Prologue, only the eusocial insects come close, and their group living is definitely not based around selfhood. Anthropology therefore has an important voice in the discussion of selfhood; and its motivating question, 'What does it mean to be human?', is key to understanding our unusual relationship with our selves.

Is there an answer?

So, after all the different turns, what is a self? I know that you are you, and not me or some other person who is not you; and I know that I am me because you tell me I am. We each recognise each other, and ourselves, as individual beings; and our society and culture are arranged around recognising these details of selfhood. I can own things, or even ideas, and you can offer me something I value if you want to use my thing or idea. If I do something of which other people do not approve, they can hold me responsible and punish me. Other people insist that I am the same person I was 50 years ago, even though I look, sound and think differently from the self I was then; and at a fundamental level, despite evidence to the contrary, I also think I am the same person. So what is this self that is so important to other people and ourselves? And where does it come from?

In this chapter, we have encountered a wide range of different viewpoints, from 'the self is the only truly real thing' to 'the self is an illusion'. Different commentators have shown the self to be a metaphysical reality, a physical reality, a cognitive reality, or a cognitive trope. It has been described as a single integrated whole, a series of nested functions, a series of separate but interrelated functions and a set of ad hoc instances. It has been analysed as a genetic phenomenon, a personal phenomenon, a social phenomenon, a cultural phenomenon and a religious phenomenon. Faced with this milling crowd of selves, it seems not at all unreasonable for us to ask, 'Would the real self please stand up?' – although, if Metzinger and Wegner are correct, this should only result in nervous muttering and shuffling of feet.

So, taking all these ideas into account, what can we say with any degree of certainty about the self? Well, we can agree that it is something that we all need if we are to be fully functioning humans, regardless of how real we believe it to be; we can accept that it is complex and multifaceted, regardless of our particular views of what the complexities are; we can recognise that it is not simply an internal thing, for our self is defined by others as well as ourselves; and we can probably concur that the self we are able to study scientifically is essentially a product of our brains, regardless of our views about the metaphysical self. This is quite a lot to be able to agree on, and it provides us with a stable enough foundation to take our investigation of the self forward.

2
Where Did Self Come From?

> 'I quite agree with you,' said the Duchess; 'and the moral of that is, "Be what you would seem to be" – or if you'd like it put more simply. – "Never imagine yourself not to be otherwise than what it might appear to others that what you were or might have been was not otherwise than what you had been would have appeared to them to be otherwise."'
>
> 'I think I should understand that better,' Alice said very politely, 'if I had it written down: but I can't quite follow it as you say it.'
>
> 'That's nothing to what I could say if I chose,' the Duchess replied, in a pleased tone.
>
> (Lewis Carroll 1865, Chapter 9: 'The Mock Turtle's Story')

The Duchess' admonition to Alice is probably indecipherable (at least, I cannot find an unambiguous meaning in it, even when written down), but it does represent an important feature of selfness: the self seems to be defined through the interaction of different external viewpoints about the self. It is not simply an internal description. This range of external viewpoints was more simply described in Chapter 1 as 'they think I am, therefore I am': I am aware of myself because I am aware of you being aware of me.

Most humans would say that they are self-aware: we feel that we can choose between alternative courses of action, and that we can be aware of ourselves choosing between those alternatives. We don't just have a feeling of personal choice, we also feel there is a self making those choices – we have an awareness of our own selfness. René Descartes (1649 [1998]) took the view that we are the only animals to have sufficient self-awareness to know there is a self to be aware of. Most modern primatologists, however, are less certain about the exclusivity of self-awareness, and point to experimental results that can only be satisfactorily explained by acknowledging some kind of self-awareness in their primate subjects (for example, Patterson and Gordon 1993). Some exceptional non-human subjects, heavily exposed to human culture, even seem to exhibit compassion and social mindfulness at levels that Cartesian philosophers would like to reserve for humans (for example, Savage-Rumbaugh et al. 1986). But does this mean that those non-humans have also reached a level of self-awareness where they are capable of asking themselves the question 'Who am I?'

Even if we allow that these exceptional non-humans have access to a certain level of self-awareness, we usually stop short of accepting that they have the same self-awareness as humans. To be human is to be, somehow, more aware of yourself than any other species can be. We can know who we were, who we are, and that our self has been changed between then and now; and we can know who we are going to be – often imagining several different future selves at the same time (Fingelkurts and Fingelkurts 2015). It is as if we were working with multiple versions of our self, emphasising different aspects of our character in each version. We also often feel that we have individual continuity, that the self I was then is somehow the same self I am now, and that the future selves are all continuations of the present self; but when we look comparatively at those different selves, it becomes hard to see what it is that continues.

The sense of not-self

Let us, for now, leave aside the question of how the human sense of self works, and look at some of the ways in which non-humans have selves – even if they are not aware of the selves they have. It turns out that, for some definitions of selfhood, having a self is far from unusual in nature; and, using the most basic definition (that self is the cause of self-preservation), it may even offer a viable definition of life itself.

When looking for evidence of any kind of selfhood, we can, in evolutionary terms, start way back with the amoeba, a single-celled animalcule endemic on this planet. The choice of the amoeba as the earliest candidate is somewhat arbitrary: it stands for any single-celled animal (a protozoan, foraminifer, bacterium or archaeon would serve just as well). What is said here about the amoeba can be said about any of these single-celled animals.

The first point to make about the amoeba is that its apparent simplicity is deceptive. An amoeba is a eukaryotic cell, the same type of cell that makes up the human body, and it is a highly efficient little machine (Cordingley and Trzyna 2008). A eukaryotic cell is composed of a series of sub-mechanisms that control movement, feeding, and cell division – and these sub-mechanisms work together in such a way that the cell appears to have a *will to survive*. The amoeba moves toward, and envelops, food items, and it moves away from threats to its survival. On the surface, this will to survive appears to work in a similar way to human choice; but it does not involve the conscious awareness needed for human choice, it is just the outcome of electro-chemical interactions between the amoeba and its environment.

The amoeboid eukaryotic cell does not seem a particularly fertile ground in which to look for any type of selfhood, but it actually demonstrates the most fundamental version of self. The amoeba is a set of mechanisms within a flexible cell membrane, and this membrane marks the boundary between the ends of existence (movement, feeding and division) and the means by which that existence is maintained. Things outside the amoeba's cell membrane have the potential to support or damage its existence; everything inside it is (theoretically) already devoted to the amoeba's existence. It is therefore useful to the amoeba to be able to detect and react differently to items outside its cell membrane than to items inside it, giving it, for all practical amoeboid purposes, a sense of not-self.

It is this sense of not-self, allied with the will to survive, that offers a viable definition for life: living things react to their environments in ways that support, or minimise damage to, their existence; non-living things do not. The sense of not-self provides a simple and natural way for organisms to enhance their personal survival; and the more sophisticated and effective the sense of not-self, the fitter the organism will be. Like any natural system, however, the weaknesses of the sense of not-self are exploitable by other organisms; and, in this case, the key weakness is that detection is focussed outward. If something can get inside the cell wall by posing as, say, food, it can wreak havoc inside the cell, undetected and unopposed by the cell. Viruses, and species of bacteria and fungi, have all adopted versions of this trick, exploiting other cells beyond their own capsid or cell membrane as part of their own 'will to survive'.

Despite this key weakness in the single-celled animal's definition of its world, the sense of not-self was sufficient to take life from the single cell to multi-cellular cooperation. The survival of genetic clones (which, because of cell division, is what neighbouring same-species cells are most likely to be) is of almost equal worth to the cell as survival of the cell itself, and this means that aggregations of single-celled clones can appear to work together to achieve common ends; and the common ends give the appearance of shared intention. Slime moulds, colonies of cloned single-celled animalcules, can appear to move as a single entity, although each cell is actually governed by only two relevant chemosensory imperatives: first, move toward food; second, move toward same-species cells, or conspecifics (Hudson et al. 2002). The cells that detect food move toward it (the first imperative), dragging along the other cells behind them (the second imperative). This gives the appearance, to human observers, of a single, amorphous, multi-cellular entity.

One of the strangest outcomes of this colony relationship is what happens when there is no food being detected. The cells aggregate, as expected under the second imperative, and begin to form what look like budding bodies. The cells in these budding bodies form spores (dormant cells that preserve their DNA cargo) and blow away. The wind carries them to new, hopefully richer, environments, where they can activate, propagate and start new colonies. These clonal slime mould colonies, with their primitive cell specialisations, provide an evolutionary template for what happens in much more complex organisms like we humans. So the sense of not-self could be seen as the beginning of an explanation for the existence of complex organisms.

The sense of almost-self

From self-organising clonal cooperatives to multi-celled organisms is a small step in terms of systemic innovation: a multi-cellular organism is just a clonal colony with extra rules – the main one being that, if enough cells of a particular type die, the whole organism dies. However, in terms of evolutionary innovation, the cell specialisms required by multicellularity involve a long series of developmental changes, and a full explanation is considerably more complex than can be given here. One developmental change that should be mentioned, though, is the electrochemical recognition by cells of their clonal relatives, allowing different reactions to clones and to alien cells. This differentiated response is an extension of the external sense of not-self, not the beginning of an internal sense of self. It can be described as a sense of almost-self (clones are good, non-clones are bad), but not almost a sense of self.

A multi-cellular organism can be described somewhat metaphorically as a clonal colony with enhanced cell specialisation: each cell in the organism has a specialist role. This means that the simple genetic programme of the eukaryotic amoeba, which produces undifferentiated copies, must have a secondary programme overlaid on it to control cell differentiation. Muscle cells have to be where muscle cells should be; and brain cells, skin cells, bone cells and all other cells also need to be in the right place. There need to be mechanisms to encourage the right sort of differentiation and to discourage the wrong sort. These mechanisms must be products of the genetic processes within the cell, but they work between the cells instead of inside them. They are essentially about intercellular communication, and it is only recently that we have begun to understand how these mechanisms work (Mittelbrunn and Sánchez-Madrid 2013).

The secondary genetic programme for cell differentiation therefore generates, and relies on, a system of communication between cells; and this, in turn, requires a cell to have a sense of almost-self about other cells in the multi-cellular organism. Each cell has to react to its clones cooperatively and to alien cells inimically – there has to be an autonomic and concerted reaction by the clonal colony to non-colony cells to prevent them invading the colony (for this purpose, an autonomic reaction can be defined as an electrochemical response that does not involve choice; it is the inevitable response to a particular stimulus). The apparently cooperative sense of almost-self at the cellular level is sufficient to generate the appearance of a sense of not-self at the colony level, as the colony itself appears to have an 'inside' and an 'outside'; and this is why we tend to refer to multi-celled clonal colonies (such as ourselves) as organisms.

Cell differentiation introduces the possibility of another type of cooperation for the organism: some cells can become more vital to the continued operation of the organism than others – or, to put it another way, a hierarchy of cells can develop. We see this in our own organism: skin cells, which sit right at the edge between the means and ends of the organism, are short-lived, and perform most of their barrier function by dying. They are on a conveyor belt of constant renewal: over three weeks, your skin completely replaces itself. The skin of your colon is replaced even faster, every four or five days. This compares to neuron cells in the brain, which can last a lifetime, and replace themselves at a much slower rate (Gage 2002) – so slow that it was once thought there was no replacement at all. In terms of the body as clonal colony, skin cells are the poor bloody infantry, sacrificed in droves so that the commanding cells in the brain can work in comparative safety. This three-stage cellular evolution (segmentation, differentiation and hierarchy) is, as we shall see, also applicable to the origins of human culture and language, and it may represent a standard strategy for dealing with the universe.

The sense of almost-self is a feature of all cells in multi-cellular organisms; and, with cellular differentiation and hierarchy, the aggregation of cell reactions gives the organism the appearance of being centrally directed. The central direction, however, is contained in the gene programme of every individual cell, and not within a particular organ of the organism. This distributed organisational template, with the appearance of being centrally directed, works very well for plants and for other organisms that have only autonomic functions. However, the introduction of automatic functions (functions under a level of control by the organism) requires actual central direction – or, as we express it in terms of the organism, a central nervous system and a brain.

Senses of other and sense of self

So far, we have seen that a sense of not-self is valuable at the cellular level: a cell has an inside, where everything is dedicated to preserving and propagating the organism; and it has an outside, where everything provides a means to achieve those ends. The sense of almost-self is similarly valuable at the organism level. The survival of the organism is paramount; but it is useful to recognise, and cooperate with, your relatives because they carry some of your genes and can pass those genes on to the future. Recognition of the existence of relatives by organisms is not as valuable as the recognition of clones at the cellular level. Clones will nearly always produce exact copies of the original cell; but relatives, especially when sexual reproduction enters the mix, will produce only partially faithful copies – and the more distant the relationship, the less similarity you have with the copy.

The sense of almost-self is therefore variable at the organism level: some almost-self organisms are more *almost self* than others. A simple rule of cooperating or competing with neighbouring cells, depending on their chemical signals, has to be replaced by a system of conditional cooperation under some kind of automatic, or cognitive, control. Response to a stimulus can no longer be divorced from the organism generating the stimulus, and different organism–stimulus combinations need different responses, depending on the context of the stimulus. A central nervous system gives this level of choice to an organism, allowing a range of stimuli to be integrated into an impression of the situation before a response happens. A central nervous system also allows the development of senses beyond the chemosensory: sound and vision become viable conduits for information-gathering and exchange, once specialist detector and transmitter systems have evolved.

All of these factors mean that it is advantageous for organisms to develop an enhanced sense of not-self that can distinguish between different types of not-self. This is, effectively, a sense of other, a sense that there are other organisms in the world with me. A simple sense of not-self combines with a variable sense of almost-self to create the environment in which this sense of other becomes possible, and also generates the fitness advantage that makes it valuable: the organism can generate variable and conditional responses to stimuli based on the context of the stimuli, where the context is other organisms.

The sense of other, however, does not lead automatically to the evolution of a sense of self; the evolutionary route to a sense of self is different. For the amoeba, sensing the outside world is useful, while sensing the internal world remains less valuable: no sense of self or selfness is needed or desirable. Once an organism's range of responses has been increased by the development of a central nervous system, however, the capacity for the individual to see their choices as personally 'good' or 'bad' becomes more valuable. To give an example: plants, without a central nervous system, can only try to ride out a worsening local environment, or produce seed on the chance that their offspring may travel beyond it; animals, on the other hand, because of their greater cell differentiation and hierarchy, can make a personal decision to move to a better environment. The introduction of a brain (alongside many other cellular specialisations) gives an organism a greater level of control over its reactivity: it can choose whether to move, where to move, how fast to move – indeed, many survival-related activities become subject to choice. It is this new activity of choosing that creates the next level of mindfulness, the sense of self.

Sense of self is a representation by the organism of the agenda of the organism. It is not a conscious representation, it is more akin to feelings of satisfaction when things are going well for the organism, and a sense of unease when they are not. The sense of self does not involve awareness that there is a self; it is more a sense of being than a knowledge of existence. There is no subjective *I* or objective *me* recognised by the organism, there is just a feeling of the integrity of the self, which is augmented by the central nervous system's ability to globalise localised phenomena in the body, such as pain and pleasure: the whole individual can feel well or ill when only a part of them is actually feeling well or ill.

Sense of self and sense of other are not directly related phenomena. Sense of other is not a product of sense of self, or vice versa; they are separate cognitive representations of the means and ends of survival and are ideationally very different. They both have their roots in the relationship between sense of not-self and sense of almost-self, but they elaborate these bases in different ways. Sense of other addresses the external differences between the organism's clonal cells and different parts of the rest of the universe; sense of self addresses the internal cohesion of the organism's cells. They both, however, rely on a central nervous system with a control node, or brain.

Brains are, themselves, very costly organs to build and maintain: the human brain, for example, takes up about 2 per cent of the body by weight, but uses about 20 per cent of the energy consumed by the body (Raichle and Gusnard 2002); for infants, the brain-to-body energy budget is over 40 per cent (Kuzawa et al. 2014). There will, therefore, always be a trade-off between an organism's energy budget and the brain's capacity to perform any cognitive task – which includes subliminal recognition of self and other. In theory, evolution should favour a minimal recognition of both self and other; but in practice the fitness advantages of a capacity can sometimes outweigh the energy costs, so the organisms who pay the energy price are more successful in terms of fitness and reproduction than those who do not. It is this simple evolutionary mechanism that drove some organisms, including our ancestors, toward the next level of cognition: awareness.

Awareness

Where sense of not-self and almost-self are autonomic chemosensory reactions that require no central nervous system, sense of other and self are cognitive processes – but they are still automatic and require no conscious attention from the organism to make them happen. Awareness, on the other hand, is a cognitive process that is all about attention. In simple stimulus–response systems, chemosensory mechanisms represent both the stimulus and its response, and the first invariably produces the second. Simple cognitive processes are more controlled and controllable, but they still rely on stimulus–response, even though the range of responses is much greater. Awareness, in contrast, introduces another dislocation between stimulus and response, creating a third way for an organism to react. A stimulus could provoke the organism into an invariant, autonomic reaction; or it could be evaluated by the brain subliminally, causing an automatic response with some variability; or it could be consciously evaluated, causing an attentional response. As humans, we like to think we are carefully evaluating our responses to all stimuli at all times, but we are actually aware of only a tiny number of the stimuli we receive (Morsella et al. 2016). This is highly convenient for us: instead of, say, trying to control the autonomic muscle interplay of walking, or the automatic process of negotiating the terrain we are walking over, we can concentrate on where we are going, or even what we will do when we get there (Arp 2007).

The presence of a complex brain means, on some level, the presence of awareness; and the amount of brain complexity is a good indicator of the complexity of awareness possible in a particular species. By this simple measure, the uniqueness of human brains in terms of relative size and complexity means there has to be something special about human awareness; but this does not mean that only humans have awareness. Contrary to what Descartes believed, we are far from being the only aware species on the planet. The rest of nature is not composed of automata, and what makes us the species we are is not a special metaphysical substance found nowhere else in nature (and, indeed, not yet identified in us). The human difference lies, instead, in a natural process of genetic and social manipulation that preferentially produces human bodies and brains; and, unlike the soul, it is a process that scientific method can discover.

Human awareness is often misinterpreted as soul-like; but it is not a substance possessed by, or produced by, the brain. It is an aspect of the way brains work – a process rather than a state. Awareness is always 'awareness of' something, it cannot exist without a focus; and, as with sensing, it is possible to be aware of both what is outside the organism and to model what is inside. This, however, raises an interesting conundrum: being aware of external objects and events gives the organism greater control over its surviving and thriving, and therefore increases evolutionary fitness; but what is the advantage of being aware of my internal mechanisms – and, particularly, my internal cognitive mechanisms? Being able to second-guess myself would seem to add an unnecessary layer of choice and delay to the decision-making process, which cannot advantage the organism: if I have already selected my response subliminally, presumably as the fittest response I can make, what advantage is there in having the capacity to change my mind? In a mixed population of deciders and ditherers, the ditherers will lose out.

The advantages of being able to second-guess others are much more obvious, and show why awareness of others is likely to have preceded awareness of self. Having a greater range of automatic responses to particular organism–stimulus contexts increases the number of strategies available to the responder; and, as long as that increase enhances surviving and thriving for the responder, it will be selected for. However, if the stimulus creator develops a wider range of alternative stimuli that plug into alternative responses (and developing this wider range does not require attention to, or awareness of, these stimuli), then the number of organism–stimulus contexts the responder has to deal with increases. And, as long as this wider range enhances surviving and thriving for the stimulus creator, it will also be selected for. For instance, the possum that first learned to play dead was able to plug into its predator's response to dead prey, and survived when its still-running conspecifics did not. This competition between range of stimulus and range of response means that members of the same species become locked into a cognitive arms race, where more strategies to anticipate stimuli require bigger brains, but bigger brains also generate more stimuli that require strategies to manage them. Matt Ridley (1993) identified this phenomenon in relation to sex and sexual signalling, referring to it as the Red Queen problem (a reference to the Red Queen in Lewis Carroll's *Through the Looking-Glass*, who had to run very fast just to stay still). It is, however, a problem that is not limited to sexual signalling; it occurs in any signalling environment where deception can happen. It is also a problem for any genetic effect that can enhance both stimulus response and stimulus production, such as increases in general cognitive capacity.

So what is the advantage of awareness for the individual, and how does that advantage make awareness valuable in fitness terms? The main fitness advantage that awareness offers is that it allows the individual to keep up in the strategy–counterstrategy competition to survive and thrive: once a single individual is using awareness to outfox its conspecifics, awareness becomes an evolutionarily fit strategy. However, the capacity to second-guess the actions of others also introduces a new, reflective and reflexive type of cognition: not only does an organism have an enhanced range of responses to others, it also has an enhanced range of responses to the responses of other organisms. It is no longer the fastest response that is most effective, it is the response with the least effective counter-response. As soon as the first glimmering of awareness appeared, the race was on, with ever-more outrageous cognitive costs being paid to keep up. As long as the fitness advantage of awareness outweighed the costs, as for any genetic trait, it was selected for; but the awareness selected for would have been other awareness, not self-awareness. As long as the self remains opaque to the self, it poses no difficulties in terms of conscious choice. So how did we become aware that we had a self? What aspect of being human made self-awareness a possibility, and what advantage did it give us that was sufficient to outweigh the disadvantage of second-guessing ourself?

Sharing information

One explanation for the origin of self-awareness is that it is an inevitable outcome of the sharing of information about relationships in our group (Edwardes 2010, Chapter 7). In production, this does not require self-knowledge, because it is all about other people; but in reception, it does. If I receive information about a social relationship in which I am a protagonist, the only way I can incorporate that information into my social calculus is to envisage a third-person view of myself, a self-as-other. This is because all the other entities in my social calculus are *theys*: identified individuals, but essentially means external to me, not ends personal to me. So awareness of self (or, at least, awareness that I am a self) is a by-product of sharing social information. As long as that sharing makes the individual fitter, the behaviour will survive and thrive; and as long as modelling myself is an inevitable consequence that does not completely whittle away the fitness advantage of sharing social information, it is along for the ride.

A secondary outcome of this awareness of self through the modelling of self-as-other is the awareness that my physical and cognitive selves are intimately correlated with that modelled self. I have a cognitive representation of a third party, which is also a representation of me: I am not only self-aware, I am aware of my own 'selfness' – that my modelled self is simultaneously a special first-person case and a mundane third-person case in my cognitive social modelling. There is a hierarchy to my self-awareness: awareness that I can be modelled by others, and awareness that I, too, can model me. This awareness of selfness is not something we are continuously aware of, but it is something that informs our relationships with other individuals: it is the *me* in 'what will they think of me?' and the *I* in 'I should'.

Sharing social information is, however, not something that appeared suddenly and holistically in our evolutionary history; it is reliant on other cognitive developments. One key development is the capacity to model others as beings with their own agendas – intentional beings rather than animate objects. To do this, we need to understand that others have minds with which they generate their own agendas;

in other words, we need a Theory of Mind (ToM). This term was first adopted by Premack and Woodruff (1978) to describe the way humans model others as intentional beings, and it can be understood as working on two levels. First, it is a theory that others have minds, so they cannot be manipulated simply by using stimulus–response sequences; second, it is a theory about the kind of minds they have, and how those kinds of minds can be manipulated by belief and expectation. Minds make decisions based on available data, so they can be biased by the type of information they possess; by selectively giving information to others, we can bias the range of responses by those others to our stimuli.

This leads us to the two major signalling dilemmas that ToM produces. The first is the sender's dilemma: why give away valuable information? If having the information advantages me, and not having it disadvantages you, why should I share it? The second problem is the receiver's dilemma: if the sender is disadvantaged by giving me true information, but advantaged by giving me false information, why should I believe the information shared? These two dilemmas do seem to dictate the limits on much natural communication, but they are not insurmountable. The answer, as with all economic dilemmas like these, is to find a condition where giving the information is more valuable to the sender than its cost, and receiving it is more valuable than costly for the receiver.

Traditionally, there are four evolutionary routes to stable sharing. The first is William Hamilton's (1964) kin-selection mechanism: I should share information with individuals who share my genes because their survival is also, in part, my own genetic survival. This mechanism explains why parents look after their offspring, and why social groupings of any species often share a close genetic history. The second evolutionary route is Robert Trivers' (1971) reciprocal altruism: I should help you today because you will help me tomorrow; and you will help me tomorrow because you will need my help the next day. If the cost to me of helping is less than the advantage to me of your being helped, and if the need for help is both random and common, reciprocally altruistic individuals will survive and thrive better than less altruistic individuals. The third evolutionary mechanism is Amotz and Avishag Zahavi's costly signalling (1997): if it is important to the receiver that a signal be true, then it is worth paying attention to the cost of the signal. Cheap signals are easily faked and unreliable; expensive signals are difficult (or costly) to fake, so are likely to be reliable. This explains a lot of signalling in nature, such as the peacock's tail, the costs of which perplexed Darwin; but it cannot help us with deliberate reduced-cost signalling, like language. Finally, the fourth route to a stable sharing mechanism is joint enterprise (Melis and Semmann 2010). If we can work together to achieve something that we cannot each achieve alone, then it is worthwhile sharing information honestly. This type of exchange is typical both in human societies, with their high degrees of specialisation, and in human language, in its conversational role; so joint enterprise would seem to play a significant role in the development of stable sharing.

These four routes to stable sharing are not mutually exclusive, and the route that humans took probably involved a mixture of them. The topic of sharing information will be examined in more detail in Chapter 3; but, for now, the development of self-awareness can be summarised in the following four steps. For whatever reason, humans became able to share social information; in the sharing of social information, we exchanged cognitive models of other members of our social group, as both senders and receivers; among the models we received there inevitably would have been models of our self; and, to incorporate these into our social calculus, we would have needed to model our self as if it were another self.

The path from sense of not-self to awareness of selfness is, in evolutionary terms, long but quite linear, as Figure 2.1 shows. Each new

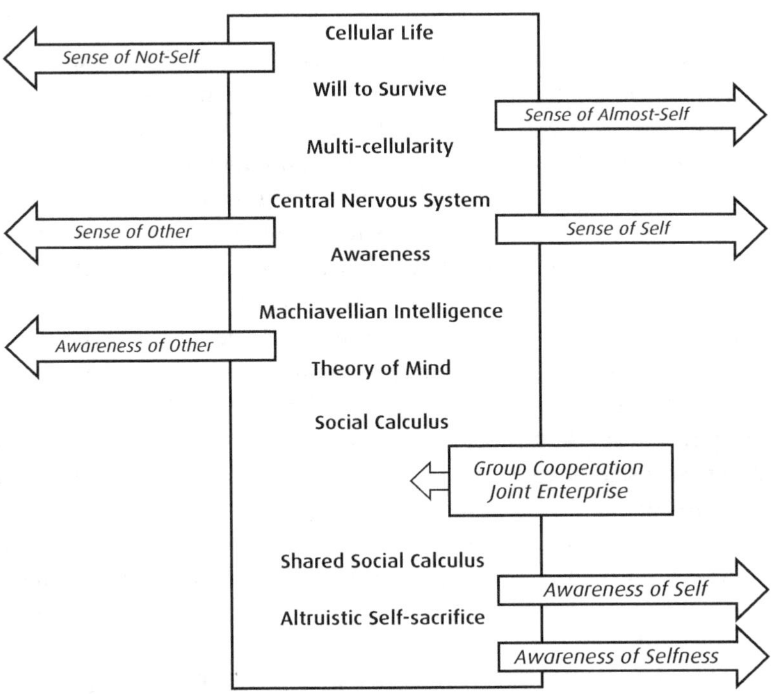

Fig 2.1 The development of selfhood

capacity develops naturally from the one before, and the senses and awarenesses of other and self emerge unremarkably from the previous capacities. The only time extra capacities were needed was at the point at which we began to share our social calculus. If there is anything special about the evolution of *Homo sapiens* then it probably occurred at this stage.

Do animals have awareness of self?

If self-awareness is a product of language, and language is a purely human capacity, can we say that other animals do not have self-awareness? The logical answer is 'yes'; but, as with all things cognitive, there is a significant 'however' to be added to that simple affirmative. We need to look at different types of awareness of self before we can say unequivocally that self-awareness does not exist in other species.

We can start with the question 'Do other animals have awareness of their physical bodies?' As we have seen, this is far from a given of being alive, and is certainly not an attribute of single-celled animals; but how complicated does a nervous system have to be before it is capable of physical self-awareness? Fortunately, we can approach this question from the other end by looking at only a small subset of animals, the primates.

In 1970, Gordon Gallup thought he had found a way to investigate physical self-awareness: he tested a small number of chimpanzees and monkeys to find out if they could recognise their own reflection in a mirror. His experiments involved familiarising his subjects with mirrors, then placing a mark on their face while they were anaesthetised and seeing how they reacted to the mark when they woke up. The chimpanzees began investigating their own faces when they saw the mark – they seemed to know that what they were seeing in the mirror was a reflection of themselves. Afro-Eurasian monkeys tended to ignore the mark, or attempted to investigate the face in the mirror – they did not recognise their physical self in a reflection (old-world monkeys were selected for testing because humans share a more recent common ancestor with them than with the new-world American monkeys). Chimpanzees who had not previously encountered mirrors did not pass the test, nor did human children younger than about 18 months old (Amsterdam 1972), but it did appear that the mirror test was identifying something significant in self-recognition.

The test has since been repeated with a range of animals, and it has become clear that mirror recognition is not even limited to mammals.

All the great apes (bonobos, chimpanzees, gorillas, orang-utans) have been shown to pass the test (de Waal et al. 2005), as have several non-primates, such as bottlenose dolphins (Reiss and Marino 2001), orcas (Delfour and Marten 2001), an Asian elephant (Plotnik et al. 2006) and European magpies (Prior et al. 2008). To complicate matters, a more recent experiment showed that rhesus monkeys can also be trained to pass the test (Chang et al. 2015). Contrary to Gallup's findings, these animals co-identify the reflection with their physical self if they are forced to pay attention to the face in the mirror and can link current sensations with current visual effects.

This does not mean the mirror test doesn't work, but it does mean we should be careful about how we interpret it. As Gallup himself has said, 'Simply because you're acting as if you recognize yourself in a mirror doesn't necessarily mean you've achieved self-recognition' (quoted in Callaway 2015). However, if the mirror test is indeed a measure of physical self-awareness (and it seems to be), then we can at least say that this capacity is not limited to humans.

How exclusively human is cognitive social modelling? This, too, seems to be a capacity we share with other animals. Dorothy Cheney and Robert Seyfarth (2007) have shown that chacma baboons (*Papio hamadryas ursinus*) maintain quite complex models of their group, allowing them to identify both hierarchies of individuals within families, and the hierarchy of families within the group. It helps that there seems to be no ranking overlap between families: the lowest-ranking individual in a high-ranking family is still higher than the highest-ranking individual in the next family down. While this social modelling is social arithmetic rather than social calculus (as it is about the relationships of others to the self rather than the relationships between others), the baboons are nonetheless able to adjust their social modelling appropriately for changes of rank both within and between families. Although social modelling has been less widely explored in other species, there are indications that great apes, dolphins, whales, elephants and some birds are capable of social arithmetic; and there are clues that they may also be capable of a form of social calculus. The similarity between the list of species capable of social arithmetic and that of animals passing the mirror test may be telling us something important about social cognition – or it may just be that these are the animals whose cognition we have studied in sufficient detail. However, the extent of social modelling beyond the human species is not something that needs to concern us here; as with physical self-awareness, it is enough to be able to say that it is not exclusively human.

So is shared social calculus exclusive to the human lineage? Here, we have something that has not yet been unequivocally detected in non-human communication. This does not mean it is exclusively human; but, until we identify the exchange of social information in other species, it seems reasonable to treat it as provisionally exclusive. Sharing social calculus requires communicative strategies that leave their mark on a communication system, and some of these we have yet to identify in non-humans – but some we *have* identified, so we cannot yet be certain either way about the exclusivity of shared social calculus.

The first of these strategies is naming, or attributing identity labels to other group members. Unlike internal social calculus, a name-label needs to reliably identify a particular member of a group to all other members of that group, so the labels must be communally shared. This type of labelling has only been reliably identified in one species of dolphin (*Tursiops truncatus*) so far: it appears that every dolphin in a pod has a signature whistle (Cook et al. 2004), and they each use that whistle to indicate their presence and position to other pod members. This signature whistle remains the same when the dolphin moves to a new group (which they do often), so it is a label the dolphin uses to identify themself, not a label given to the dolphin by each group (King et al. 2018). Even more interestingly, they also use the signature whistles of other pod members to attract the attention of those others. By itself, this does not mean dolphins are sharing social calculus, but it does indicate that this group of species is worthy of further investigation.

The second requirement for sharing social calculus is signal combinatoriality: you must be able to consolidate individuals into a group by linking their names to a particular relationship; and you must have the communicative mechanisms to bring this relationship to the attention of the listeners. To put it simply, your signal must be able to indicate two individuals and the relationship between them. So, for social calculus, combinatoriality requires both segmentation (a signal must be capable of containing more than one meaning-unit) and differentiation (the meaning-units have to represent different things – individuals and relationships). This type of combinatorial social sharing has not yet been identified in non-humans, but other forms of combinatorial signalling have. For instance, Campbell's monkeys were found to use distinctive calls for eagle or leopard predator alert calls, but they also used a suffix, the same suffix for both calls, to change their meanings to more general alerts (Ouattara et al. 2009). In contrast, the sound-units in the calls of putty-nosed monkeys seem to have no individual meaning, but the way they are combined can create warning signals of ground predators or aerial predators, or can be used to coordinate group movement to new feeding grounds (Arnold and Zuberbühler 2006).

However, these combinatorial calls may not offer sufficient proof: the interpersonal referentiality in shared social calculus is very different from that in other combinatorial signalling. In contrast to social calculus, which is explicitly about other in-group individuals as third persons, other combinatorial signals seem to reference in-group members only as receivers, or second persons, and this (except for the dolphins) only implicitly; the presence of receivers justifies the making of the signal, but the signal is *for* them, not *about* them. Other combinatorial signalling, like most signalling (including the dolphins), involves attracting attention; but any third-person reference is to out-group individuals, which can be treated as events or things rather than individuals. Shared social calculus has its origins in, and remains today, largely third-person reference about in-group individuals.

So what of the capacity to model the self – to be aware of your own selfness? Is this limited to humans? In terms of their natural social and communication systems, there seems to be no sign of awareness of selfness in non-humans; but then, because of the disadvantages that self-modelling brings for the modeller, we would expect to see it only if there were identifiable advantages to possessing it. This may be why, when we look at animals exposed to human language, we do see some indication of awareness of self: experiments in which we have tried to teach human language to non-humans have shown that, the more we expose them to a human communication system, the more humanlike their behaviour seems to become.

Non-humans using human language

From the mid-twentieth century onward, a series of scientific experiments were undertaken to teach a range of animals to use human language. The earliest experiment, an attempt to socialise a baby chimpanzee called Gua by bringing it up with a human child, was a qualified success in terms of showing an intellectual and empathic potential in the young chimpanzee, but a failure in terms of language: in the nine months of the experiment, Gua produced no language-like sounds (Kellogg and Kellogg 1933). A second, longer experiment (six years), involving a young chimpanzee but no human child, concentrated on language. This too, was a failure; the chimpanzee, Viki, mastered only four words (Hayes 1951). We now know that chimpanzees cannot vocalise like humans because they do not have the vocal equipment or muscle control to do so. For this reason, later experiments used non-vocal modes of communication.

One famous experiment involved teaching a chimpanzee, Washoe, to use American Sign Language. By the time of her death in 2007, aged 42, she knew several hundred signs and combined them to make simple messages, such as [DRINK SODAPOP], [BALL CATCH], [ROGER TICKLE], [YOU DRINK], [RED ICE-CREAM] and [HOT DRINK]. She had also passed on her signing skills by teaching her adopted son, Loulis (Fouts and Mills 1997).

Another experiment trained several chimpanzees to communicate using magnetic symbol-shapes placed on a metal board. Each symbol represented a word, while a rule that the order of the symbols on the board affected meaning provided an element of syntax. The star pupil, Sarah, was able to produce quite complex instructions (such as [MARY GIVE FIG SARAH]), and she responded to more complex instructions (such as [SARAH TAKE BANANA THEN MARY NOT GIVE CHOCOLATE]). However, some of the chimpanzees in the group never fully understood what they were supposed to do (Premack and Premack 1983).

Other species have also been involved in language-learning experiments. Bonobos (a species very similar to chimpanzees) were trained with a type of 'keyboard' – a series of symbols on a grid; each symbol represented a word, and the bonobos selected symbols to make meaningful sentences. Once again there was a star pupil, a male called Kanzi, whose output and humanlike skills continue to surprise and amaze. As well as giving and responding to quite complex instructions, he has learned how to make controlled fires for cooking and how to make stone tools, and he has taught some of what he knows to his son, Teco. However, once again, some other members of the trained bonobo team only vaguely understood the purpose of the keyboard, and some never mastered it (Segerdahl et al. 2005).

A female gorilla called Koko (Patterson and Gordon 1993) and an orang-utan called Chantek (Miles 2011) were, like Washoe, both trained in American Sign Language. When Chantek died in 2017, he had a vocabulary of 150 signs, knew how to use simple tools and, perhaps most interestingly, was able to refer to events that had happened years ago. Meanwhile, Koko, who died in 2018, apparently surpassed all the other signing apes. Her carer, Francine Patterson, claims that she could understand a thousand different signs. While it is difficult for outsiders to verify the linguistic claims, there is a tentative view that Koko did seem to be using a humanlike communication system (Genty et al. 2009).

Two other species have been involved in humanlike communication experiments. A grey parrot called Alex (Pepperberg 1999) was taught to recognise words for colours, shapes and materials, and was able to pick out items with the correct attributes ([RED WOOD SQUARE], for instance). He was also able to recognise the symbols for numbers, and was able to describe quite large groups of objects with the appropriate number symbol. Of course, Alex had an advantage that other animals do not: he could mimic human speech, and there is some evidence that he used it communicatively and conversationally.

While dogs would seem a poor source of evidence for linguistic competence, they have nonetheless proved themselves capable of linguistic innovation. Two collie dogs, Rico (Kaminski et al. 2004) and Chaser (Pilley and Reid 2011), were trained to recognise their toys by name. Rico was able to retain 200 names for items, while Chaser had over a thousand named toys. Both dogs were able to infer that a new name should be matched with a new item, and Chaser could also identify items by a type label (for example, BALL) as well as by a name-label (the over one hundred individual names for his ball toys). That is, there was a hierarchy to his cognitive labelling.

All of these experiments show that some aspects of language use are not beyond non-humans, and we should be careful about laying exclusive claim to the capacity. However, even where a particular linguistic competence has been demonstrated by the non-human, there remains an important difference between human and non-human language use: the vast majority of non-human utterances are instrumental (asking for something) rather than interpersonal (exchanging social information), and only a few are about third parties. Nonetheless, the star non-human language users, Washoe the chimpanzee, Kanzi the bonobo, Koko the gorilla and Alex the parrot, do seem to be aware, on some level, that they are a self; and, while their conversational efforts do not reveal that they are aware of their own selfness, some of their other behaviours do demonstrate an awareness of self that is not typical among their species.

For instance, Washoe maintained unusual interpersonal relationships with both humans and other chimpanzees, acting as interspecies interlocutor on several occasions. Roger Fouts also recounted several stories of Washoe's empathic responses when her human carers were injured (Fouts and Mills 1997). Although empathy by itself is not a reliable sign of self-modelling, it does mean that the empathic individual is able to model, and relate to, what another individual is feeling. Koko is famous for her interspecies associations with kittens and cats, with which she had a recognisable owner–pet relationship (Patterson 1987).

This required her to have the capacity to model herself in the novel role of carer for another species. While this may just have been an emotional substitute for her frequently expressed desire for a child, her consistently benevolent treatment of the felines implies that she does not see herself as a standard female gorilla – and that, on some level, she did see herself as a self. Kanzi maintains friendships with non-bonobo primates at the Yerkes Primate Centre where he lives. He asks for visits and takes gifts to the apes he visits, indicating that he seems to be relating to them in an unusually human way (Savage-Rumbaugh and Lewin 1994).

It is tempting to over-interpret these examples as evidence that there is no real difference between the capacities of the different ape species: we are all people, under the hair. However, there is still no evidence for awareness of selfness in non-humans, and empathy alone is not sufficient to show that it exists. Unlike humans, other apes do not seem to share their empathic concerns about others with third parties; unlike humans, other apes do not share irreal versions of the world (versions of the world that are real simply because people agree they are real, even though they know they are not real – like the value of Bitcoin); and, unlike humans, other apes do not seem to be capable of joint enterprise beyond grooming, hunting and going to war. This should not, however, cause us to compare non-humans unfavourably to humans: chimpanzees are good at being chimpanzees, and it is unreasonable to expect them to be good humans, too. The fact that they can confound our expectations in even small ways is a comment on their versatility, not on our superiority.

What is special about human self-awareness?

It seems that, while other animals may have different levels of self-awareness, only we humans seem to be aware of our own selfness (Edwardes 2014), that we are both physical objects with our own agendas and cognitive systems with recursive recognition. So what? Only peacocks have those magnificent tails; but the only reason they have them is that peahens have preferentially mated with well-endowed peacocks. Is a sense of self a similar costly signal? 'Mate with me, I can bear the costs of awareness of selfness and still survive.' Surprisingly, the attributes that awareness of selfness brings, which are mostly costs for the individual, do seem to be seen as social advantages by other humans. The individual with awareness of selfness is 'intelligent', 'enlightened', 'wise'; their behaviour is 'generous', 'social' and, perhaps most tellingly, 'unselfish'. Lack of awareness of selfness makes the individual 'ruthless', ‘unsympathetic’ or, at the extreme, ‘sociopathic’. There are plenty of examples in the modern world of what happens when we give the selfness-unaware individuals unrestrained freedom: greed may be good for the individual, but the tragedy of the commons means that if too many are greedy then everybody loses. Not only is awareness of selfness considered a good thing to have, our society seems to be arranged around it – and when we forget that, our social systems break.

This seems to imply that human awareness of selfness has driven human social evolution; but we have to remember that selfness is an emergent feature of the sharing of social models – disadvantageous by itself, but piggy-backing on the advantages that sharing gives. By itself, and for the individual, awareness of selfness is just a concomitant disadvantage of sharing social models; but for the group it provides a reliable indicator of the individual's capacity and willingness to share social models honestly – to cooperate in the tribe's information network. And this, in turn, is an indicator of the individual's capacity and willingness to cooperate in joint enterprise. Good citizens cooperate; and good citizens can be identified by their self-effacing willingness to cooperate, share and inform.

At the level of the individual, human awareness of selfness is a problem; but the things that cause it – joint enterprise and information-sharing – are just too good to give up. So the fact that it can signal the presence of the things that cause it converts it from a negative quality to a positive one. The peacock's tail display is, in itself, a *Bad Thing*, as it makes it easier for predators to catch the peacock; but because it shows the individual can bear the costs of the tail and still thrive, it becomes a *Good Thing*. Similarly, awareness of selfness shows that the human individual can bear the cost of their awareness and still thrive – and, additionally, enhance the survival of others in the group and therefore the survival of the group itself.

Human self-awareness is special, and makes us humans the peculiar animal we are; but it is not beyond explanation, nor is it in need of a special dispensation from normal evolutionary processes. We may be the only species in which the necessary prerequisites have come together, but that does not make it miraculous.

Does having an awareness of selfness mean there is a self to be aware of?

One final question we need to address in this chapter is whether awareness of selfness is awareness of the existence of a cognitive self, or an illusion caused by the existence of the cognitive self. As we saw in Chapter 1, this is a serious argument currently being pursued in a range of disciplines; and, just as the SSMH presented here deconstructs self-awareness into physical self-awareness and awareness of selfness, we need to similarly deconstruct the question of the existence of self.

This is not as complex an endeavour as it seems. The existence of physical self-awareness is not really disputed: everyone accepts that there is a physically cohesive self – despite the fact that experiments on deceptive sensation (the rubber hand illusion (Rohde et al. 2011), visual illusions (Carbon 2014), phantom limb syndrome (Giummarra and Moseley 2011) and so on) do seem to indicate that this physical self-awareness can be fooled. The big problem, however, is not with physical self-awareness, it is with awareness of selfness: if the cognitive self is a deception, is it possible to be aware of something that does not, itself, exist? There are only three possible answers to this question:

1. An individual can be aware of their selfness because there is a self to have selfness.
2. An individual can be aware of their selfness even though there is no self; they are aware of the illusion that they have a self.
3. An individual cannot be aware of their selfness because being aware is itself the illusion.

The strange thing is that the choice of answer seems not to matter in terms of awareness of selfness. Whether or not my awareness or my selfness is real or imagined, human social systems – which is the only place where my awareness of selfness has worth – continue to work. They rely on everyone accepting the selfhood of others, not necessarily their own selfhood. Just as the Catholic Church cannot be interpreted properly without acknowledging its belief in transubstantiation (the idea that the consecrated bread and wine of the communion service are, on some level of reality, really the body and blood of Christ), so human society cannot be fully interpreted without acknowledging the need for belief in the selfhood of others. The selfness of the self remains a by-product of that belief.

Yet awareness of selfness remains an important part of our social calculus. To use another metaphor, now that we have Einsteinian mechanics we know that Newtonian mechanics are fundamentally flawed, an inadequate description of the laws of physics; but we also know that they are considerably simpler to compute than Einsteinian mechanics, and, in the vast majority of cases, they are accurate enough. The logical thing to do is to use Einsteinian mechanics every time for accuracy; the sensible thing to do is to use whichever is accurate *enough*. Selfness may, indeed, be an illusion; but that does not help us when we are computing our social calculus of who is doing what to whom.

3
The Modelled Self

> '… And I haven't sent the two Messengers, either. They're both gone to the town. Just look along the road, and tell me if you can see either of them.'
>
> 'I see nobody on the road,' said Alice.
>
> 'I only wish I had such eyes,' the King remarked in a fretful tone. 'To be able to see Nobody! And at that distance, too! Why, it's as much as I can do to see real people, by this light!'
>
> (Lewis Carroll 1872, Chapter 7: 'The Lion and the Unicorn')

What is happening in this quote? Is the White King just playing with words, or does this dialogue represent an important aspect of self-awareness – at least, in language? The king asks Alice if she can see a specific thing (either of the two messengers); Alice's reply, though, is ambiguous: is she saying that she *cannot* see the specific thing (either messenger), or that she *can* see a generic thing that doesn't actually exist ('nobody')? Either way, she has not answered the king's question directly and clearly enough, prompting his counter-response about the capacity to see things that are not there.

And yet we tend to consider Alice's contribution to the conversation as normal, and the king's response abnormal. Practically and pragmatically, there is no difference in meaning between 'I don't see anybody' and 'I see nobody'. In fact, it is only when the presence of absence and the absence of presence are different states that the king's problem appears: 'I don't see any *me*' and 'I see no *me*' can be the difference between having a self you cannot identify in the current context and not having an identifiable self at all. It is this difference that lies at the heart of the modern debate about selfhood.

So which approach is right? Is it difficult, or impossible, to see my self myself, or is there no self to see? It depends, as we saw in Chapter 1, on which theory of self you start with. Is a self a collection of predictable responses that produce selfhood as an identifiably individual thing? Or is self a process of responding predictably that allows others to see you as an identifiably individual thing? And, if the second is true, does this mean that my self is an actual thing, a thing we can agree is real, or a convenient illusion?

As Chapter 2 made clear, having a self you can be aware of is problematic in evolutionary terms: it seems to reduce the fitness of the organism by allowing it to adopt some very un-Darwinian strategies. Yet not having a self does not fit well with the cultures we live in: even the most self-denying human cultures believe that the self can be called to account and punished. We may not actually have a self we can be aware of, but we still have to act as if we do! So, between these contradictions, is there a middle road that can explain both the problematic unfitness of being self-aware and the social insistence on continuous selves? The modelled self may give us just such a middle way.

How to make models of others

To discover how we make models of ourselves, we must start with our capacity to make models of others. This is a capacity that lends itself well to an evolutionary explanation, and which seems to be widespread among our fellow primates and beyond. The individual who can anticipate the actions of their conspecifics, their predators and their prey will have an advantage over the individual who cannot, and they should therefore be better at surviving and thriving (Seyfarth and Cheney 2013). Of course, an advantage often comes with some countervailing disadvantage; and, in this case, the capacity to make social models comes with the significant energy costs that the necessary enhancement of cognition requires. However, as long as the advantages of a capacity outweigh the disadvantages, that capacity will be selected for in evolutionary terms; and, as the capacity to anticipate the actions of others has become commonplace in many species, it clearly must be advantageous.

The advantages of social modelling in the predator–prey dyad are different from those between conspecifics. Between predator and prey there is an evolutionary war of strategy and counter-strategy to get an individual's genes into the future. Usually, a single strategy and a single counter-strategy define the relationship, and both are emphasised and enhanced by natural selection over the generations. While it does not involve social modelling, an example of the strategy and counter-strategy process is the golden poison arrow frog, *Phyllobates terribilis*, which is in an arms race with its only predator, the *Liophis epinephelus* snake. The frog has a skin neurotoxin that is so powerful that it can kill a human just through contact, which seems like a massive overkill (literally). However, over time, the snake (whose diet comprises largely golden poison arrow frogs) has developed a tolerance of the toxin. So the frogs with higher toxicity survive better than the less toxic, while the snakes better able to deal with the poison survive better than the less capable. This is Matt Ridley's (1993) Red Queen problem in action: in evolutionary terms, both the frog and the snake are running as fast as they can just to stay still.

The social modelling strategy, in contrast, gives humans an advantage that is difficult for both our predators and our prey to counter: the advantage of group cooperation. Because social modelling allows humans to anticipate each other's actions, both offensive action against prey and defensive action against predators can be coordinated. However, coordinated action against predators and prey is not an unusual capacity in nature, and is not limited to socially clever species: babbler finches coordinate mobbing effectively against predators (Zahavi and Zahavi 1997, 5–6) and wolves coordinate the killing of a range of prey (Baan et al. 2014). Even eusocial insects like ants and bees show a high level of group cooperation in defending against threats to their nests (Whitehouse and Jaffe 1996). It does not take a high level of cognitive sophistication to produce the social cohesion needed for tactical defensive or offensive cooperation.

Between conspecifics, though, the attack/defence arms race needs a more sophisticated competitive process, because the bidding war between a single strategy and a single counter-strategy is less efficient. For instance, the poison arrow frog has to have a tolerance to its own toxin, so its conspecifics will also have this tolerance: the toxin is useless in a competition with another poison arrow frog. For competition between conspecifics, it is better to have a range of strategies and a capacity to switch to a new strategy if the first one doesn't work. In this case, communicative strategies become more significant. For instance, one of these new strategies will be submission, a signal indicating that the losing party in a contest is giving up. As a general rule in conflicts between conspecifics, it is to neither party's advantage to continue a fight beyond victory; so it is in the interests of the victor to recognise a surrender – and, therefore, in the interests of the vanquished to be able to signal surrender.

This is an example of what Thom Scott-Phillips (2015) describes as a code model of communication: there is a signal that is advantageous for the sender to make and for the receiver to acknowledge, so the sender and receiver evolve toward each other in terms of signal and response. If the surrender is to work, though, the sender and receiver must both be able to model the likely reactions of the other party. It is important to the sender that this particular receiver will recognise and act on the signal, and it is important to the receiver that this particular sender is honest in their surrender. The reliability of the signal is founded on the intentions of the sender and receiver, so it becomes useful for both parties to be able to model each other's motivation, and to have volitional control over when to signal and how to react to a signal. This is what Scott-Phillips describes as the ostensive–inferential model of communication, which 'involves the provision and interpretation of evidence for the meaning that the speaker intends to convey' (2010, 95). Or, to put it another way, human communication is an immediate negotiation toward meaning between two people, not a slow, evolutionary negotiation of signal and response.

If a signal is volitional, however, it can be subverted. Richard Byrne (1995, 125–6) tells of an adolescent baboon, Melton, who had played with an infant too roughly. The infant, naturally, screamed for its mother; and she, with several other adults, began to chase the hapless adolescent. However, instead of trying to outrun the adults, Melton stood up and began to scan the horizon – a signal to other baboons that a predator has been spotted in the distance. The adults ceased chasing and also began scanning, looking for the threat that had cued Melton's behaviour. Melton had distracted the adults from their punishment detail with a more serious – although non-existent – threat. His behaviour could be read as a deliberate subversion of the predator signal, and a deliberate deception of the adults; or it could be read as a transferred fear reaction, causing him to adopt a pose that had helped reduce his fear in the past. Either way, the predator warning had been subverted and the adults deceived.

Melton shows us that, in primates at least, the link between the mental state and the external signal produced by that mental state is more complicated than just a simple stimulus–response system: the external signal is made only if the signaller decides (deliberately or automatically) to make it. The external stimulus has to become an internal perception, and a judgement has to be made about its relevance. This judgement may be faulty, leading to a signal being made inappropriately, even if it is not under deliberate control; but, if the sender has deliberate control over producing the signal then an extra level of deception, intentional deception, becomes possible.

This intentional deception relies on the signaller understanding, on some level, the effect the signal will have on the recipient. The signaller has to be able to model the recipient as a motivated object – not necessarily a being with its own agenda, but an object that is likely to respond to a signal in a reliable way. The signaller must also understand the advantage that the deception will give them over the recipient, and how to capitalise on that advantage. It requires the signaller to have a versatile understanding of the likely responses to the signal, and of the various ways to exploit those responses.

The ability to model others as motivated objects is not limited to humans, or even primates; it seems to be an ancient faculty, occurring in many different species (Stiles 2000). It certainly seems to be present in most mammals, and its level of sophistication in any species seems to be related to the level of socialisation in that species, not just cognitive capacity (Stevens and King 2012; Borrego and Gaines 2016). Knowing how others in your social group are likely to react to you allows you to plan your day, avoiding enemies and staying close to friends. It also allows you to map your social environment, to understand who is on your side and who is against you. However, the modeller themself does not need to be attentionally present as an entity in their own modelling – they are the unacknowledged constant with which all relationships are formed, the invisible hub around which their social model revolves.

How to make models of relationships between others

Modelling others in relation to an unmodelled self requires a simple social arithmetic, in which friends count as positives and foes as negatives. In this first-level social modelling, the individual maintains a cognitive register of their relationships with other members of their group. It is a simple and direct mechanism whereby the emotion the individual feels toward another group member *is* their relationship with that group member; so this type of social modelling does not need to be attentional. We can describe this as one-argument Relationship-A modelling, because the modeller needs to identify another individual (the 'argument', A) and remember their emotional relationship to that individual.

Relationship-A modelling is not uncommon in nature, but it is not the only type of social modelling we see. A second, more complex, level is also present in primates and some other animals. This second-level social modelling works because it enhances the knowledge that an individual has about their group, allowing them to more effectively navigate and manipulate the relationships in that group. It is sometimes equated with Machiavellian Intelligence (Whiten and Byrne 1988), although that is an extension of Relationship-A modelling in a different direction: the Machiavellian individual is able to use their relationships with others against those others. It is characterised by strategic alliances and vendettas, misdirection and misinformation, and a lack of vigilant sharing and other social rules for alpha suppression.

Second-level social modelling is quite different from first-level: it involves the modelling of relationships *between* others, which we can describe as two-argument A-Relationship-B modelling. The modeller's feelings toward each of the modelled others are not informative about the emotional relationship between those others; in fact, the modeller's own feelings can interfere with effective modelling. So, to properly understand an A-Relationship-B model, the modeller has to ignore their own emotional relationships with A and B. As well as a more complex social grammar, the modeller needs a more complex *emotional* grammar – they need to understand their emotions as meta-references, where understanding is not the same as currently experiencing the emotions (Edwardes 2010, 98–9).

A-Relationship-B modelling requires a considerably more sophisticated cognitive capacity than Relationship-A modelling: the modeller has to model others, as before, but they also have to accurately model the relationships between those others. I can like, or dislike, or fear Alf, and my emotion represents and dictates my relationship with him: what I feel directly affects my behaviour. However, the relationship between Alf and Beth is not the same as my relationship with either of them, so I cannot let my own feelings toward either of them influence my understanding of their relationship with each other. For instance, my relationship with Alf is bad, while my relationship with Beth is good; but I also know that the relationship between Alf and Beth is also good; so, if I wish to ally with Beth, I need to accommodate her relationship with Alf, which is contrary to my own relationship with Alf. This social calculus may be employed by chimpanzees and bonobos as well as humans, and something like it has been observed in other primates (Whiten and van Schaik 2007), which makes the characterisation of non-human primates as unrepentant Machiavellians seem somewhat unfair. However, A-Relationship-B modelling is considerably less common in nature than the Relationship-A modelling of social arithmetic.

Does A-Relationship-B modelling also require a new type of selfhood? Probably not. This would only be needed if the two-argument form of social calculus replaced the one-argument form of social arithmetic;

but why would it do so? The new social calculus just needs to interface with the already-effective old system, it does not need to replace it. This incremental approach corresponds with what we know about evolution (Futuyma 2015) and also with what we know about social calculus in the human brain: there seem to be at least two systems of social modelling at work, one to experience affective reactions, and one to model them (Lucas et al. 2015).

A-Relationship-B modelling has implications for ToM (Baron-Cohen 1995). This is the knowledge that others have their own minds with their own agendas, and, by adapting my actions to accommodate the agendas of others, I am able to achieve my aims with less conflict than if I ignore them. ToM also seems to allow the individual to plan their own relationships with others, based on the relationships between those others and the modeller's own relationships with them; it therefore implies a level of conscious control over the modelling process itself. In contrast, the Machiavellian intelligence of Relationship-A modelling does not need the level of awareness that we usually associate with ToM – it is all about automatic modelling of what is happening with objects 'out there', beyond the edge of the self, in a selfhood-free zone. Machiavellian intelligence is not about accommodating the agendas of others, it is about using the relationships of others to advantage the unmodelled self.

The existence of ToM in human social modelling implies that there must be a merging of the individual's Relationship-A modelling with their A-Relationship-B modelling. This allows the modelling individual to begin to treat the modelled others as subjects with their own agendas, and opens the way for enhanced cooperation and joint enterprise. These, in turn, create an environment where communicative cooperation becomes useful; and this pushes human social modelling to a new, third level, where we are sharing our models of others with those others.

Sharing models of others

To progress from a system of internal social modelling to externally communicated modelling, ToM has to become a conscious activity. We cannot share our internal models until we are aware that we are making them; and we cannot become aware that we are modelling other individuals until we can see them fully as individuals. The automatic modelling of Machiavellian intelligence is insufficient to provide us with this awareness. However, we have only primitive methods, at present, to interrogate extinct species for signs of conscious social modelling (and methods for detecting it in living species are not much better); so we cannot know with certainty when human ToM began. What we can do, though, is try to identify the mechanism that made social modelling a conscious activity, such that it could be communicated to others.

In fact, the processes of communication and awareness of social modelling are probably two halves of a single, ratcheting evolutionary effect. Early species of *Homo* are likely to have had primitive communication mechanisms based around vigilant sharing – see David Erdal and Andrew Whiten's (1994) idea that everyone in a group makes sure that everyone else is not taking more than their fair share. This process is both an external expression of internal modelling and evidence to others that the vigilant individuals are using social modelling. It is not a direct, referential signal (although the sanctioning of the greedy would be), but it is inferentially communicative: other individuals become aware that social modelling is not a capacity available just to them, it is being used by those around them. Or, to put it another way, it is evidence that other individuals in the group have intentional awareness of others. If the gains that this awareness of other-awareness gives to cooperative individuals are smaller than those it gives to Machiavellian individuals, then the species will tend to become more Machiavellian; and this seems to be the path that the patriarchal chimpanzees have taken. If, however, the net gain is the other way, the species will tend to develop a more informed social cooperation; and this seems to be the path taken by the matriarchal bonobos and early humans. Vigilant sharing does not automatically lead to sharing of social models, but it can be an important impetus in that direction.

Sharing models of others using A-Relationship-B constructs requires a complex interface between social cognition and signalling cognition. Both signaller and receiver must maintain a modelled set of other individuals in their group, and a modelled set of their own relationships with those others; and they also have to keep an attentional tally of all the A-Relationship-B constructs in their group that are relevant to them. This is a very language-like system: objects (the individuals) are associated through relationships, producing propositional, or sentence-like, meta-knowledge of the social structure of the group. To exchange these models, individuals must negotiate to sound–meaning pairings, both as name-signs to represent members of the group and as representations of the relationships between the name-signs. It seems like a problem with many levels of complexity. If neither individual has sound–meaning pairings in their own internal social modelling, how are they both able to generate them? And, even if both individuals have already created their own sound–meaning pairings, how do they merge them into a single system? Even if these two problems are solved, there remains a third: how does the single system adapt for new social group members, new relationship types, new communicators and new conventions? The process of bringing social models into communication is not a natural given, and will be discussed in more detail in Chapter 5.

Fortunately, however we got here, there is evidence that modern humans do use language to exchange social models: we, unlike all other living primates, are natural social communicators – or gossips, as Robin Dunbar (1996) expresses it. A large part of language involves exchanging social information about shared acquaintances, and sometimes about individuals known to only one of the correspondents in a dialogue. At first glance, this social information exchange appears to be highly advantageous to all parties: it creates an environment in which cheats find it difficult to prosper because their cheating can be shared by the cheated, and so become universally known by all the other group members; it allows the non-cheating group members to unite against the cheater and cooperate in sanctioning and excluding them; and it therefore rewards the virtuous and punishes transgressors. However, while this is a good description of how successful human groups organise themselves, it is also an insufficient evolutionary explanation of how we reached this position.

The problem with social communication, as Camilla Power (1998) shows, is that it is, itself, wide open to cheating. As we saw in Chapter 2, first, there is the sender's dilemma: I know something you don't know, which gives me an advantage over you; why should I give away that information, and thus my advantage, to you? Second is the receiver's dilemma: if the sender has control over the information they give me, why should they give me true information? True information costs them and advantages me, while false information advantages them and costs me; so, if it is to their advantage to lie, why should I believe any volitional information they offer me?

The sender's and receiver's dilemmas are common to all volitional signalling; but there is one further dilemma for the receiver that is a product of the particular nature of social communication: the confirmation dilemma. When a vervet monkey gives the leopard call, it is best for other vervets to act first and ask questions later; but what happens if the call is false? Cheney and Seyfarth (1990, 213–15) provide a case in evidence involving Kitui, a low-ranking older male vervet. His age meant that he was heading down the ranks, and any new male joining the group was likely to push him down even lower. This stressful existence may have made his signalling less reliable, as it did for Melton. Kitui was recorded giving a false leopard alarm call on three separate occasions; in each case there was no leopard, but there was an unaffiliated male vervet trying to join the group. Kitui's call kept the new male in one tree, away from the main group in another tree. Unfortunately, Kitui did not understand that, for the deception to be fully effective, his own behaviour should correspond with his call; his failure to climb a tree himself while calling gave the game away, and the other vervets began ignoring his deceitful calls.

From this we can see that vervets' responses to leopard calls are subject to confirmation after reaction: if they are not confirmed, then the call – or, at least, the call–caller pairing – loses its value and becomes meaningless. However, shared models of the relationships between others, unlike warning calls, are not immediately verifiable: they are mostly internalised interpretations of observed events, and rely on evidence that is usually in the past. They are also opinions, not facts, and they are heavily biased by the sender's point of view. It is virtually impossible to confirm the truth of shared social models; so why should the receiver pay any attention to them?

There are two possible solutions to these trustworthiness dilemmas. The first is that social communication is not about explicit meanings, it is about implicit meanings: it is an attempt to engage the receiver in a social activity, in the same way that grooming does. The primary purpose of sharing a social model is to build alliances: to identify whether the receiver has the same views, and therefore the same intra-group objectives, as the sender. The sender is only superficially offering their own view of a particular social relationship; more importantly, they are actually attempting to negotiate to an agreed social calculus surrounding that relationship. When a sender offers the model 'Alf likes Beth', they are inviting the receiver to participate in a negotiation toward meaning in which the sender, as well as the receiver, is open to revising their social calculus.

The second solution is that social communication does not need to be truthful to be valuable. When I offer my interpretation of a social relationship, I have to make it consistent with the social calculus you already have, if it is to be believable; and the only model I have for your social calculus is my own social calculus. So when a sender offers the model 'Alf likes Beth', they are telling the receiver more about their own relationships with Alf and with Beth than about the actual relationship between Alf and Beth. Each individual message is like a piece of jigsaw; and the more pieces the receiver has, the better their understanding of the sender's worldview (or group-view, at least) and of the network of relationships surrounding the sender. Even if a sender deliberately tries to give false information, pre-acquired social communication means that almost everything can be cross-checked; it cannot be confirmed as true or false, but a message that does not fit properly into the jigsaw is probably false.

Both of these solutions are dialogic: they work because individual signals only have value as part of a continuing social exchange. The dialogue between individuals is not comprehensible in terms of individual messages, only in terms of the whole communicative experience. The message in an utterance no longer needs to stand or fall by its correspondence with the real world. It represents only a single data point in a much larger dataset; and that dataset, in turn, relies on opinion and viewpoint, not existential truth.

Both solutions also benefit from a more complex form of social modelling, in which the receiver is able to tag each received *A-Relationship-B* model with the identity of its sender. This gives an *A-Relationship-B-by-C* form, in which the truth in a shared social model is not absolute but nuanced by what the receiver knows about the sender. This modelling is therefore hierarchical: the identity C 'governs' the natures of A, B and the relationship between them – their natures are real only in terms of C's utterance. When this new form of social modelling is shared with others as a 'C-said-A-Relationship-B' utterance, two things happen. First, the sender gains deniability over the truth of the utterance: the sender is not saying A-Relationship-B, they are only reporting C's utterance. Second, the receiver can tag this new message in their social calculus with the identity of the new sender, creating an *A-Relationship-B-by-C-by-D* form (Edwardes 2014). Sharing social models does not just enrich the receiver's social calculus, it also introduces a new level of sophistication to modelling, one that has the potential for recursive cognition – and recursive communication.

Shakespeare uses this sharing of social calculus to great effect in *Much Ado about Nothing*, in which Benedick and Beatrice change their views of each other because of two conversations that are staged by their friends so that they overhear them: Benedick overhears that Beatrice 'loves him with an enraged affection', but will not admit it (Act 2, Scene 3); and Beatrice overhears 'that Benedick loves Beatrice so entirely', but Beatrice is 'self-endeared' (Act 3, Scene 1). Both decide to act upon these staged social calculus models, believing them to be true because they were overheard; and it is their resulting alliance that brings the play to a happy conclusion.

Making models of my self

Once the gossip machine is up and running, communication itself begins to introduce new features to social modelling. Social communication relies on individuals having an awareness of the intentionality of others: communicable social modelling requires an understanding that others have minds, which means that minds are possessed by both the individuals being gossiped about and the individuals being gossiped to. The process of social modelling is, by definition, the capacity to model others, which can be managed without conscious attention; but the extra complexity involved in the communication of those models means that they have to become consciously managed. Additionally, while cognitive social modelling is completely about third-person models of other people, communication introduces an extra complication: it is possible for the sender to offer their model of the receiver to the receiver. Talking to the receiver about the speaker's model of the receiver brings to the attention of the speaker the receiver's role as listener, and the particular interest of the listener in the model being shared. Thus, the model takes on a second-person significance for the sender. This new significance does not make the model different from that of any other third-person model, but it changes the pragmatics of the communication act. Informationally, you need to tell the listener honestly what they need to hear; but pragmatically, you also need to present the information in a way that makes the listener want to hear it. Sharing models of an individual with that individual means that the model has to be subjectively comfortable as well as objectively accurate to the listener.

If this seems like a big task, consider what happens when the listener receives a model of themself. First, they have to be able to incorporate that model into their social calculus; and the only way they can do that is to treat the model like any other received third-person model: they have to model themself as a third-person entity in their own social modelling. Second, and more significantly, what the listener has received is somebody else's third-person model, which happens to co-identify with their own model of themself; except that, in the pre-communicative unshared state of social modelling, there was no need for a consciously available model of themself. So the received model is simultaneously the only conscious evidence that the individual has about themself, and a second-hand opinion. It is likely that, as the individual adds more third-person models to their self-model, they will begin to develop an awareness of themself as a first-person entity. However, this is an awareness of an amalgam of other people's third-person models. We each end up with a certainty that we have a self, but the self that we have is actually a model, and not a true awareness of a real self. We are back to the position of Metzinger, Wegner, Nørretranders and Hood (see Chapter 1), that there is no actual self behind the modelled self that we insist is us. So when we make a model of ourself, do we not see anybody, as Alice believes? Or do we see nobody, as Alice says?

This awareness of self, regardless of how inaccurate or irreal it may be, does generate an important new cognitive awareness: that there is a personal self to be had. Awareness of the modelled self, and awareness that it is a model, generate the awareness that I have selfness –a *me*-ness, a *myself*-ness and an *I*-ness.

Me, myself and I

As we saw in Chapter 1, Freud asserted that we all have three selves: the id, a largely subliminal self that enacts all the basic instincts of being human; the super-ego, the conscious self which enacts all the social and cultural activity of trying to be the best human we can be; and the ego, which enacts all the aware cognitive activity of being human, and which tries to choose the best path between the demands of the id and the aspirations of the super-ego. For Freud, none of these were modelled selves, they were all real; but, while the id clearly has no awareness of itself, the super-ego seems to be aware of itself as a social entity, while the ego is aware of all three selves. We now recognise that this image of the individual at war with itself is a useful metaphor for many psychological disorders, but it does not reflect the reality of the psychologically well-ordered person. It is little wonder that this definition of selfhood led Freudian psychologists to see psychological disorder everywhere.

Language, like Freud, gives us three views of our selfhood: the subjective *I*, which instigates activity; the objective *me*, the recipient of activity; and the reflexive *myself*, the *me* as visualised by the *I*. This linguistic representation also reflects how our self-modelling works: the subjective *I* makes a model of the objective *me* to generate the reflexive *myself*. We may feel that, like Freud's id, the subjective *I* provides a subliminal basis for selfhood; but the linguistic view means we can also step outside the model to view all three as irreal, consciously represented models, with the objective *me* being a model made by a model, and the reflexive *myself* being a model of a model made by a model. As with all words in our language, the first-person pronouns *me*, *myself* and *I* are metaphors for realities. Usually, the realities represented by words are external to the person generating the words; but in the case of first-person pronouns they appear to be internal realities. This, however, is just another feature of the selfhood illusion: first-person pronouns are functionally external in that they are models of internal reality projected onto the real world. Modelling is always a cognitively internal activity, but its products are externalised; which is what allows us to see our models as models of *something*.

Our relationship with our pronouns is complex. For Émile Benveniste (1970 [1996]), there is an important attentional difference between the different persons: the third person represents an object outside the communicative act, so is fundamentally different from the first and second persons, which are inside the communicative act; and the first person itself creates a subjectivity in language, allowing the speaker to simultaneously represent themself as the subject, or ego, of an utterance and the producer of it (Benveniste 1958 [1971]). It also seems that there is a significant difference in usage between *me* and *myself*, at least in terms of what is being modelled. Usages of *me* and *myself* in the constructs *I love/like/dislike/hate me/myself* seem to reflect the distance of the model from the self: *me* is, relative to *myself*, more loved and liked than disliked and hated by *I*, and more loved and liked in the present tense than in the past (Edwardes 2003). James Pennebaker (2011) shows that the way we use our pronouns (and other small function words) can also be a window onto our personality and intentions. For instance, how frequently we use first-person pronouns is an indicator of how formal we are being – in the terminology used here, how formal we want our relationship with our conversation-partner to be. In formal discourse, we model our own self more as a remote *myself* and less as a familiar *I*, and we model our conversation-partner as *they* rather than *you*. The whole conversational model has been moved a step back from intimacy by depersonalising the models of the speaker and listener. The role of pronouns in selfhood will be further explored in Chapter 6.

These are just some of the ways in which language is both the progenitor of conscious selfness, and acts to define how we model our own selfness and the selfhood of others. Selfness exists because we began to share our cognitive models of others, and then had to deal with the cognitive complexity that sharing produced. *Me*, *myself* and *I* are the products of a highly cooperative communication strategy overlaid on a sophisticated pre-existing other-modelling capacity.

Awareness of selfness: for humans only?

The fortuitous confluence of events that led to awareness of selfness in our species raises an important but often glossed-over question: why has it only happened to humans? The answers we can give to this question are helpful in defining us as a species, and in understanding the nature of our differences from other species. So what answers are we able to give?

It turns out that the view of language as a Great Leap Forward in evolutionary terms (Smith and Szathmáry 1999) may not be as justifiable as we once believed. Language is not the pot of gold at the end of the cognitive developmental rainbow; instead, like all species-specific traits, it opens up new ways of being by closing down other ways that still work effectively for other species. The cognitive developments that led to language and awareness of selfness bring problems as well as solving them.

The first big disadvantage lies in cognitive development itself: as discussed in Chapter 2, having a big brain is incredibly costly, consuming about 20% of the human energy budget (which means that every fifth doughnut goes straight to the brain and not to the hips, as some dietary pundits would have us believe). This disproportionate energy consumption is not caused by complex or conscious thinking, however; our brain's energy usage seems to remain the same whether we are awake or asleep, solving quadratic equations or daydreaming, modelling complex interpersonal relationships or gazing at clouds. The energy consumption is not caused by how we think or what we are thinking about, it is simply a product of maintaining the big brain itself; it is the Red Queen, running as fast as she can just to stay still.

Yet the role that this big, expensive brain plays in our species remains opaque. Clearly there are some types of complex thinking that our species needs to do; but what are they? If we look at many other large-brained species (such as cetaceans, other apes or elephants) we find that, like us, they are highly social; so is the evolution of big brains associated with social living in large groups? Robin Dunbar (2010) thinks this is the case, and points to a correlation between brain size and group size, a correlation that seems to approximately work for most primates. However, the correlation breaks down when applied as a general evolutionary rule: the most social animals on this planet are eusocial insects (ants, bees, wasps and termites), which can live in communities numbering tens of thousands; yet their individual brains are tiny. At the other extreme there are many species of octopi: clever, problem-solving animals with relatively large brains but no social life to speak of. Other than territorial aggression, the only same-species communicative act in the life of an octopus is an act of coitus, which is followed by death for both sexes – within weeks for males and within months for females (Godfrey-Smith 2016, Chapter 8). So whether group size is proposed as the driver for brain size or brain size as the driver for group size, there seem to be significant examples in nature arguing against both positions. Additionally, while Dunbar predicts a human group size of 150 based on brain size, human joint enterprises can involve much larger groups without clearly demonstrating the group fission that Dunbar predicts. It seems that, somehow, humans have sidestepped the group-size limits, just as they seem to have circumvented the natural limits on brain size and communication complexity.

The products of the large brain are even harder to justify. We have already seen the communicative problems involved in a volitional communication system like language: the sender's problem of sharing information that is actually most valuable to them when only they know it; and the receiver's problem of trusting information that is most valuable to the sender when it is a lie. When a communication system becomes volitional, it should collapse into meaninglessness, not transform the species' socio-cultural organisation.

These problems are insignificant, though, compared to the socialisation problem: if bigger brains make for bigger groups, or vice versa, what is the fitness mechanism that favours bigger groups? Large groups face more challenges than just the socio-cognitive need to keep track of more individuals; there are the problems of environmental load-bearing, fission–fusion and shared enterprise, all of which also have to be overcome. The environmental load-bearing problems are: first, that larger groups will exhaust local resources much quicker than smaller groups, so they need to be more mobile than smaller groups; second, that larger groups will exhaust larger territories, so will have to move further to escape their own depredations; and third, that a species with a small number of large groups is more vulnerable than a species with a large number of small groups to epidemics that wipe out whole groups. The fission–fusion problems are: when a group exceeds its maximum size and has to split, there have to be enough individuals in both new groups to ensure their survival; and when two small sub-optimal groups meet, they need to have strategies to help them join together to make a more optimal group. The shared enterprise problem is: the larger the group, the more enterprises there will be to be shared; but how are the individual needs and skills matched efficiently? All of these aspects of the socialisation problem can be mitigated by effective communication; but that only weaves the communication problems into the socialisation problem, making the co-evolution of large brains and large groups even more perplexing.

So if awareness of selfness relies on language, and language is a product of brain size and group size dynamics, and human brain size and group size are both difficult to explain using evolutionary calculus, then we should not be surprised if only humans have an awareness of selfness. If, in addition, we can show that an awareness of selfness is, itself, problematic in evolutionary terms, then the question changes from 'why do only humans have awareness of selfness?' to 'why does any species have awareness of selfness?' The answer to this may lie in the development of another product of language, this time from the non-personal meanings generated by negotiation: human culture.

Language, culture and the self

Human culture, like human communication, is simultaneously continuous with the rest of nature and quite distinct from the cultures of other species: it has a different approach to what counts as information – and, therefore, what counts as knowledge. Donald Brown (2004) describes human knowledge as consisting of two types of information: *etic facts*, which are true[1] by their nature but not necessarily consciously appreciated (such as 'a tapir usually has four legs; roasted tapir is good food'); and *emic facts*, which are true because we agree they are true (such as 'the tapir is the national animal of Belize; it is wrong to kill and eat tapir because they are endangered'). Etic facts are common throughout nature and, if they enhance individual fitness, can become genetic facts (for example, the fact that snakes bite and can kill has been encoded into our genome, justifying a healthy anxiousness around snakelike objects). They should not be confused with mind-independent facts: etic facts are etic because they reflect the external world, but they are facts because they are ideas commonly shared among humans.

As well as becoming genetic facts, however, etic facts can also be conventionalised as cultural facts. For instance, a link has been established in chimpanzees between self-medication with rough leaves swallowed whole and the increased expulsion of gut worms. Desmodium leaves are used by the chimpanzee group at Gashaka, Nigeria, but other leaves are used by different groups elsewhere (Fowler et al. 2007). This behaviour is cultural: different chimpanzee groups have found similar, but not identical, solutions to the same problem. However, it is also a cultural solution based on etic facts; and, because it is based on such facts, it actually works. Compare this to facts that have informed recent human medical culture: in the late 1800s, cigarette smoking was touted in Europe as a treatment for asthma, on the basis that inhaling smoke dried up the excessive mucus thought to cause asthma (Jackson 2010); mercury remained the main treatment for syphilis throughout the 1800s, until it was replaced by arsenic in 1910, and, finally, penicillin in 1943 (Frith 2012); and, even today, the biggest threat to tigers across the world is the trade in animal parts for 'medicine' (Byard 2016). All of these are emic medical facts, based on local cultural beliefs that have no basis in etic facts, or which rely on coincidences of success as evidence.

Etic facts, therefore, are not the same as natural facts, and they can include cultural facts; what they all share in common is that they do not rely on a belief system to enforce them, which means they have to be intrinsically valuable to the knower. This is in contrast to emic facts, whose worth lies in the solidarity they create in the group: they are extrinsically valuable to the knower because they help the knower navigate their society by conforming to its culture. A culture based on etic facts is qualitatively different from an emic culture; but, because etic facts do not need to be genetically encoded, non-human cultures based on etic facts can, and do, exist. However, emic facts form the basis of most human cultures. Humans are outstandingly good at creating and enforcing emic facts, basing them on agreement rather than evidence. This becomes unsurprising if we accept the proposition that human communication is itself based on emic facts: our languages work not because there is a special 'language mechanism' inside each of us, but because we are able to negotiate toward meaning. This willingness may well be genetic, but the negotiation itself requires the ability to consciously accept another person's imaginings as valid on some level. As Lewis Carroll puts it:

> 'But she must have a prize herself, you know,' said the Mouse.
>
> 'Of course,' the Dodo replied very gravely. 'What else have you got in your pocket?' he went on, turning to Alice.
>
> 'Only a thimble,' said Alice sadly.
>
> 'Hand it over here,' said the Dodo.
>
> Then they all crowded round her once more, while the Dodo solemnly presented the thimble, saying 'We beg your acceptance of this elegant thimble'; and, when it had finished this short speech, they all cheered.
>
> Alice thought the whole thing very absurd, but they all looked so grave that she did not dare to laugh; and, as she could not think

of anything to say, she simply bowed, and took the thimble, looking as solemn as she could.

(Lewis Carroll 1865, Chapter 3: 'A Caucus-Race and a Long Tale')

Like language, exchanging social models also requires negotiation toward meaning: we each accept and use the unverified models of the social relationships of others when they are offered to us, even though we know them to be emic opinions and not etic facts. This acceptance of the opinions and beliefs of others about others unlocks all kinds of useful linguistic and modelling tricks and devices, such as referencing non-current events (temporality), referencing possible but not yet actual events (modality), and using shared imagination. It also has an effect on how we model ourselves. Social modelling gives me access to what other people think (or say they think) about me, allowing me to build a model of myself as a social being. This social self-model is an emic fact, a third-person representation of my self as an entity in my social calculus; but I can treat it as an etic model inasmuch as it represents an objective view of me as an other; it's the best understanding of my self available to me.

While human culture is an outcome of human socialisation and language, it nonetheless generates yet another, and very different, self-model. With its emphasis on emic facts, human culture presents me with an ideal model of what an individual should be in the particular culture in which I find myself. It is an aspirational self-model – still external to (and different from) the Actual self (which remains unknowable by direct introspective methods), but also different from the third-person self-model provided by the sharing of social calculus (or social communication). The Cultural self is based on the emic social expectations of others rather than their mostly emic social knowledge – and, as I am a member of the same culture, they are probably expectations that I (my social self-model) have about myself.

This emphasis on emic facts in human culture creates a very odd inversion in the social strategies of our species. Like eusocial animals, we have societies with high levels of organisation, complexity, cooperation, individual specialisation, task-sharing and self-sacrifice; but where the eusocial lifestyle involves a physical culture bound by genetic imperatives, human society is governed by symbolic culture. Eusocial societies work because of the high level of relatedness in a nest and the fact that there are few fertile females – usually only one per nest. The only way for the sterile nest members to get their genes into the future is to protect the queen, their mother, and her fertile offspring, their sisters and brothers. This means that the range of cultures possible is severely limited, because they have to be based on etic realities, not emic beliefs. In contrast, the high levels of organisation, complexity, cooperation, individual specialisation, task-sharing and self-sacrifice in human cultures are all generated emically, through group expectations and shared beliefs. The correspondences between the needs of eusocial and human societies help to explain why humans seem to have adopted a pseudo-eusocial social system;[2] but, where reliance on etic facts makes the cultural range available to eusocial animals extremely small, the human range of cultures, based on emic facts, is bewilderingly large: any set of shared beliefs can become the basis for a culture.

An outcome of relying on emic facts is that, whereas eusocial cultural systems are stable and durable, human cultures are vulnerable to collapse and elimination when key beliefs are challenged. There is little durability in human cultures, which tend to last only hundreds of years rather than the millions of years for eusocial animals; but this lack of durability does have a surprising genetic effect. The constant turnover of cultures means that there is a process of succession: cultures that place a greater reliance on etic facts have a survival advantage over more emic cultures. History has shown us that cultures with greater reliance on etic facts tend to win in any competition against cultures relying on emic facts (Diamond 2005). So any genes that favour reliance on etic over emic facts become more common in etic human cultures, and the greater survival rate of etic cultures spreads those genes across the species.

One example of this process is the spread of lactose tolerance. Ingram et al. (2009) show that 13,000 years ago there was no significant ability to digest cow's milk in any adult human population. Children produce an enzyme, lactase, which lets them drink milk (from a range of mammals, not just other humans), but production of lactase stopped at puberty. However, the domestication of cattle about 12,500 years ago led to a rise in digestive tolerance of lactose, the indigestible factor in cow milk: genetic changes extended the production of lactase through puberty and beyond. The domestication of cattle happened piecemeal, as a series of local events; and the abandonment of hunting and gathering in favour of pastoralism occurred over a very few thousand years. We can therefore say that cattle domestication was a cultural event; but it enhanced group survival by providing a reliable and regular food source, so it was also an etic event. Lactose tolerance spread as an etic fact that favoured domestication, but it remains a cultural event: adult intolerance remains high in some Asian populations where milk did not become a food staple; and, across the species, two thirds of adult humans are still lactose intolerant.

Unlike lactose tolerance, however, the ideal Cultural self is a completely emic fact: it has no existence outside the minds of the members of the culture. Yet it does have one important effect on the individual: being aspirational, the cultural self-model seems to have worth as a shortcut to social self-modelling. Instead of trying to cobble together a composite self-model from the opinions about me provided by others, I can simply try to conform to the self-model that others around me treat as a cultural template for being an ideal human. A series of children's books, *The Best Me I Can Be* (Parker 2007), indicates that, far from being a poor alternative to social self-modelling, cultural self-modelling is a common view of how effective models of self are produced, and is commonly used around children. As we will find out in Chapter 4, cultural self-modelling may be an effective way to activate self-modelling in children before they develop the capacity for effective social self-modelling. The existence of fairy stories, moral tales and mythic systems in almost all human cultures indicates that sharing exemplars of cultural morality is common, while the recorded age of some of these stories indicates that they represent an ancient human tradition.

However, the emic nature of the cultural facts in these stories means that their worth is negotiable, unlike the etic social facts that social self-modelling provides. The cultural self-model is not a product of how I am seen or how I see myself; it reflects how I believe I should be. It does not provide accuracy, but it does provide acceptability.

One final feature of the cultural self-model should be highlighted: the reasons why self-modelling is a fit strategy today are different from the reasons why it was a fit strategy when it first appeared. Ernst Haeckel (1866) is famous for the statement that 'ontogeny recapitulates phylogeny', which encapsulates his belief that every human embryo goes through the same developmental forms that produced our species, from single-celled creatures through intermediate species-like forms up to modern humans. This idea, known as Recapitulation Theory, has been rejected since the middle of the twentieth century as a plausible genetic explanation (Blechschmidt 1977, 32). It also seems to be unworkable as an explanation for self-modelling. At the species level, cultural self-modelling only became possible because sharing social models led to social self-modelling; and this, in turn, established a generalised cognitive potential to self-model. Human culture, with its emic belief in ideals, then created the shared ideal self, which the individual could then own as a cultural self-model. In contrast, at the individual level, the human child initially seems to adopt the cultural self-model to define themselves, only later replacing it with their own personal self-model, which they build from their social calculus exchanges. Ontogenically, at the level of the individual, we seem to start with the generic ideal cultural self-model because it is cognitively simpler – even though, phylogenically, at the level of the species, it is an emergent feature of social calculus and language.

The disadvantages of a modelled self: deficient self and self-deception

It seems to be a common belief that the capacity to accurately model yourself is a *Good Thing*. The self-modelling individual is able to map themself into their social calculus accurately and mindfully, allowing them to manipulate their group in ways that less enlightened individuals (perhaps those still relying on a cultural self-model rather than a social self-model) cannot manage. Indeed, human history is full of comments promoting and praising this level of self-awareness: the Oracle at Delphi had the maxim 'Know thyself' over its entrance; the fifth-century BCE philosopher Lao Tzu, the founder of Taoism, said 'He who knows others is wise; he who knows himself is enlightened'; and Pythagoras said 'No one is free who has not obtained the empire of himself', to which Socrates added, 'True wisdom comes when we know how little we know about life, ourselves, and the world around us'. In Hindu doctrine, knowing your eternal self, or *atman*, is the route to enlightenment; and in more modern times, Robert Burns said 'O wad some Pow'r the giftie gie us, to see oursels as ithers see us!'; while Oscar Wilde advised against taking the cultural-self shortcut to self-knowledge, with: 'Be yourself; everyone else is taken'.

Yet, as we have seen, the only conscious representation of our self that we have available is what we have cobbled together from the social and cultural models offered to us by others. When we model our self we are modelling ourself from the outside looking in; but our unmodelled selfhood is imposed on the world from the inside looking out. The self-knowledge that language allows us is not reflexive but reflective, creating an image of our self that is recognisable and acceptable to others, and which we can then use to define and refine our self-model. This externalised vision of our self is, therefore, not so much what we are but what others believe and want us to be; it is a model of the socialised and enculturated self, a representation we advertise or aim for rather than actually are.

Social and cultural self-modelling means that we are constantly trying to meet expectations imposed on us by others: human socialisation requires us to see self-promotion and hubris as vices, while human culture promotes humility, self-effacement and modesty as virtues. We also cannot avoid comparing our own third-person modelled selfhood with the other third-person models in our social calculus, and with the ideal self that symbolic culture imposes on us – all of which means that we are always finding ourselves wanting. Indeed, the human cultural view, at least in the West, seems to be that everyone is incomplete and improvable: whatever we are, we could be better.

Several apparently unfit evolutionary strategies are generated by our self-modelling: conversational and social turn-taking, generosity to strangers, acquiescence to group norms and so on. These are all strategies that, in a Machiavellian society, disadvantage the individual by allowing others to exploit their naivety. However, these individually unfit strategies are precisely what make us successful as a pseudo-eusocial species, as they encourage high levels of organisation, complexity, cooperation, individual specialisation, task-sharing and self-sacrifice.

Our self-models even allow us to deceive ourselves about the personal value of self-sacrifice – which remains, in all cases except very occasional kin-saving actions (Hamilton 1964), inexplicable in selfish gene terms (Dawkins 1989). Honoré de Balzac (1835 [1991], 125) identified one reason why this may be so, when his character Père Goriot said, 'Some day you will find out that there is far more happiness in another's happiness than in your own': it seems that self-sacrifice has become so common that we may even get a genetically directed emotional reward from it. It is certainly encoded in our culture, where emic 'evidence' offers us rewards beyond the physical. At the end of Charles Dickens' *A Tale of Two Cities* (1859 [2000]), Sidney Carton saves Charles Darnay from the guillotine by taking his place. His final utterance, 'It is a far, far better thing that I do than I have ever done; it is a far, far better rest that I go to than I have ever known', summarises the two great emic rewards for self-sacrifice: reputation and survival after death.

It seems, therefore, that awareness of selfness – like human-sized brains or human-sized groups or human language – poses yet another evolutionary conundrum. How has a species become so unusual and apparently evolutionarily unfit without going extinct? And why, despite all these unfit aspects of our species, have we become so dominant on this planet? These are questions that will be tackled in Chapter 5; but we will first take a step back from the evolutionary improbability of our species and look at how we turn small humans into adult humans. We will review the innate mechanisms that can be activated to make us conventionally human, and the external mechanisms that we impose on trainee humans to ensure their assimilation into human societies. It is time for the nature–nurture debate.

Notes

1. The word 'fact' is used for emic and etic facts because they are not true or false in a conventionally logical way. For instance, 'elm trees are taller than oaks' is a logical proposition, capable of being proved or disproved from evidence; 'this bonsai tree is tall' is an etic fact, if particular definitions of the words 'tree' and 'tall' are accepted; 'tall trees are better' is a value judgement, which is true if people agree it is true.
2. Eusocial in its cooperation, but not eusocial in its reproduction.

4
How Do We Become Selves?

> 'I'm sure I didn't mean –' Alice was beginning, but the Red Queen interrupted her impatiently.
>
> 'That's just what I complain of! You should have meant! What do you suppose is the use of a child without any meaning? Even a joke should have some meaning – and a child's more important than a joke, I hope. You couldn't deny that, even if you tried with both hands.'
>
> 'I don't deny things with my hands,' Alice objected.
>
> 'Nobody said you did,' said the Red Queen. 'I said you couldn't if you tried.'
>
> (Lewis Carroll 1865, Chapter 9: 'Queen Alice')

Human children are unusual: we are born helpless in ways that would ensure the extinction of a less social species. We also require phenomenal levels of support and input in the early years of our life, probably more than any other animal on the planet. And, of course, as adults, we have also evolved with the complementary capacity and willingness to meet the needs of our helpless children. Throughout nature, the division of a parent's resources between itself and its offspring is the outcome of an evolutionary fitness competition. The parent–offspring conflict, a term first used by Robert Trivers (1974), determines whether a species does better by caring for its offspring after birth, or by abandoning them to their fate. If a species gets more copies of itself into the future by abandoning its offspring, fitness constraints mean that it will evolve to do so. Parental investment in each individual progeny will be small; but if this is to be an evolutionarily stable strategy for the species, reproduction has to become a numbers game. While each individual is a negligible resource cost to the parents, a new reproductive generation can only be brought about by producing young in large volumes. Survival to adulthood may be rare, but population stability can be maintained if only a fraction of the many offspring survive to reproduce.

Humans are at the other end of the parent–offspring conflict continuum. In humans, the need for extended breastfeeding usually suppresses fertility (Chao 1987), so our species reproductive rate is unimpressive: a pre-industrial-age human female was capable of bringing perhaps eight children to adulthood during her reproductive lifetime (White 2013). Larger numbers of children have occasionally been recorded in industrial cultures – Queen Victoria being a case in point – but eight seems to be the limit for modern hunter-gatherers. This slow rate of reproduction is offset by an increased lifespan that includes, for females, a post-menopausal non-reproductive stage. The extra non-reproductive time allows mothers to raise the last of their own brood or to contribute to raising their daughters' children.

This, however, is just one of the ways in which human mothers are advantaged in their reproduction; they also receive a significant contribution from their mates. Because the species reproduction rate is slow, it becomes valuable for males to defend and support their reproductive successes rather than leaving things to fate. Reproductive success for human males is not really about reproduction opportunities, it is mostly about getting offspring to the point where they can begin their own reproduction. Human mothers are also supported in their reproductive success by their pre-adult offspring, who learn their cultural and biological reproductive roles from the adults around them. This alloparenting (acting as a surrogate parent) by the previous generation, the current generation and the next allows human mothers to wean their infants relatively early (early, that is, compared to other long-lived mammals). However, the advantages for the parents of extended life and alloparenting are countered by altriciality (our young are born helpless and dependent) and an extended childhood (humans do not reach reproductive maturity until about age 16, and do not reach cognitive maturity until about age 25 – Arain et al. 2013). In the evolutionary battle for resources between parents and their offspring, human offspring seem to be winning hands-down.

If we compare human hunter-gatherer reproduction with chimpanzee reproduction, however, we can see that we are an unusual, but not isolated, case. Death from age-related conditions happens at about 80 for human females, while for chimpanzee females it is about 55. In that time, chimpanzees can bring about six young to adulthood, compared to the human eight; and, while evidence of alloparenting is indisputable in humans, there is also anecdotal evidence of chimpanzee alloparenting by other adult females, although it is less frequent: if weaned offspring are left motherless, then other mature females sometimes adopt them. Chimpanzee offspring are born only slightly more capable than human babies, but their period of helplessness is shorter; and chimpanzee childhood is also shorter, at about 11 years compared to the human 16. Evidence for the existence of a chimpanzee menopause is patchy; it seems to occur only in ancient females, sometime after age 55, and is associated with generally failing health, unlike in humans (Thompson et al. 2007).

So we can say that humans are unusual in nature, but not extreme; and altriciality, alloparenting, late onset of fertility, long life and early menopause all contribute to the unusualness of our species. Sarah Hrdy (2009) has shown that the high level of human inter-female cooperation is made possible by extended childhood, during which the young female can build a network of alliances as well as learning her parenting skills. These alliances become valuable in later life because, unlike chimpanzees, human females maintain close contact with their family groups, while human males tend to move away into other groups. This matrilocal aspect of human nature (whereby females remain with their birth-group) contrasts with the patrilocal nature of chimpanzees (whereby it is males who remain with their birth-group): there is no value for chimpanzee females in building relationships in early life, because they will be moving to other groups in adolescence. This picture is, however, complicated by power relationships. Bonobos, like chimpanzees, are patrilocal, but unlike chimpanzees they are matrifocal: females dominate in bonobo groups. It is, therefore, important for a newly immigrated bonobo female to build relationships with the existing females in the group; and practising relationship-building in pre-adolescence can help.

Although they shared a common ancestor only six million years ago, humans, chimpanzees and bonobos organise their societies in different ways, and these differences seem to be related to the environmental niches they both live in and construct. We used to believe that the chimpanzee was a good proxy for the common ancestor of all three species, but we now have evidence that, genetically (Prüfer et al. 2012) and physically (Diogo et al. 2017), bonobos may resemble the common ancestor better than chimpanzees; in which case, the common ancestor species – and early humans – are likely to have been more matrifocal than we have so far believed. However, the existence of three very different social models in three very closely related species does show how social differences can, over a number of generations, have major effects on the behaviours and genome of a species.

Power and Aiello (1997) have linked the social features of human reproduction with two genetically based human traits: concealed ovulation and ostensive menstruation. They propose that the usual signal of 'fertility now' (ostensive ovulation) used by most primates was replaced in humans by 'fertility soon' (ostensive menstruation). This encouraged males to mate-guard their females and led to longer-term male–female bond-building. It may also have been accompanied by synchronised female fertility (all females in a group come into oestrus at the same time; Power et al. 2013), which makes it difficult for a single alpha male to dominate breeding, and further encourages non-alphas to selectively mate-guard. Eventually, this led to a human culture in the Palaeolithic in which matrilocality created matrifocality and matrilineal inheritance; and the most successful males were those who worked with, and accommodated, females – not those who tried to dominate (Boehm 1999). Human females called the reproductive shots, creating a symbolic culture that probably shared many features with Chris Knight's (1991) model of a Palaeolithic matrilineal human culture.

The effect of altriciality, alloparenting, late fertility, long life and menopause in human evolution laid the foundations for a childhood in which learning and teaching are significant factors. Most species' childhoods are a matter of supplementing their genetic capacities with osmotic learning from those around them (osmotic learning involves no direct teaching, so things can only be learned if they are noticed and attended-to by the learner). In contrast, human childhoods involve the constant presentation of new skills and challenges to the child, with active interventions by adults to ensure learning happens in a timely and appropriate way. How children learn is a vital topic for humans, and we are constantly reviewing our models and theories of how human babies become human adults; and particularly how human children develop language and selfhood.

The developing child: traditional approaches

Human childhood is unusual, because we enter it in an underdeveloped state, and because it is so long; but these two features do mean we are eminently trainable. Our underdeveloped brains are ready to be moulded by our experiences as well as by our genes; and our extended childhood gives us the time to pick up skills and culture in a credulous way, before the reproductive demands of adulthood impose their own realities (Sisk and Zehr 2005). Is the unusual nature of our childhood the reason why we, and maybe no other species, are able to develop a sense of selfness, an ability to objectify our own existence? And, if selfness develops as we mature, then what kind of selves are we when we are born?

No scientist today would say that our mind at birth is a blank slate, as John Locke (1689 [1836])[1] is supposed to have described it; we come into the world with an in-built set of behaviours that make us human babies and not chimpanzee or bonobo infants. It does seem, however, that those behaviours include the expectation of a long period of nurturing after birth, a service that adults around us are usually able and willing to supply. This nurturing means that, when we consider human childhood, we are looking at it from inside our own nurtured experiences; and these, in turn, were produced by the trilogy of our parents' natural desire to nurture their offspring, the cultural expectations placed on our parents by their own nurtured childhood and the cultural self-models we are offered as we grow. Human childhood relies on the pre-existence of human adulthood, which is a product of human childhood; and this leads to a chicken-and-egg problem of how both ends of the fitness equation evolved simultaneously.

If we follow childhood through its stages, we can begin to understand how human adults are made out of human children. Even here, however, where evidence is plentiful and current, the process of childhood has, until recently, remained largely theory-based and not information-based. The two best-known traditional theories of childhood came from people with very different ideologies: Jean Piaget and Lev Vygotsky. Both were born in 1896, but their observations on human childhood produced markedly different views on what it means to be a child, and, indeed, what it means to be a scientist who studies children.

Piaget was born in Switzerland to an academic family, and spent most of his life in France and Switzerland, working as a career academic. He lived to be 84 and, at his death, his theories formed the core of many educational methods in the West. In contrast, Vygotsky was born in Tsarist Russia, but lived most of his adult life in the Soviet Union. His academic career was, in its way, as promising as that of Piaget, but it was affected by two events. First was his contraction of tuberculosis (TB), probably during the German occupation of West Russia from 1915 to 1918; this meant his academic life was interrupted several times by prolonged bouts of illness, and TB caused his early death in 1934, aged 37. The second event was the Soviet revolution of 1917 to 1920, which meant that Vygotsky's theories suffered from an unofficial embargo by the West on any product of communism. Contemporary Russian scientific texts were, by default, considered unworthy of the effort of translation: they were seen as politically biased at best, and at worst mere propaganda.

Piaget's ideas on education only became influential in the 1960s, when the efficacy of the late-Victorian educational model (based on rote-learning, memorisation, regular testing, punishments rather than rewards and convention over invention) finally began to face informed challenges. Piaget (1959) had recently published his own ideas on how children develop through childhood, including his educational proposals based on those ideas. He saw the development of the child as occurring in four stages:

- In the sensorimotor stage, from birth to age 2 years, children experience the world through movement and their senses, and they learn about object permanence. The language they use is basic: they identify objects by naming, and use some simple object–action constructs that have no syntactic regularity.
- In the pre-operational stage, from ages 2 to 7, the child acquires semiosis (sign-meaning combinations) and attentional awareness. Initially, they can only take an egocentric viewpoint ('I am the only self in the universe'), but during this period they develop the understanding that other viewpoints exist. Their language becomes more complex, allowing two- and three-argument forms, but it is still not fully conversational; the skills of turn-taking and building a dialogue through negotiation toward meaning are still underdeveloped.
- In the concrete operational stage, from ages 7 to 11, children begin to think logically about concrete events – things they know or feel to be real. At this stage, language is complex, analytical and conversational; but it does not yet involve metacognition: there is little or no thinking about their own thinking.
- In the formal operational stage, after age 11, the child develops abstract reasoning. This permits full language and the development of the interpersonal skills needed for adulthood.

In the 1960s and 1970s, several national educational systems across Europe began to use versions of the Piagetian approach. For instance, Finland adopted an unusual three-level model (pre-school to age seven, comprehensive school to age 16 and voluntary vocational school to age 19), still in place today. It has no formal streaming based on skills or IQ; and it is now considered one of the best systems in the world. France and Germany have similar systems, although pre-school ends at age 6, and schooling is divided into two age cohorts, up to 11 and beyond 11. Germany also has some skills-streaming beyond age 11. The UK and the USA maintained their old Victorian principles of bringing children into the state school system at age 5. They also test and stream pupils by IQ (rather than by skills) at age 10–11, and (in the UK) encourage subject specialisation after age 14, and again after age 16. Both of these systems are also increasingly succumbing to an apparently Anglo-Saxon preoccupation with testing and streaming: in England, testing occurs at ages 6–7 and 10–11 (SATS tests), 13–14 (streaming tests), 15–16 (GCSEs), 16–17 (AS-Levels) and 17–18 (A-Levels). Other than Finland (and, possibly, Singapore), no Western national education system can be said to work consistently better than the others; the key factors in the success of a national system seem to be logistic (that is, money spent and the level of bureaucracy imposed) and not ideological.

In contrast with Piaget, Vygotsky's work was not published in the West until the 1980s, and the publications have become an area of controversy all of their own: there are disputes about whether the works published in English reflect the original Soviet texts, and whether the Soviet texts reflect the original thinking of Vygotsky. His key work on childhood (1934 [1986]) is actually a collection of papers and writings put together by his students after his death; so, even if it remains true to Vygotsky's vision, it is not something he intended to publish in that form. However, its English publication occurred at just the time that doubts were being expressed about the Piagetian approach, a timely coincidence. Max Planck said that 'science advances one funeral at a time', and the death of Piaget in 1980 certainly removed the unquestioning academic seal of approval that seemed to have developed around his theories. In the search for new paradigms, Vygotsky's ideas seemed to offer a viable alternative, and they had what was seen as an added advantage in the 1980s: they came from a non-Western source.

Vygotsky's theory divides childhood into two halves. He called the period up to age 2 the pre-linguistic stage, and everything after became the linguistic stage. This corresponds, in terms of developmental timing at least, with Piaget's division between the sensorimotor stage and the preoperational stage. But, while the sensorimotor and pre-linguistic stages in the two models are broadly comparable, Vygotsky's single linguistic stage is considerably different from Piaget's multi-stage model of the rest of childhood. Where Piaget saw learning as biologically incremental, Vygotsky saw it as culturally incremental: he viewed what is learned after age two as socially driven, not developmentally driven. Vygotsky described learning as happening in a Zone of Proximal Development (ZPD): each piece of learning dictated what could be learned next, and it was pointless trying to hurry or subvert the process by teaching ahead or outside of the ZPD. This process has been described as scaffolding, a term first used in 1976 to describe the more focussed activity of tutoring (Wood et al. 1976) but never actually used by Vygotsky.

Both Piaget and Vygotsky treat language learning up to age 2 as driven by instinct, while after that age it is driven by the ego-free mechanisms of either genetic imperatives or social conditioning through cultural self-modelling. Neither seems to see a role for the child in their own learning: there is no place in either theory for the child to negotiate toward meaning. Yet, if language is involved in the process of creating a self (or selves), there has to be input from the child.

The developing child: modern approaches

More recent studies that have looked at the development of the self in childhood seem to support the idea that the child plays a role in building their own ego. Even before the age of 2 they are learning about interpersonal relationships and engaging with their world through their carers; but it is at around the age of 2 that ego-building, self-awareness and awareness of selfness begin to take off. One symptom of this has long been recognised as *the terrible twos*, when the child begins to assert their own agenda of wants; and it is unlikely to be a coincidence that this is also the time when they develop a communicative competency sufficient to express those wants. However, this does not tell us whether it is egotistical desire driving the appearance of language, or language permitting egotistical desire. We can look at studies of childhood development to answer this.

In 1970, Walter Mischel wrote of experiments he had conducted on children's capacity to defer immediate reward for future gains (Mischel and Ebbesen 1970). He offered children aged 41 months to 66 months the choice of a marshmallow now or two or more marshmallows (or cookies, or pretzels or other edible treats) after a period of waiting. The child was sometimes told the length of the waiting time, and sometimes just told there would be a wait. The experiments are now grouped under the title of The Marshmallow Test (Mischel 2014). Mischel found that the capacity to wait for a reward was a product of three things: what the child was encouraged to think about during the wait, the presence of distracting objects and the visibility of the rewards. Varying the size of the delayed gratification or the period of delay did not seem to be particularly significant. However, a follow-up study 40 years later (Casey et al. 2011) found that the children who were able to delay gratification in the original tests tended to be more self-controlling and able to moderate their emotions as adults.

Sarah Brewer and Alex Cutting (2001) carried out similar experiments in 2000 for the UK Channel 4 TV series, *A Child's World*, but with a slightly different question in mind: how and when do children learn delayed gratification? They tested 2-year-olds and 4-year-olds to see what differences there were in their decision to delay gratification and their capacities to wait. The experiment was slightly different from Mischel's in that they offered the children a piece of chocolate now or a bar of chocolate (six pieces) in ten minutes. They found that 2-year-olds were much more likely to opt for one piece now – although some went on to lobby for the whole bar as well as the single piece! By contrast, 4-year-olds were willing to wait, although they filled the time differently: as Mischel had earlier found, the girls tended to distract themselves by singing or engaging in other activities, while the boys tended to distance themselves from temptation by moving the chocolate away, or moving away from the chocolate.

What do these experiments tell us about children? The first, and most important, point is that human children do not think in the same ways as adults. There are processes of cognitive change and learning going on throughout childhood, altering the child's perceptions of self and time. The second point is that young children do not have an innate sense of time on which to build a concept of delayed gratification: this is something that develops, or is learned, with age. The third point is that humans are individuals, even as children, and personality traits can be relatively stable through a lifetime.

Another set of experiments on childhood social cognition are the Sally-Anne tests, originally designed by Baron-Cohen et al. (1985) to identify children's capacity to model what others are thinking. The children were presented with a story (or sometimes took part in the story) scripted as follows:

> There are two dolls, Sally and Anne, and two containers, a basket and a box. Sally puts a marble in the basket and leaves the room. Anne moves the marble from the basket to the box and leaves the room. Sally comes back for the marble. Where will she look for it, in the basket or in the box?

While typical 4-year-olds will say 'in the basket', correctly modelling that their knowledge is different from Sally's, 2-year-olds and older autistic children will say 'in the box', modelling Sally's knowledge as the same as their own. A second version of the test was used by Perner et al. (1987) to test the comparison between self-belief and other-belief at ages 3–4. They divided their subjects into two groups by age: 3–3.5 years; and 3.5–4 years. The test used the direct knowledge of the data subjects themselves, rather than their models of what dolls knew, and it was scripted as follows:

> The subject is shown a Smarties tube and asked what they think is inside the tube. They usually say 'Smarties', and they are then shown that the tube actually contains a pencil. The subject is then told that another child (whom they know and who is a similar age) will be coming in, and the subject is asked three things: what they remember being in the tube (a pencil); what they originally thought was in the tube (Smarties); and what they think the new child will think is in the tube.

The accuracy of all three responses was greater for the older age group, but the responses indicated something significant about children's capacity to attribute false belief. For some of the younger group, there was a marked difficulty in expressing the idea that they themselves could be mistaken: they insisted that they originally thought the Smarties tube contained a pencil rather than Smarties. Not only did they have the expected difficulty in attributing their former false knowledge to another, they also had difficulty attributing it to their former self. It was as if an idealised cultural self-model, in the absence of an effective social self-model, were dictating the nature of both the present and past modelled selves. This difficulty was noticeably reduced for the older group.

The Sally-Anne and Smarties Tube experiments have been repeated many times and with many variations, but the results all point in the same direction. First, children below age 4 tend to have difficulties understanding that others may not have the same knowledge as they do: it is as if, for these children, there were a single gestalt mind in the universe, so if they know something then everyone knows it. Second, the idea that the knowledge of the self-now can be different from that of the self-then is also difficult for children under the age of 4; there is a 'nowness' to their knowledge that makes their self-image impervious to error. Third, there is a developmental or learning trajectory behind understanding false beliefs; typical children develop an understanding around age 4, but false beliefs can remain problematic long after age 4 for some individuals on the autistic spectrum.

All of these experiments are about the particular version of ToM that humans are able to develop: the capacity to model others not just as intentional beings but as beings with their own agendas and models. We are not born with a ToM, it is something we build through exposure to other people. Initially, we have limited needs and few wants, and if we survive it is through the provisioning of our needs by our carers. We have no use for an id with its own agenda; our agenda is met by those around us (and if it is not met, there is little we ourselves can do to remedy the situation). Around the age of 2, our innate sense of autonomy – the survival instinct, if you wish – begins to encounter resistance from our caregivers, causing us to learn how to push back. Our language skills begin to take off, our self-serving capacity to deceive begins to develop sophistication, and our other-modelling skills develop depth – we begin to understand other individuals better – and breadth – we begin to understand interpersonal relationships. Unfortunately, the only effective tools we have available at the start of this journey are our emotions, hence the temper tantrums described as the terrible twos. When these don't work, however, we begin to expand our alternative communication strategies (evidential persuasion, non-evidential nagging, stubbornness, acquiescence and so on), and our argumentation skills begin to take off. What is driving an increasing communicative engagement with the other humans around us is our ego-based desire for social inclusion through cooperation and language acquisition.

Simon Baron-Cohen (1995, Chapters 4–5) takes the view that ToM is something that develops as we grow, not something we are born with. He proposes that children are born with two basic interpersonal detectors, which develop through the first 9 months of life as the first two steps on the path to a Theory of Mind Mechanism (ToMM). With the development of the first detector, the Intentionality Detector (ID), the child begins to model the desires and goals of others: if an object moves to avoid things or to achieve things, it has intention. Developing soon after the ID is the Eye Direction Detector (EDD), the ability to understand what another person is looking at and why they may be looking at it. It could also be described as an Attentionality Detector, discerning another's desires and goals from what they are interested in. These two detectors each give what Baron-Cohen describes as dyadic representation: the representation of another as an *object* with *intentions*. However, their real strength begins when, from 9 to 18 months, they combine together in what Baron-Cohen calls the Shared Attention Module (SAM): the SAM generates the capacity to understand triadic relationships between the agent, their goal and the self as observer. The child becomes aware of the observational role they play in understanding the objects and intentions around them, but they also become aware that the other is an individual who may not share their intentions. SAM sets the stage for ToMM, allowing Baron-Cohen to say that ID, EDD and SAM make ToMM. The development of ToMM is slow, however, and it takes another 30 months (until age 4) to reach basic effectiveness.

ToM continues to develop throughout most of our lives (if we let it), mapping our relationships onto our social environment in increasingly complex ways. As babies we have no need for a concept of ToM, and as infants we are interested only in subverting the agendas of others to meet our own needs. However, by age 4 we are beginning to understand the peculiarly human social aspects of ToM: if I accommodate the needs of others and work with them, then we can both gain; but if I continue to act selfishly when most others are being reciprocally accommodating, sanctions will be imposed on me to restrain or reform my selfish agenda. In terms of interpersonal social modelling, we become much more aware of the need to negotiate our enterprises – not just on an ad hoc basis but systematically throughout our life. In terms of self-modelling, we become aware that successful negotiation involves an honesty reliant on accurate models of both self and other, and that our cultural self-model is not really up to the task. An outcome of these new awarenesses is that our social calculus and social self-modelling become a complex, perpetually on cognitive relationship with the universe; we begin to comprehend the relationship between the other minds out there and our own mind.

The developing child: deception

Our capacity for deception also becomes more subtle from age 4 onward. We begin to understand that some of the nostrums we have been offered in early childhood concerning truthfulness are advisory rather than absolute. We learn about opinion, that it is possible for someone to believe they are right when we believe otherwise; we learn about white lies, that sometimes the truth is neither productive nor appropriate; we learn about meta-realities, that some things can be believed in the absence of, or even despite, evidence to the contrary; we learn that we ourselves can believe these meta-realities, and that our local culture may require us to do so; and we learn that if you go by what is actually said then language is overwhelmingly deceptive, but if you negotiate toward meaning then language becomes overwhelmingly honest. As Ursula Le Guin (1969) expresses it, 'I talk about the gods, I am an atheist. But I am an artist too, and therefore a liar. Distrust everything I say. I am telling the truth. The only truth I can understand or express is, logically defined, a lie. Psychologically defined, a symbol. Aesthetically defined, a metaphor.'

We negotiate toward meaning not just with every utterance we make; we are in a constant negotiation toward social meaning, which dictates the level of our acceptance into the social groups and mechanisms around us. Deception becomes less a matter of deceiving and more a matter of modelling meta-realities that differ from our own, so that we can share in them. Indeed, we may define our social limits on deception by the meta-realities that surround us. Santos et al. (2017) showed that heavy exposure of a child to what is known as 'parenting by lying' can result in an adult more willing to lie themselves.

Brewer and Cutting (2001, 73–6) conducted a hand-hiding game experiment with children of different ages. The adult hides a coin in one hand and then offers the child the choice of two closed hands to guess where the coin is. Correct choice is a matter of chance; but things get interesting when a younger child of about age 2 is invited to offer the same choice to the adult. The child will offer two open hands, or one open hand (with or without the coin). Their logic appears to be: 'I know where the coin is, so everyone must know where the coin is, and deception is impossible'. The child does not have full ToM, so the idea that there might be a knowledge of the universe different from their own is beyond them. There is no understanding that they own their own knowledge, so no concept of their own mind, or of self-modelling. Slightly older children (about age 3) have the rudiments of ToM and offer two closed hands; but they often try to misdirect by telling the adult the coin is in the wrong hand, or they shouldn't look in the correct hand. Their art of deception may be inexperienced and ineffective, but they now understand that there is more than one mind in the universe. However, their approach to the task indicates that, for them, it is still a pastime with no competitive element: there is no developed model of the self to 'win' or 'lose' the choice. Even at age 8, children often have particular body language that they use when they lie, giving away the fact they are lying: for example, they may fidget in a particular way, or refuse eye contact. Effective deception requires both an effective model of the person in front of you and an effective model of your self. Cultural self-modelling does not provide us with an etic enough model of the self to help us to lie effectively, and it is only as we approach puberty, having built an effective social-self-model, that we begin to lie well.

Our social calculus becomes more sophisticated as we master deception and its detection, and therefore become more competent in our negotiation toward meaning. The models we make of others come to include their intentions and beliefs, the model we make of ourself becomes more nuanced and less monolithic, and our knowledge of the relationships between our modelled self and others turns our social calculus into a network of what-ifs. Our modelling becomes truly modal: it is no longer just a representation of what is likely to happen in an X-therefore-Y Darwinian logic. We now become able to model the impossible, Y-despite-never-X. Compared to that formulation, the unlikely – possibly X-therefore-Y and X-therefore-possibly Y – are simple to model.

By the time human children enter adolescence, they are usually accomplished modellers and competent liars. They can model the minds of others, not just as agentive beings but as intentional beings who can also model. They can model themselves as third persons – and, therefore, as intentional beings. They can use language not just as a meaning-exchange system but as a meaning-making system; and they can share any meanings they wish to make by negotiating toward meaning. They can persuade by making use of other people's what-ifs to skew the meanings being negotiated: they can flatter, cajole, frighten and inspire. They can understand the relative and contextual worth of truth, and use it appropriately. In short, the childhood exposure to language has changed the child from *Homo credulans* to *Homo sapiens*. It is not the innate presence of language that makes us the apes we are; it is the continuous use of it in childhood that changes how we can think and work with other people: through the process of languaging, the innocent human child becomes the political adult.

Timescales for self in childhood

What does it feel like to be a human baby? If we are honest with ourselves, then the answer has to be that we can never know. It is a state we have all lived through (we were all born and went through the same stages of helplessness); we can imagine how a baby must feel (we have all encountered the idea of babies, even if we have not met a real one); and we can even attribute our today-me feelings about being a baby to the modelled baby-me idea in our heads; but that is not remembering my baby-me, nor is it even feeling like a human baby. Babies are clearly significantly aware of the world (unlike comatose people); yet no retrievable memories were laid down when we were babies, and there is no sense of continuity between any imagining of our infancy and our current self-definition. How can a period in life when so much learning is happening leave no conscious trace of that learning in our brains and minds?

It is almost as if our life were compartmentalised into two different states. When we are self-unaware as babies, we can have no knowledge of what being self-aware feels like; and when we are self-aware as older humans, we can have no knowledge of what being self-unaware feels like. These mutually exclusive states of selfness are not just stages in our life-story, they also happen on a daily basis in the sleep–wake cycle. We now know that the brain is active throughout the sleep cycle, and we dream several times a night; but we only remember a dream if we are dreaming it when we wake up – and often not even then (Becchetti and Amadeo 2016). The human brain seems to be quite efficient at keeping our aware and unaware selves separated, but we are only just beginning to understand why this should be so.

The unconscious–conscious sleep–wake cycle is a big mystery that is not going to be solved here. We are only interested in what it can tell us about human infancy; and on that subject it is quite eloquent. It provides evidence that nobody is actually a cohesive, single self. We have no way of being sure whether our separate aware and unaware selves are mutually or independently cohesive – although remembered dreams indicate that either could be true. We may feel that we are a single self, but the inaccessibility of the one-third of our life that we spend asleep indicates that we may not be.

As well as the major division into conscious and unconscious selves, our conscious selfhood is also often seen as divisible. Sigmund Freud (1923 [2010]) split the holistic psyche into the unconscious id and a conscious selfhood; but he further split the conscious self into an ego and a super-ego. The ego is the self-as-actor, the self that gets things done, while the super-ego is the self-as-modeller, the self that plans and interprets. According to Freud, neither of these conscious selves truly exists when we are infants, although a rudimentary cognition that will develop into an ego is detectable. The ego forms in early childhood and begins exerting itself from about age 4 (Freud does not give a developmental timescale, but the ego-affected self he describes fits with what we know about 4-year-olds). The super-ego is more difficult to pin down, but by age 11 we have effective models of our social environment and our possible roles in it; we also have a clear understanding that there are social expectations we must meet and social taboos we should not break.

Jerome Bruner divided our conscious selfhood into Episodic selves and a Narrative self. The Narrative self establishes and maintains continuity, or narrative force, between our Episodic selves, our memories of who we were at different times in the past and our models of who we could be at different times in the future. The Narrative self is not a given at birth, it is the product of our social interactions in early life; and it only begins to create our life-narrative from our memories and plans when we own our experiences and treat our core modelled self as a *conceptual self*. This is not an automatic process. It requires social input to give the self context and purpose:

> Narrative accrual is not foundational in the scientist's sense. Yet narratives do accrue, and, as anthropologists insist, the accruals eventually create something variously called a 'culture' or a 'history' or, more loosely, a 'tradition.' Even our own homely accounts of happenings in our own lives are eventually converted into more or less coherent autobiographies centered around a Self acting more or less purposefully in a social world.
>
> (Bruner 1991, 18)

The conceptual self that is created by this process is, at the time of creation, the core self; but it is also a now-self, and it changes through time. Past and future core selves can be narratively associated with the now-self, but they cannot *be* the now-self. Bruner (1990, 100–2) describes the negotiation with others toward a conceptual self as being the product of a series of transactional selves, selves negotiated with those around us. He gives no developmental timescale for this process, but he does say that 'Four-year-olds may not know much about the culture, but they know what's canonical and are eager to provide a tale to account for what is not' (1990, 82–3). At age 5, humans are usually capable of cultural narrativisation, which means they are able, or almost able, to describe their own lives as a story, and create a conceptual self they can describe to others (Benson 1993).

As we have seen in previous chapters, other selves and theories of selfhood are available. However, despite the importance of the contribution of childhood to an understanding of selfhood, discussion of timescales for the development of selfhood in childhood is sparse. This is, in part, because we are still learning the story of human childhood, so speculation about what cognition a child is capable of at a particular stage or age could be seen as premature. However, our understanding of our selfhood in childhood, alongside our understanding of our cognition in childhood, form the bases of our personal development and inform our self-modelling in adulthood.

How to make a human adult (start with other human adults)

From this discussion, it would seem that the recipe for a human adult consists of five ingredients. First, we need a sense of other, an innate ability to model our relationships with others. This seems to be an ancient capacity, something we inherited long ago from an unknown ancestor; and we know this is the case because we can see it at work in the relationships between many different species, including our fellow primates. However, as it is innate, we have no need to be explicitly aware of our modelling for it to work: simple, affective mechanisms of liking and disliking are enough for this relationship modelling (Bault et al. 2017). Human children seem to come into the world with this faculty already working.

The second ingredient we need is an awareness of other, explicit knowledge that others in the group have intentions. This is a product of Machiavellian intelligence, which we have already identified as a capacity present in many primates. Awareness of others as intentional beings leads on to ToM, and then to the ability to explicitly model the relationships between others. It may be that the journey from social arithmetic to social calculus had already been started by the *Pan-Homo* common ancestor; from the evidence, it seems that chimpanzees and bonobos have at least begun the journey (Call and Tomasello 2008). By age 2, though, human children are already beginning to show signs of social calculus in their relationships.

The third ingredient is where we seem to part company from the rest of nature: our need and willingness to share our cognitive models. This seems to have occurred long after the split with chimpanzees, but it may not be limited to just *Homo sapiens*; it could have evolved in early *Homo*, or even the australopithecines. It seems likely that it is one of several cooperative strategies that form a continuum from *Pan* species to modern humans (Vanutelli et al. 2016). The willingness to cooperate in information-sharing is constrained by the sender's and receiver's dilemmas, which only our group of species has overcome in a useful way. Modern human children are sharing social models by age 4, both by calling adult attention to their peers' social violations (tattling) and in sharing stories about others (gossiping).

The fourth ingredient of the human adult recipe is an inevitable outcome of sharing social calculus: a need to accommodate third-party models of ourself in our social calculus (as we saw in Chapter 3). Developmentally, this is a more gradual process than the first three: we begin to model ourselves as third-party objects at around age 4, but we understand compassion (modelling others as equal to the self) at around age 6, and we develop emotional empathy (experiencing the emotions of others) during adolescence (Allemand et al. 2015). However, we do not develop a full adult awareness of our selfhood until our early twenties – and sometimes even later.

The final ingredient in making a human adult is a capacity to accommodate opinions as well as facts in our cognition and communication. Not everything we receive from others is a reference to the actual world – a lot is a personalised version of that world; I do not need to adopt your opinion of the world to understand what that opinion is, and why you hold it. The capacity to treat the same information in two ways simultaneously – as true for you but not necessarily for me – is another product of sharing social models, and relies on the capacity to take the viewpoint of another (Tormala 2016). By paying attention to both your and my viewpoints, I am able to negotiate toward meaning with you; and this negotiation can be based on persuasion (I try to make you change your viewpoint) or compromise (we both change our viewpoints) (La Rocca et al. 2014). This is a complex interpersonal task, and the fact that it is quite difficult for a significant minority of individuals (such as the 17-in-1,000 people on the autism spectrum – CDC 2018) indicates that, genetically, this capacity to effectively negotiate toward meaning must be quite recent and has not yet stabilised in the species.

These five ingredients rely on three cognitive tools we generated to handle aspects of our socialisation. The first of these is the simple syntax of A-Relationship-B modelling, the engine behind the cognition of social calculus; the second is negotiation toward meaning, a product of the sharing of social calculus models; and the third is complex language grammar, the engine behind the cognition and communication of opinion, persuasion, compromise and deception. The first of these, simple syntax, may not be exclusive to the *Homo* clade, but it provided the base on which the other two tools could build. The second, negotiation toward meaning, is likely to be exclusive to humans, but it is not necessarily limited to just *Homo sapiens*. The third, complex language grammar, may indeed be a species-specific strategy, at least in its more complex forms; but it is unlikely to be genetically instantiated – and, because of its fast-changing nature, may never become so (Christiansen and Chater 2008).

Because the fourth and fifth ingredients (shared social calculus and opinion-accommodation) do not seem to be genetically driven, there is no need to search for genetic explanations for cooperative communication or complex language grammar. This does not mean that they have no explanation – a willingness to be complicit in deception, in particular, needs more than a *Just-So* story to explain it as a fit survival strategy– but it does indicate that cultural explanations may prove to be sufficient.

As children, we are faced with a complex environment in which a reputation for cooperation is more important than the capacity to coerce; we need to know not just how we feel about others but how others feel about others, and how others feel about us. We cannot rely on introspection to define our self, we need to model how others define us; which means that we are not looking at our self in our social calculus, we are looking at models of our self, so we have to rely on what other people are telling us about us to decide who, and what, we are. To become human adults, we need other adults to provide input: *Cogitant ut sum, ergo sum.*

Note

1. What Locke actually said was, 'Let us then suppose the mind to be, as we say, white paper, void of all characters, without any ideas – How comes it to be furnished? Whence comes it by that vast store which the busy and boundless fancy of man has painted on it with an almost endless variety? Whence has it all the materials of reason and knowledge? To this I answer, in one word, from EXPERIENCE. In that all our knowledge is founded; and from that it ultimately derives itself. Our observation employed either, about external sensible objects, or about the internal operations of our minds perceived and reflected on by ourselves, is that which supplies our understandings with all the materials of thinking. These two are the fountains of knowledge, from whence all the ideas we have, or can naturally have, do spring' (John Locke, 1689 [1836], 51).

5
Where Did Social Calculus Come From?

> 'I couldn't afford to learn it,' said the Mock Turtle with a sigh. 'I only took the regular course.'
>
> 'What was that?' inquired Alice.
>
> 'Reeling and Writhing, of course, to begin with,' the Mock Turtle replied; 'and then the different branches of Arithmetic – Ambition, Distraction, Uglification, and Derision.'
>
> 'I never heard of "Uglification,"' Alice ventured to say. 'What is it?'
>
> The Gryphon lifted up both its paws in surprise. 'Never heard of uglifying!' it exclaimed. 'You know what to beautify is, I suppose?'
>
> 'Yes,' said Alice doubtfully: 'it means – to – make – anything – prettier.'
>
> 'Well, then,' the Gryphon went on, 'if you don't know what to uglify is, you *are* a simpleton.'
>
> (Lewis Carroll 1865, Chapter 9: 'The Mock Turtle's Story')

So far in this book, much has been made of social calculus, the capacity to model the relationships between other members in a group. When this capacity is inside our heads and not out in the world, it is rather unremarkable; it may even be a feature of cognition we share with apes and perhaps other social species. It does allow us to understand our social groups better, and maybe gain an edge over other individuals with less competence at social modelling; but it does not act as a significant marker of difference in either our individual or species lifestyles. However, when it is shared, social calculus becomes a powerful motor driving social and cultural cohesion and change. It provides the A-Relationship-B syntax that seems to form the basis of language grammar; it allows cliques and cabals of like-minded individuals to form subgroups within the social group, and in that way it determines the systems of socialisation in the group; it establishes commonality and variation in the culture of the social group while helping that culture to become increasingly arbitrary (that is, governed less by genetically and economically effective choices and more by contingency and fashion); and it allows opinion to be expressed and understood, and therefore lets a range of cognitive capacities (modality, imagination, story-telling, deception, modelled futures and pasts, and negotiation toward meaning) out of the Pandora's box of the brain and into the world. Shared social calculus also provides the mechanism by which I can begin to understand that my self is a real objective thing for other people, just as their selves are real objective things for me; and I can therefore understand my self in the same way I understand their selves: my self modelled as a third person is a by-product of social calculus plus sharing.

Social calculus is, strictly speaking, computational and not arithmetical; it behaves like an iterative nodal network with multiple connections between the nodes, rather than an arithmetical calculation with a single answer. Networks are notoriously difficult to represent arithmetically, but simple to build computationally. However, and completely coincidentally, the Mock Turtle's different branches of arithmetic do unexpectedly map to social calculus: Ambition is a product of being able to model my self as better than my current state, a natural comparison between my social and cultural self-models; Distraction maps to story-telling, or shared productive imagination; Uglification can be viewed as anti social deception, the downside of shared social calculus; and Derision is one way of sharing my models of others with those others. All these 'branches of arithmetic' require a language-like communication system to work: story-telling, lying and sharing models are primary functions of human language; and self-modelling is only possible if others are sharing their models of me with me. Human language is driven by, and drives, the sharing of social calculus; and, even today, social gossip remains a significant feature of human language exchanges. However, if sharing social calculus is impossible without a language-like communication system, and self-modelling is impossible without shared social calculus, then my third-person social model of my self has to be a by-product of social calculus shared through language.

If knowledge of selfness relies on social calculus, then understanding how social calculus evolved becomes significant if we are to understand the origins of self. As we saw in Chapter 3, social cognition is not an automatic product of large brains: some cephalopod species like octopi are highly encephalised, yet they have no society and therefore no need for social calculus. Social cognition is also not an automatic product of organised societies: eusocial insect species live in nests numbering up to hundreds of thousands of individuals, with each individual having a defined social role; but these roles are genetically encoded, hence require no negotiation toward meaning to generate shared enterprise. The shared enterprise emerges from each individual carrying out a task that happens to coordinate with the tasks of other individuals. The individuals do not need to bargain their way through a complex social web of self-interests to work together, because they are sterile workers who rely on their queen to get their genes into the future. For eusocial insects, the division between means and ends is between the nest and the world, not the individual and the world.

Social networks, genes and brains

Because social calculus requires a particular type of cognition, it also requires a particular type of brain able to carry out that cognition. All cognition has an energy cost – for instance, the large amount of the body's energy that the brain uses (see Chapter 2) means that there must be an evolutionary explanation as to why bearing the cost of social cognition is a fit strategy for a species; and there must be species-specific genetic mechanisms behind that strategy. In a currently non-extinct species we should be able to identify strategies of social calculus in the behaviour of that species; and, nowadays, we may even understand the genetic mechanisms affecting those strategies.

Using costly brainpower to navigate the complexities of social calculus is only valuable to a species that lives in large groups of cooperating individuals, all of whom retain control over their own reproductive agendas. This is something of a contradiction in evolutionary terms: individual reproductive agendas, by default, generate competition rather than cooperation. If I have a choice between my reproductive agenda and yours, mine should always win – because, in the past, individuals who didn't put their reproductive agenda first didn't get their genes into the future. In the absence of other examples from the rest of nature, humans cooperatively sharing social calculus would seem to be an inexplicable contradiction. However, while we may be the only species that brings them together, cooperative sharing is not limited to just our species, and social calculus may not be exclusive to the *Homo* clade, either. Looking at how social knowledge and cooperation work in other socialised species will give us a better understanding of how our particular habit of sharing social calculus may have evolved.

The birds (Avifauna) are a group of animals separated from us by over 300 million years of evolution; but we are increasingly becoming aware that some species are also highly intelligent (Gutiérrez-Ibáñez et al. 2018). Some species of parrots (psittaciformes) and some crows (corvids) are also known for the size of their social networks, and they seem to have developed the necessary brainpower to handle those networks (Emery 2016). Bird brains are organised differently from mammal brains: our cerebrum is composed of a relatively thin folded layer of grey matter (the cortex, the part of the brain that does most of the planning, modelling and choosing) over the top of a network of white matter (which shuttles information between different areas of grey matter and other parts of the brain); in contrast, the bird brain has an area of grey matter (the pallium) which is more concentrated than the human cortex and which requires fewer and shorter white-matter connections. Where the human cortex is almost two-dimensional, like a wrinkled sheet of paper, the bird pallium is a three-dimensional mass. The organisation of the bird brain seems to lend itself well to both innate and learned behaviours, so much so that some species of bird can learn to mimic behaviours (such as calls and songs) that were originally generated by another species, allowing them to deceive individuals of that other species to their advantage (Flower et al. 2014).

In terms of cooperation, the avian brain supports a wide range of social behaviours: solitary nesting, pair-bonded nesting, communal nesting, flocking, large breeding colonies, cooperative breeding, parasitism and male-dominated harems (Collias and Collias 1984). These different breeding strategies are supported by a range of different communication strategies, such as territorial and mate-seeking displays and vocalisations, threats and alarm calls, and social integration signals (Bradbury and Vehrencamp 1998, 358–63). Social integration signals are particularly interesting: there is evidence for individual identity calls in several bird species (Sewall et al. 2016), indicating that they do not just identify different individuals cognitively, they can signal those identities, too. There is currently no evidence that they share their social cognition models with each other, but they may maintain something approximating a cognitive social calculus system using labels that, if vocalised, could be recognised by the individuals labelled.

Genetically closer to home, mammals also have a wide range of socialisation strategies. Naked mole rats (*Heterocephalus glaber*) are an unusual mammal in that they have adopted a eusocial mode of existence.

A nest comprises about 80 individuals, but may house as many as 300. It contains a single queen, two or more fertile males, some larger soldier workers and many smaller tunneller workers. In addition, the workers are divided into frequent workers, who do more work but consume more resources, and infrequent workers, who do less work, consume fewer resources and may live longer. Individual workers can move between the different roles as needed, adopting the size and lifestyle appropriate for the new role. The queen has an unusually long gestation period for a rodent, and only produces one litter a year in the wild. However, the size of the litter (sometimes more than 20 pups) means that the single queen produces about the same number of offspring as would be produced if the nest reproduced in a more conventionally rodent-like way (Roellig et al. 2011).

Naked mole rats have a complex communication system that we do not fully understand; but, just as for the eusocial ants whom naked mole rats most resemble in terms of their subterranean lifestyle, smell is a key communicative tool. Faeces are particularly important: they are either smeared on or eaten to generate a shared *nest scent*; and pups are fed with a softened form of faeces known as faecal pap. As well as olfactory signalling, naked mole rats vocalise extensively, as Jarvis and Sherman (2002) show:

> Vocalizations include food recruitment calls, high-pitched contact and aggressive chirps, a mating call, toilet-assembly call, and vocalizations specific to pups, such as squawks when pups are stepped on and caecotroph-solicitation chirps. Many calls are associated with alarm … If a small maintenance worker encounters a foreign object in a tunnel, it usually 'taps' or 'sneezes,' which recruits other small workers from nearby. However, if the worker encounters a snake or a member of a foreign colony, it rushes off toward the nest 'screaming'. This mobilizes large-bodied defenders, who begin chirping and running to the site … There, they threaten the intruder with open mouths and snapping teeth and make either grunting sounds (predators) or hisses and aggressive trills (foreign colonies).
>
> (Jarvis and Sherman 2002, 5).

Naked mole rats are unusual mammals in several other ways: they require much less oxygen than other mammals; they seem to be highly resistant to cancers; they can live for up to 32 years – and, unlike other mammal species, the fertile queens often live longer than non-fertiles

(Bens et al. 2018); their basic food sources are tubers they find in their tunnelling activity; and they 'farm' the tuber by eating it from the inside out, so ensuring it continues to grow while it is being consumed (the outer skin of the tuber is where most growth occurs). However, the surprising feature of their social system is that, unlike other social mammals, they do not seem to need social calculus: individuality is suppressed, as it is for other eusocial species, and there is little evidence of individual personality or cognitive modelling of other individuals. Each individual has its role and performs it as and when needed, working not as an individual but as an element of a super-organism.

Meerkats (*Suricata suricatta*, a type of mongoose) have a social system closer to the pseudo-eusociality of humans than the full eusociality of naked mole rats; but it is still a social network dominated by alpha breeders. While each individual does seem to have its own agenda, and personality does play a small role in their society, individual agendas and non-alpha reproduction in a group are suppressed by the current alpha male and female. This is accomplished partly by bullying, which suppresses fertility chemically, and partly by consuming the offspring of non-alphas.

This does still leave the sub-alpha individual with three routes to fertility. The first route is to replace the alpha male or female and become a gang leader. Take-over fights are rare, although not unknown; but alpha meerkats are not guarded by the group in the same way as alpha naked mole rats, so natural attrition is relatively frequent. Only individuals who have migrated into the gang from outside will be accepted as new alphas, however, so meerkats have to leave their birth-gang and seek out a new gang if they are to have a chance of becoming an alpha using this route. The second route is to leave the birth-gang and found your own gang. It is a risky strategy in that new groups have to compete for territory with larger, older groups; but, if successful, the reproductive rewards for the new alphas are immediate. The third route is to encounter a fertile and receptive member of the other sex while out foraging; alphas are often amenable to extending the genetic pool of their offspring behind their partner's back, and subordinates seldom forego an opportunity to attempt furtive reproduction.

Meerkats, however, do not seem to be very effective at social calculus. They do seem able to differentiate between calls made by different individuals (Townsend et al. 2012), but there is no evidence they understand a call as authored by a particular individual (Tibbetts et al. 2008). This may be because they don't seem to recognise other gang-members visually; instead, they rely on a group scent, generated by repetitive scent-marking exchanges, to identify gang-mates. If an individual who has become separated from their gang makes their way back after a week or so, acceptance back into the gang is far from automatic. Unless some lingering group scent is detected on the prodigal meerkat, they will be treated as a stranger. Female meerkats are not able to reliably identify even their own offspring. Occasionally, a beta female who has been impregnated by a lone male will give birth and then attempt to sneak her pups into the 'royal' crèche. If the alpha female detects them, they will be eaten; but this happens seldom enough to make the sneak adoption tactic viable.

Meerkat foraging and feeding are lone activities: unlike humans and eusocial animals, they do not indulge in joint provisioning enterprises. Meerkat pups are fed in a crèche for about two months, first with their mother's milk and later by carer provisioning; and during the latter part of their childhood they learn their foraging skills, both from personal practice and from carer teaching. Their success in foraging practice at this point in their life dictates their future fitness and likelihood of reaching alpha status (Thornton 2008). Adults who are unable to forage efficiently will have poorer condition and less time to undertake furtive reproduction, as well as being unlikely to achieve alpha status. Meerkats, like humans and unlike naked mole rats, therefore appear to have a pseudo-eusocial society; but, unlike humans, their pseudo-eusociality seems to be based on suppression of (or, at least, lack of recognition of) individuality and not on cooperation and joint enterprise. This aspect of their behaviour makes meerkat social networking more like that of naked mole rats than that of humans.

Although meerkats don't seem to need it, complex social cognition in the mammalian clade is not limited to humans, or even to primates. For instance, bottlenose dolphins (*Tursiops truncatus*) live in pods of up to 15 individuals; and these pods often come together to make larger fission–fusion groups of up to a thousand individuals. The groups separate again into pods after a short period (hours rather than days), but individuals may not necessarily leave the group in the same pod with which they arrived. We still do not fully understand the details of this fission–fusion social system, but it does seem to involve a flexible and hierarchical view of social group membership, as well as individual and changeable association preferences. Like other social mammals, dolphins have large and complex brains. In fact, if brain size and complexity are correlated with intelligence, then the large and complex brains of dolphins make them the second-most (possibly the most) intelligent species on the planet (Foer 2015).

Bottlenose dolphins use a range of communicative behaviours. They seem to use click communication to synchronise activity and to establish and maintain alliances (Connor et al. 2006); they use gentle physical contact for the same purpose; and, in the same way as most primates, they recruit each other's attention toward salient events and objects – and joint attention is a key ingredient of social cognition (Pack and Herman 2006). Their vocal communication is complex and seems capable of carrying organised and complex meanings (although we currently have no real evidence that it does so). They may have the capacity to use grammatical utterances in the same way as humans (Herman and Uyeyama 1999), and there is even a controversial suggestion that their vocalisations seem to have the same sound structure as human words and sentences (Ryabov 2016), although this may be more a coincidence than evidence of language-like communication. They also seem to have definable and differentiated group cultures, which they maintain even when the culture becomes maladaptive (Whitehead et al. 2004). This is a behaviour to be expected in emic belief-based systems but not in etic definition-based systems.

Bottlenose dolphins, like humans, seem to have the capacity to recognise and label other individuals. Cook et al. (2004) showed that dolphin signature whistles are used frequently by individuals to identify themselves to other members of a pod; and King et al. (2013) showed that other dolphins use slightly modified versions of an individual's signature whistle to indicate they recognise the individual. Because of the fission–fusion society, it seems likely that identification and recognition of individuals extends beyond the ad hoc grouping of the pod: bottlenose dolphins seem to maintain at least a Relationship-A form of social modelling; and their capacity for complex social alliances (Connor 2007) indicates they could be maintaining an A-Relationship-B social calculus. What we can say with certainty is that the communication of signature whistles indicates that a facility for shared social calculus is a distinct possibility for these animals.

However, all cetaceans differ from humans in one important respect: without an equivalent of manual proficiency, making and using complex tools is impossible. Dolphins do conduct joint enterprises for hunting; they turn-take when consuming prey that they have worked together to corral and trap; males work together to impress or coerce females; pods work together to protect their young from sharks or to hunt and kill sharks; but there is only one good instance recorded of tool use. Dolphins in Shark Bay, Australia, have been recorded using sponges to protect their rostra while foraging for buried prey (Patterson and Mann 2011). It is a rather basic example of tool use: the tool does not enhance the foraging itself, but only makes it less uncomfortable; and the tool does not need to be modified for use. There is no evidence of tool curation – but the sponge is often worn away in the foraging activity, so there is often nothing to curate. We can say that this tool-use is cultural because, based on current observations, it is limited to a single group; but we cannot yet say whether it is an emic or etic activity.

What do all these examples of social cognition tell us about our own social calculus? The birds tell us that social cognition is not limited to just primates or even just mammals; it seems to be a common response to social living for a non-eusocial species. Naked mole rats tell us that eusociality is not limited to the insect clade, but it always seems to rely on a suppression of individual agendas; this makes social calculus pointless for a fully eusocial species. Meerkats show us that there is more than one way to be pseudo-eusocial: humans seem to rely on eusocial levels of cooperation and joint enterprise while retaining non-eusocial levels of individualism; meerkats reverse this equation, with disindividuation approaching eusocial levels while their cooperative behaviour is limited. Bottlenose dolphins tell us that complex social modelling does not rely on tool use, tool-making or other technological ability. We cannot know whether dolphins are sharing social calculus models, so we cannot know whether they have social self-models; but shared signature whistles and communicative complexity indicate that it is possible we are not the only self-modelling species on the planet; and, if that is the case, we can say that self-modelling may be necessary for human culture to exist, but it is not exclusive to humans.

Different species have taken different routes to socialisation, and the social modelling they use is accordingly varied. For humans, social calculus is the key to understanding the relationships around us; but social calculus is only one of many ways of handling relationships with conspecifics. Social calculus gives us the ability to model a network of complex social relationships; but it is cognitively costly and not necessarily the most efficient method for managing social organisation: eusocial animals don't need it, and it is not a necessary requirement or product of pseudo-eusociality. As an unlikely outcome of what must be an evolutionary process, it needs a convincing evolutionary origins story.

Machiavellianism

The story of social modelling does not start with genus *Homo*, or even with our precursor clade, genus *Australopithecus*. We need to start with an unknown ancestor, the first species in the human lineage capable of Machiavellian intelligence. This is a trait we share with our closest relatives, so the proposed unknown ancestor is likely to be quite ancient, a precursor of chimpanzees and bonobos as well as humans. As a proxy for this creature we can look at modern chimpanzees and bonobos, but we need to remain aware that a modern animal is not a precursor animal, or even necessarily the best exemplar for a precursor animal.

Chimpanzees and bonobos seem to be the current Machiavellian masters; but what does that mean? In the hypothesis set out in this book, it means that they are capable of modelling the Relationship-A associations around them: they maintain cognitive models of the members of the social group in which they live, and the relationships they have with those others in the group. It is now 40 years since Premack and Woodruff (1978) addressed the question of whether chimpanzees have ToM, and they proposed a series of skills that could be tested to provide evidence for or against its presence. Could chimpanzees understand that other individuals had different knowledge and beliefs? Could they understand the difference between knowing something and guessing something? Could they differentiate lies from truths? Could they separate 'pretend' from 'real'? And finally, do chimpanzees have self-knowledge? Premack and Woodruff recognised that some of these are skills that even humans possess only erratically; and self-knowledge is, as we have seen so far, a slippery concept that may involve neither a known self nor a self to be known.

Nevertheless, a lot has been discovered about chimpanzee awareness since Premack and Woodruff's study, providing both direct and indirect answers to their questions. In terms of cognitive similarity, Call and Tomasello (1999) showed that chimpanzees have no problems understanding that other individuals have beliefs about third parties, but they have difficulty understanding that those beliefs can be false: they cannot fully comprehend that another individual does not automatically know what they themself know. In this respect they are like human 2-year-olds, who have similar problems understanding what others know; but they are unlike human 4-year-olds, who are usually adept at attributing false belief appropriately.

Mercader et al. (2007) provided evidence that chimpanzees make stone tools for specific purposes, as our ancestors did; and the cognitive skills for physical modelling that allowed us to enter the human stone age are present in chimpanzees, too. Bianchi et al. (2013) compared the brain development of chimpanzees with that of humans and found that we follow a similar developmental path: not only do the two types of brain develop to the same schedule, they seem to have a similar capacity for plasticity, which is vital for learned processes like social calculus. However, while the schedule may be the same, the timescale is not; and longer timescales mean that human brains develop more than chimpanzee brains.

In terms of social communication, Slocombe and Zuberbühler (2005) looked at chimpanzee food grunts (produced when a chimpanzee is eating), and they identified subtle variations that seem to indicate to others the type of food being eaten; these calls are, therefore, functionally referential, informing listening chimpanzees about food sources that others have found and what they should be looking for themselves. In another study, Davila-Ross et al. (2011) looked at laughter, and showed that chimpanzees' replicated laughter – laughing at others' laughter – is different from their spontaneous laughter; they seem to differentiate between being amused and being entertained. Roberts and Roberts (2016) looked at the different communicative roles of grooming, gesture and vocalisation for chimpanzees in terms of social proximity. They found that there seems to be a hierarchy of signals, with grooming reserved for simultaneous social and physical proximity, gesture being used mainly for physical proximity, and vocalisation (especially synchronised calls) being used for social proximity. This resembles the way humans use the different communication channels of grooming, gesture and vocalisation.

In terms of social awareness, Carpenter and Tomasello (1995) conducted imitative learning tasks with human children, chimpanzees raised in a human environment (commonly described as enculturated animals) and chimpanzees raised by other chimpanzees (wild animals). They found that the enculturated chimpanzees behaved more like human children than their conspecifics. They concluded that 'a human-like sociocultural environment is an essential component in the development of human-like social-cognitive and joint attentional skills for chimpanzees, and perhaps for human beings as well' – or, to put it another way, what separates humans and chimpanzees is not our different cultural capacities, but our early exposure to human culture. Human socialisation is different from chimpanzee socialisation in that we have an evolutionary use for human culture; but that does not mean we are the only species able to operate successfully within human culture.

Call et al. (2004) showed that chimpanzees can differentiate between humans who are able but unwilling to give them food and those who are willing but unable to do so: they persist in begging longer with the unable than with the unwilling. Lonsdorf et al. (2004) showed that, like humans, chimpanzee priorities are gendered: females tend to pay greater attention to self- and other-supporting activities like feeding, while males place a higher value on socialisation; the psychosocial gender differences are not highly marked, but they do seem to be common to both species. Webb et al. (2017) showed that, in terms of consolation after conflict, different chimpanzees, like humans, have different personalities: some individuals console much more readily than others, and the 'maxi-consolers' also seem to be more social.

Brosnan et al. (2010) discovered another interesting comparison between chimpanzees and humans. We are both aware of inequity of reward, and we both react to it; however, chimpanzees react less extremely than humans, seeming to treat inequity as disappointing but expected. Humans seem to have a complex moral sense of fairness and egalitarianism, although with a wide range of individual variation (Artinger et al. 2014).

All of these comparisons add up to a conclusion that there is a genetic distance between genus *Pan* and genus *Homo*, but it is not as great as we used to believe: we are beginning to understand that, cognitively, we share more with the species genetically closest to us than we once thought. Call and Tomasello (2008) have now reviewed the idea that chimpanzees have ToM, and concluded that it all depends on the accepted definition of ToM:

> In a broad construal of the phrase 'theory of mind', then, the answer to Premack and Woodruff's pregnant question of 30 years ago is a definite yes, chimpanzees do have a theory of mind. But chimpanzees probably do not understand others in terms of a fully human-like belief–desire psychology in which they appreciate that others have mental representations of the world that drive their actions even when those do not correspond to reality. And so in a more narrow definition of theory of mind as an understanding of false beliefs, the answer to Premack and Woodruff's question might be no, they do not.
>
> (Call and Tomasello 2008, 191)

Despite the fact that the study of both primates and ToM are rapidly evolving fields, this quote still holds true today. Does this mean, however, that chimpanzees are just a short step away from humanlike selfhood? Or does chimpanzee Machiavellianism provide a formidable barrier to self-modelling?

As far as we know, the social arithmetic of Machiavellian intelligence is the dominant type of social modelling used by our closest relatives; and it seems likely that an evolutionary race toward

Machiavellian intelligence is what started our own evolutionary development toward social calculus in the first place. An individual with a more sophisticated social modelling would be able to manipulate less sophisticated individuals to gain a reproductive advantage; and when the manipulation itself becomes sophisticated enough, we can label it Machiavellian. This raises the question as to why humans, who clearly use sophisticated social calculus communicatively as well as cognitively, seem to be less Machiavellian than chimpanzees and bonobos. We are a species accomplished in confabulation, so we clearly have the capacity to plot, dissemble and deceive. It seems, however, that we have taken Machiavellian intelligence in a new direction, allowing us to treat confabulation in a nuanced and sophisticated way. The lie the receiver knows to be a lie is treated as an acceptable fiction, and the capacity to generate acceptable fictions (story-telling) is seen in human society as a valuable skill. The ability to conceal other truths within the lies is seen as an even more valuable skill, so the capacity to read a message on multiple levels becomes correspondingly useful. However, this multi-level communication also means that meaning in human language is seldom simple or direct.

The tragedy of the commons

The social manipulation that Machiavellian intelligence makes possible poses a problem for communication systems that rely on simple and direct signals: if an individual has conscious control over a signal, then they can use it to lie. And, because signals in a non-language environment are usually simple and direct, to lie is to attempt to deceive. If the lie works, then the signal begins to lose meaning, as we saw in Chapter 3 with Kitui the vervet; and if the lie works often enough, then the signal becomes meaningless. This is the tragedy of the commons, originally proposed by Garrett Hardin (1968): a shared resource not subject to sanction, as is often the case with signalling, can be monopolised or subverted, thus advantaging the few – or the one – by disadvantaging the many.

Nature has its own way of preventing the tragedy of the commons in signalling: the involuntary signal. If a signal can only be made when the context is right, and if there is no voluntary control over the signal, then it cannot be used deceptively. It is a simple solution common throughout nature – and we do not need to search beyond modern humans for examples of difficult-to-fake involuntary signals.

Darwin himself (1897) noted the role that involuntary emotional expressions play in human social exchange, and how we share many of these involuntary signals with other species. However, Darwin was also interested in the wide range of involuntary signals that seem to be produced only by humans. These include: weeping (other animals get watery eyes, but they do not seem to relate external events back to the self or indulge in the self-absorbed process of treating future possible difficulties as current problems – and then getting upset about them); sulkiness (other animals express their current hormonal emotion, but only humans express their intellectual distaste at the current state of a relationship); a guilty expression (only humans seem to be concerned about any ill-effect their actions have had on conspecifics); and blushing (an unintended indicator to others of current unease or social discomfort). All these are signals that are difficult for us to suppress, and which inform others about our current cognitive mood. They are honest signs of our current psychological state.

However, involuntary signalling is not how human language works. Instead, we have three mechanisms to mitigate the effects of the tragedy of the commons in language:

1. We use other-identification (naming) to tag signals with their source. This transfers unreliability in the signal from the current signaller onto the original signaller; for example, in an A-Relationship-B-by-C signal, it is the original signaller's (C's) reputation for reliability that is at risk, not that of the current signaller.
2. We sanction deceptive individuals to make deception unprofitable; and this sanctioning of the deceiver is carried out by the group, not just the deceived.
3. We use the versatility of multi-level signalling to encode deception on one level, while offering useful information on a different level. Linguistic truth is not an all-or-nothing representation of the world, it is nuanced.

All these mitigators rely on the availability of a language-like communication system: the first relies on signal complexity, the second on reputation-sharing, and the third on complex semanticity. Behind them all is a social contract of trust: as signal-receiver, we provisionally trust the signal and the signaller. If, however, we detect deliberate and anti-social deception, then we are ready and willing to sanction the signaller, even if the deception is aimed at another individual. The willingness to trust is usually referred to as altruism, and the willingness to punish any deception (not just personal deception) has become known as altruistic punishment. Between them, these signal responses make antisocial deception costly for the deceiver.

Altruism

For decades after Darwin published *On the Origin of the Species*, many people believed it to be a treatise on 'nature, red in tooth and claw'.[1] This understanding was emphasised by Herbert Spencer's view that Darwinian biology could be summarised by the phrase 'survival of the fittest' (Spencer 1864, 444), rather than Darwin's own – more moderate – phrase, 'descent with modification' (Darwin 1859 [2001], 123) (although Darwin later adopted Spencer's phrase). Unfortunately, 'survival of the fittest' was a somewhat inaccurate and emotive phrase that generated all kinds of religious proto-scientific attempts to show that Darwin was wrong (for example, Løvtrup 1987), or that humans were a special case in nature, or that humans had nothing to do with nature. And all of these attempts to discredit Darwinism were based on an obvious truism: human activity is not usually dominated by self-serving emotions, because humans cooperate in complex and mutually supportive ways. We now know that this high level of cooperation without personal gain, or altruism, does not disprove Darwinian evolution or distance humans from the rest of nature; it merely shows that Spencer's dictum tells only part of the story.

Using just the bare bones of evolutionary theory, human cooperation is indeed difficult to justify. In any species where descent with modification dictates which traits are passed to the next generation, Machiavellian intelligence would seem to be the pinnacle of social organisation. The individual who does not exploit the ignorance and weaknesses of their conspecifics will nonetheless have their own ignorance and weaknesses exploited by others. Nice guys finish last and, more importantly, get fewer of their genes into the future. Over time, genes that enhance Machiavellian intelligence become more commonplace in the population, and the modifications produced by descent become more Machiavellian and less naively cooperative.

The reverse seems to have happened with humans. If our lineage had started out as Machiavellian as chimpanzees are now, then we must somehow have reined in our self-interest and enhanced our cooperativeness. There is now some evidence (Diogo et al. 2017) that the modern chimpanzee is not a good proxy for the common ancestor, and that both chimpanzees and humans diverged from a common ancestor that had more in common with bonobos. Of course, chimpanzees are not completely Machiavellian and we are not completely cooperative, and individuals of both species vary quite widely in their socialisation; the possibility for a species to move up or down the cooperative scale certainly exists. Yet, somehow, the strategies that worked for chimpanzee ancestors did not work for our ancestors. There are many possible causes for this: environment, socialisation, diet, group size and reproductive strategies are all possibilities, and it is likely that becoming human involved more than one of them. Even technology could be implicated: Dessalles (2014) points out that, once we had the capacity to make sharp stones that could be thrown, the reign of an alpha could easily be cut short by a good or lucky throw. To stay in control, you need allies, not dominance. With humans, we have to revise our ideas of what counts as 'fittest': altruism is as important as, or perhaps more important than, nature-red-in-tooth-and-claw competition.

Altruism does not disprove evolution, but it does require an evolutionary explanation. Richard Dawkins' Selfish Gene theory (1989) tells us that, at the level of individual strands of DNA, the capacity to replicate must generate competition between strands for the raw materials of replication. When the strands combine to make a single-celled organism, there are two levels of competition: individual genes, or versions of genes, are in competition not just for themselves, they are competing in terms of their contribution to the organism. Those that improve the surviving and thriving of their organism are likely to replicate at a faster rate than those that do not. John Maynard Smith and Eörs Szathmáry (1995) have extended this 'levels of competition' model all the way up to inter-societal conflict; but they also show that cooperation is, at times, more effective at getting genes into the future.

So what causes altruism? We have already encountered some of the mechanisms in Chapter 2, in relation to sharing information. William Hamilton's kin-selection theory (1964) was the first to describe an evolutionarily coherent cause for altruistic behaviour: an individual should be willing to forego an advantage if two siblings or children gain equal or greater advantage; or if four grandchildren or children of siblings gain equal or greater advantage; and so on. Kin-selection theory says that your child or sibling has half your genes, so their survival is worth the same to you as half of your own survival; so if dying will save three or more children or siblings, it's worthwhile. Kin-selection theory provides a bleak but realistic explanation for altruistic behaviour, although it only works between related individuals.

Hamilton (1964) also proposed that kin selection would favour the appearance of visible signs of relatedness, such as pelt markings or colours, or distinctive scents. These signs would identify close relatives, allowing a cheap shortcut around the costly alternative of cognitively maintaining a family tree. Dawkins (1989, 89–90) labelled this 'green-beard altruism', but he dismissed it as unlikely: how probable is it that a single gene would both enhance altruism and provide a clear signal of relatedness? Not very, was his conclusion. However, the two genetic effects can be decoupled quite easily, so they do not require a single genetic change or even a single gene to be involved. Recognition of relatives serves many functions, not least in preventing incest. There is clearly a disadvantage in incestuous reproduction (Lumsden and Wilson 1980), and individuals who are able to recognise, and avoid reproduction with, close relatives will have more successful offspring than those who do not. The green beard can therefore already be in place before kin-selection altruism evolves; and it helps us to see how altruism can be both parochial and generous.

The second coherent solution was reciprocal altruism, as proposed by Robert Trivers (1971). This says that, if favours are offered to other individuals to form long-term relationships, then each favour raises the worth of the giving individual to the receiving individual. If the favour is returned at a later time, then the two individuals enter a virtuous cycle where they each continually raise their worth to each other, changing engagement to friendship, and friendship to alliance. If the favour is not returned, then the worth of the receiver to the giver is reduced, and no further favours are likely to be offered. Unlike kin selection, reciprocal altruism is not expressible as a simple mathematical formula; but that may be to its advantage. Kin selection assumes a knowable future, which makes it unrealistic; reciprocal altruism involves speculation about alternative futures, which is much closer to what humans actually do. However, neither of them captures the indirect reciprocity that we humans rely on as a foundational feature of our culture: we help each other because we can, not because we expect a return on our investment.

Two further solutions have attempted to address this. The first is indirect reciprocity, the idea that we do good deeds to enhance our reputation (Nowak and Sigmund 2005); reputation acts as a general group 'currency', meaning that favours may be returned indirectly by others in the group, not directly by the original receiver. Indirect reciprocity, however, merely transfers the mystery from altruism to reputation. It does not explain why maintaining, and acting on, a cognitive register of reputations should become a stable evolutionary strategy (although it clearly did: without it, the honest sharing of social models becomes virtually impossible).

The second solution is costly signalling (Zahavi and Zahavi 1997), which holds that every favour offered carries the signal that the giver can do these favours without compromising their own fitness; favours are not currency, they are ostentatious gift-giving. Marcel Mauss (1950) found that this was a common feature of pre-Columbian cultures in North-West America, and ostentatious generosity remains a tool of social elites in modern capitalist economies. Costly signalling was originally proposed as a mechanism to explain the evolution of ostentatious displays like the peacock's tail, a problem of evolutionary fitness that perplexed Darwin; but it was soon realised that it also explains a lot about the extremes of human altruism. In costly signalling we have a theory that models human behaviour, and which solves the problem of how altruism can occur without pre-existing cooperation: costly signalling promotes cooperative behaviour, reciprocal altruism and reputation-building without relying on any of them to pre-exist. It also explains how altruism could have emerged out of self-serving behaviour. However, costly signalling does not explain how the human attitude to non-cooperation evolved: our complex moral sense of fairness and egalitarianism acts as a back-stop to arrest back-sliding non-cooperative behaviours. It does not always work (as illustrated by the election of Adolf Hitler in 1933, and continuing popular support for many corrupt politicians around the world), but it does inevitably impose itself as social moral outrage builds in a group against an individual's excesses. It may take generations before a sufficient 'head of steam' builds, but humans do seem willing to address social inequalities in ways that no other species does. We punish our social transgressors in an organised fashion, labelling the transgressions in ways that would be incomprehensible to other species: hypocrisy, bullying, greed, treachery, sociopathy … the list goes on. This willingness to punish transgressors is a key step in the development of a willingness to share social models.

Altruistic punishment and free-riders

Taking revenge against the perpetrator of an act that disadvantaged you is known in the study of altruism as punishment. Chimpanzees have been seen to take personal revenge for actions that directly disadvantaged them (Jensen et al. 2007), so punishment of individuals by wronged individuals is not a novel feature of being human. However, humans also work together to punish miscreants, even where only some of the group have been disadvantaged; this is something that chimpanzees do not do (Riedl et al. 2012). Yet even this level of altruistic punishment is not sufficient for our species: we take things one step further and punish those who do not themselves cooperate in punishing miscreants. We even have the pejorative term, freeloader, for non-cooperators in both joint enterprises and joint punishment (although a more neutral term, free-rider, is used in academic literature). It seems that humans are not just altruistic, we are also enforcers of altruism: we take a moral stance not only against those who flout the social compact but also against those who attempt to avoid their socially imposed duty to sanction the flouters.

An example of this sanctioning of free-riders occurred in Britain at the start of the 1914–18 conflict: some women began pinning white feathers to the jackets of men who were not in uniform, to shame them into joining up. This was before conscription imposed a legal duty to enlist, and it caused many men who were needed on the home front to 'run away to war'. However misguided, the white feather encapsulated the view that those not directly punishing the enemy were somehow social free-riders, and therefore deserved to be punished themselves.

So how does a species become so willing to punish both non-cooperators and free-riders? Several computer simulations have been produced since the turn of the century, showing how altruistic punishment could arise as a species-wide capacity. Avilés (2002) showed that free-riding is a risky business, and only works if it remains below a critical threshold. She found that, when it is rare, it becomes more common; but, as it reduces the capacity of the group to compete with other groups, it cannot exceed a critical threshold without causing the group to collapse. This reduces the reproductive success of the free-riders, limiting their genetic access to the future. Free-riding only works as a parasitic strategy, and it relies on the majority of others not adopting it.

Fehr and Gächter (2002) showed that altruistic punishment is not just conducive to cooperation, it is necessary if cooperation is not to be overrun by cheats and free-riders. In support of this, Gardner and West (2004) showed that kin selection works against non-partisan cooperation, and relatedness may actually get in the way of effective altruistic punishment. Instead, altruistically punishing relies on cooperation at the group level to remain a stable strategy; at the group level, the costs of punishing are shared and therefore individual costs are reduced, which favours group-level cooperation over individual altruistic punishers. Boyd et al. (2010) showed that this sharing of costs means that punishment can proliferate in a cooperating group; and Fowler (2005) found that, in a mixed population of contributors, defectors and nonparticipants, the appearance of altruistic punishers led to their dominating the population. Additionally, he found that punishment does not work unless the net payoff for the population is positive.

However, all these simulations can only show what should logically happen. What is the situation in the actual world? Riehl and Frederickson (2016) looked at the evidence from a range of cooperative animals and noticed that cheating and punishment are both uncommon. Instead, they found that uncooperative animals are usually not cheating to gain advantage, but just to survive: they do not cooperate because they do not have the spare resources to cooperate. However, failure to cooperate in a cooperative species is likely to disadvantage the non-cooperator even further:

> Contrary to what is typically assumed, not cooperating is rarely an adaptive strategy for social animals; when cooperation generates direct or inclusive fitness benefits, a failure to cooperate lowers an animal's lifetime fitness. In these societies, cheating is not selectively favoured in the first place and non-cooperative phenotypes may be maintained only in mutation-selection balance. If cheaters are therefore rare, they are unlikely to impose much selection for punishment. These results are consistent with recent theory, which has increasingly shown that punishment—even in humans—can be evolutionarily stable only under limited circumstances, and that cooperation is unlikely to evolve when cheating is truly advantageous.
>
> (Riehl and Frederickson 2016, 9)

In this situation, punishment of cheats is overkill and has disadvantages for the group. Where altruistic punishment does exist, it is usually punishment for a positive action, not for negative inaction. Riehl and Frederickson propose that altruistic punishment of active cheats, non-cooperators and free-riders evolves separately in each case, and that the evolution of punishment probably precedes the evolution of cooperation. The occurrence of all three in a single species is, therefore, quite unusual. Yet, somehow, humans have moved from vengeful individual punishment to organised altruistic punishment of cheats (using a sense of fairness), of non-cooperators (using social morality) and of free-riders (using cultural prescription).

From altruistic punishment to social model-sharing

The path from vengeful to altruistic punishers likely involved many small steps, most of which we have no hope of recreating or understanding. However, three known steps do stand out, and between them they tell a cohesive – albeit not comprehensive – story of our route toward enforced cooperation.

The first of these steps is vigilant sharing, as proposed by Erdal and Whiten (1994). Looking for an evolutionary explanation for human cooperation, they proposed that the first step, the shift from vengeful individual punishment to organised altruistic punishment of cheats, was a product of counter-dominance ('nobody should get more than me'); if enough *me*'s felt that *you* were hogging a resource, then they would gang up on you to restore the balance. The Darwinian pursuit of self-interest by everyone, accompanied by the shifting alliances of Machiavellianism, means that no individual can hope to preserve exclusive access to a resource, so sharing becomes the sensible default position. If I don't share, the others gang up on me and I lose the resource I was trying to dominate, and perhaps more; if I share but keep a fair proportion for myself, the others will have enough reason to leave me alone with my portion. Nothing un-Darwinian needs to be invoked for this to be a stable scenario: being fair is being fit; so survival of the fittest collocates with survival of the fairest, and a sense of fairness therefore becomes part of our genome.

The second step, punishment of non-cooperators, was originally set out as reverse dominance by Boehm (1993), ironically in a paper that Erdal and Whiten were responding to in their 1994 paper. In a response to Erdal and Whiten's vigilant-sharing model (see Erdal and Whiten 1994, replies), Boehm makes a distinction between earlier foraging groups, for whom vigilant sharing would be necessary to preserve group cohesion, and later large-game hunting groups, where cooperation in the hunt created a new level of socialisation. Boehm expanded on reverse dominance in 1999, arguing that it does not represent the removal of hierarchical tendencies, but is instead the equalisation of hierarchy: everyone is kept at the same level by group-enforced sanctions. If the sanctioning mechanism breaks down then hierarchy will reappear. This makes it a social mechanism and gives it more reach than vigilant sharing. Imagine a group that share vigilantly, thus ensuring any windfalls in their foraging efforts help everyone; now imagine an individual who never forages as long, or as effectively, as the others. This individual is not a complete cheat, attempting to subvert the shared enterprise; they are a partial non-cooperator, attempting to use the shared enterprise for personal advantage. But how can they be policed by vigilant sharing alone? They are sharing, and forcing others to share with them; just less of the former and more of the latter.

In large-game hunting, the individuals who hold back are more obvious, and the disadvantage for the rest of the group is more stark: large-game hunting is dangerous. Reverse dominance can be used to police this non-cooperative behaviour because it is not about being left behind in the share-out, it is about being socially moral in the shared enterprise. With reverse dominance, the individual's agenda ceases to be the primary source of their fitness; instead, the cohesion and cooperation of the group – first the hunting group and later the social group – make commitment to the group agenda the key fitness indicator for the individual. The reproductive success of the individual relies, in large part, on the success of the group's shared enterprises.

The third step in our route toward enforced cooperation is the strangest of all: self-sacrifice. How can self-sacrifice ever be a viable and evolutionarily stable strategy? Surely the self-sacrificers are removing their genes from the future, so how does a genetic tendency to self-sacrifice get off the ground? The 10 million military casualties in World War I and the 27 million in World War II (more than 1% of the world population at the time) show that self-sacrifice is not the vanishingly rare phenomenon that evolutionary calculus indicates it should be.

Self-sacrifice represents the extreme end of altruism, the maximal version of the small, everyday sacrifices (giving resources, time and knowledge to strangers without expectation of a quid pro quo) that are not just frequent, they are a commonplace expectation in our human social systems. Like everyday altruism, self-sacrifice is unexpected in evolutionary terms; but it is not unknown, and it is common in eusocial species. Anyone who has witnessed a conflict between two ant colonies will know the suicidal tenacity that individual ants display in defence of their nests. However, the reason that individual ants are willing to sacrifice their lives is because it is not their life that gets their genes into the future, it is that of their queen; this is not the case for *Homo sapiens*, who are usually individually fertile.

We have only recently begun to look at the human psychology of self-sacrifice as non-aberrant behaviour, and what we are finding is that sociality, morality and culture provide an overlay to human genetic imperatives; it is almost as if we had a dispassionate self, allowing us to treat our Actual self as an insignificant factor in being a self. Huebner and Hauser (2011) look at self-sacrifice in terms of a variant of the trolley problem, a hypothetical dilemma that requires a subject to choose between inaction, which will kill five people, and action, which will kill one person. The basic problem is that a runaway trolley (tram) is going to kill five people who are on the track, unless it is diverted; but if it is diverted, it will kill one person on the alternative track. The dilemma is, should you divert the trolley? There are variants of this problem, and the one Huebner and Hauser are interested in involves a choice between inaction (five anonymous people die), self-preserving action (one anonymous person dies) or self-sacrifice (the subject dies by throwing themself in front of the trolley, thus stopping it). They looked at a *folk-morality* scenario (the choice that people believe others should make) and a *self-sacrifice* scenario (the choice an individual should make when their own life is part of the equation). In the folk-morality scenario, 18.7 per cent believed inaction was best, 43 per cent judged that the lone stranger should die, and 38.3 per cent thought the choosing individual should sacrifice themself. In the self-sacrifice scenario, 18.2 per cent chose inaction, 48 per cent chose the lone stranger, and 33.7 per cent chose to sacrifice themself.

The response to a hypothetical case may not be a good indicator of what would happen in a real case, and the difference between hypothesis and reality is probably much greater in the self-sacrifice scenario than in the folk-morality scenario. So the responses do not really inform us about self-sacrifice itself; but they do indicate the moral stance we take about self-sacrifice: a third of the population may not actually be willing to sacrifice themselves to save strangers, but they do seem to have a dispassionate self that believes they should be willing to do so.

A similar study by Sachdeva et al. (2015) looked at a variation of the trolley problem, in which the trolley is stopped by either throwing a person off a bridge over the track, or throwing yourself off. It offers the same choice between inaction, self-preserving action and self-sacrifice. The study was cross-cultural, pitching US students against Indian and Iranian students; and it found that people from the USA were more likely than the other nationalities to see self-sacrifice as preferable to other-sacrifice – which does not indicate the people in the US are braver, only that they think they should be seen to be so. However, unlike Huebner and Hauser, Sachdeva et al. found that subjects were more likely to sacrifice themselves rather than the other when the problem was expressed from a first-person perspective; and, contrary to the logic of kin-selection theory, self-sacrifice was much more popular than relative sacrifice.

Atran and Ginges (2012) looked at the role of religion in the definition of self and self-sacrifice. They found that religious adherence seems to enhance the worth of fellow adherents, and therefore increases the likelihood of self-sacrifice to support the in-group. However, it also decreases the worth of (dehumanises) out-group individuals, and it increases mistrust and conflict. Atran and Ginges observe that 'moralizing gods emerged over the last few millennia, enabling large-scale cooperation, and sociopolitical conquest even without war'; but if the timescale is only millennia, then religious self-sacrifice has not had enough time to become fixed in the genome, and it must therefore be working with pre-existing self-sacrificial tendencies. Their conclusion is apposite: the role of religion in self-sacrifice needs to be studied further and clarified; but they do not themselves provide much further clarification on what is a topic of vital interest in the modern world.

Dugas et al. (2016) looked at an internal measure of self-worth rather than an external hypothetical, or group-defined, measure of self-worth: a person's sense of significance, as measured by the Meaning in Life Questionnaire (Steger et al. 2006).[2] In six separate experiments, they found that individuals were more willing to self-sacrifice when their sense of significance was low, and that self-sacrifice was seen as a way to increase sense of significance. They also found that self-sacrifice increased a sense of significance more than pleasurable experiences did.

Prinz (2006) shows that there is an important link between human moral judgements and emotion: humans seem to be genetically programmed to feel bad when they are violating the cultural norms of their society. Humans are not constrained to behave in a selfless way just by their need for socialisation; over time, the constraint has, itself, become genetically fixed in the species. Being bad (opposing the cultural norms with which we are faced) makes us *feel* bad – as most toddlers understand. This means that, genetically, it is very difficult for most humans to be dispassionate over moral matters; which is odd, as the cultural norms are not themselves genetically programmed. Everett (2016) makes the argument that the range of human cultures is remarkably wide – so wide that human culture is of a different order to that of other animals; this means that the possibility of any particular cultural norm becoming genetically fixed in the species is vanishingly small. However, as Prinz shows, the will to abide by whatever rules a culture imposes on an individual does seem to be innate; which means that, if a culture encourages self-sacrifice, then the individuals in that culture will feel impelled to conform and to self-sacrifice; but if it does not, they will not.

What these studies tell us is that self-sacrifice seems to be an emic reaction to expectations enshrined in the cultural self-model – the ideal self we are expected by others to strive to be. Whether it is adherence to cultural morality, as Huebner and Hauser and Sachdeva et al. argue, being demonstrably devout, as Atran and Ginges propose, or proving your worth to the group, as Dugas et al. say, the dispassionate self seems to make etic self-preservation negotiable for humans.

So where *did* social calculus come from?

We have covered a lot of ground in this chapter, in terms of genetic biology, evolutionary time and human evolution itself; but have we got any closer to the origins of social calculus? It depends on what we see as significant in human social calculus: if we are only interested in the cognitive capacity to model others in our group and the relationships between them, then a lot of this chapter may have been a waste of time. We started by finding that social calculus as cognition may not be limited to humans, and 'before us' could have been sufficient explanation for how and when social calculus evolved. However, it is the sharing of social calculus that makes us interesting as a species, and that story takes a lot more telling. From Machiavellian intelligence, through vigilant sharing and reverse dominance, and on to self-sacrifice, we are beginning to understand the path we took to our particularly human recipe of pseudo-eusociality. It is like a jigsaw in which all the corners have been found, and we're getting a lot of the edges in place. We may not yet see all of what it means to be human, but we have framed the picture; and we are completing more of the puzzle and revealing more of the story every day.

Notes

1. Taken from Alfred Lord Tennyson's poem, *In Memoriam A. H. H.*, canto 56. Published 1850, nine years before Darwin's *On the Origin of Species*.
2. See www.michaelfsteger.com/?page_id=13 for a copy of the questionnaire.

6
The Language of Self

> 'Come, there's no use in crying like that!' said Alice to herself, rather sharply; 'I advise you to leave off this minute!' She generally gave herself very good advice (though she very seldom followed it), and sometimes she scolded herself so severely as to bring tears into her eyes; and once she remembered trying to box her own ears for having cheated herself in a game of croquet she was playing against herself, for this curious child was very fond of pretending to be two people. 'But it's no use now,' thought poor Alice, 'to pretend to be two people! Why, there's hardly enough of me left to make *one* respectable person!'
>
> (Lewis Carroll 1865, Chapter 1: 'Down the Rabbit-Hole')

In 1871, Charles Darwin published *The Descent of Man, and Selection in Relation to Sex*, the second book of his evolutionary duology. In this book, he set out to show that humans, with all their cultural accoutrements, descended from ape ancestors. He took the view that we should expect no great novelty in human cultural tools – including language, despite its apparent difference from other communication systems in nature. Darwin proposed a series of routes from natural sound-making to meaningful language-making: imitation, both of the sounds of other animals and of things, and by replication of physical actions (such as waving), but using the tongue and mouth; emotional sounds; and the sounds of work and play (Darwin 1874). Jespersen (1922, 114–17) later dismissed these as insufficient explanations, and they have become known as the bow-wow, ding-dong, ta-ta, pooh-pooh, yo-he-ho and la-la theories of language origins. They all remain possible routes to language, but none has yet been evidenced beyond the level of hypothesis.

Charles Hockett (1960) made the first modern attempt to identify what made human language different from other communication systems, and he devised a set of 13 (later 16) *design features* of communication. The first 13 features were:

- A vocal-auditory channel, or speaking and listening (1); broadcast transmission and directional reception (2); and transitoriness or rapid fading (3): we now recognise that these are useful but not necessary for language, or for any communication system.
- Interchangeability (4): we can receive as well as transmit.
- Total feedback (5); and specialisation (6): speakers can control their speech because language is communicative and intentional.
- Semanticity (7); and arbitrariness (8): sounds have meanings, but the sound–meaning correspondence is arbitrary.
- Discreteness (9): small differences in sound can represent big differences in meaning, and vice versa.
- Displacement (10): speech can refer to non-present events, treating the irreal as real.
- Productivity (11): language allows the creation of novel utterances to represent new ideas.
- Traditional transmission (12): language is a negotiated convention; language and culture are intertwined.
- Duality of patterning (13): meaningful messages are made up of several distinct meaningful units (words and morphemes), which themselves are made up of distinct but meaningless units (phonemes).

The last three design features were added by Hockett in 1963:

- Prevarication (14): language can be used to deceive.
- Reflexiveness (15): language can be used to talk about language.
- Learnability (16): language is teachable and learnable.

Of these, Hockett initially believed that displacement, productivity, traditional transmission and duality of pattern were exclusive to language. He later added prevarication, reflexiveness and learnability to this exclusive list, but then removed displacement, traditional transmission and prevarication. Unfortunately, this attempt to identify the specialness of language as a communication system relies on a belief that there is a specialness to be identified; this remains to be proved and, indeed, may not be the case. Of the four design features Hockett initially reserved to language, we now know that honeybee communication uses displacement (von Frisch 1973), although not productivity, traditional transmission or duality of patterning; but many primates are now known to have local cultures within their species, and they use traditional transmission to pass on their cultural memes (Horner et al. 2006). Looking at the other two original 'exclusive to humans' features, chimpanzees who have been taught to communicate with humans using a hybrid gesture system have shown spontaneous productivity in their signals (Savage-Rumbaugh and Lewin 1994), while prairie dogs (Slobodchikoff 2002) and marmosets (Pomberger et al. 2018) have been found to use duality of patterning. Dolphin communication may use all four – at this stage we do not have enough evidence to know, but the indicators are positive (Herman and Uyeyama 1999). Of the final three additions, prevarication (deception) is common throughout nature (for example, Kirkpatrick 2011), and osmotic learning is common in mammals (Crockford et al. 2004). This leaves reflexiveness, the status of which is unknowable because it is ill-defined – we cannot even say whether our own capacity to use language to talk about language is truly reflexive or just a subset of modelling: when we appear to be using language to talk about language, are we really referring to language, or are we just making a model of language that we can talk about? The belief in grammar as a fixed rule system behind our utterances – among some linguists, at least – indicates this may well be so.

Wacewicz and Żywiczyński (2014) indicate that Hockett's problems with his design features stem from his treatment of language as an identifiable 'thing', with the design features as components or subsystems of the 'thing'. This misses the point that language, like any communication system, is a cognitive tool for achieving objectives, and it only remains an effective system while it continues to achieve those objectives. Just as a description of a screwdriver tells you nothing about the vital role of screws in woodworking, so a reductive description of language ignores its most important function: it is a way of doing things, and the things that get done are more important than how they are done.

Daniel Everett (2017) adds a 17th entry to Hockett's list – or, perhaps, it would be fairer to say that Everett's single characteristic underlies the other 16. Everett calls this characteristic:

> 'underdeterminacy' – saying less than what is intended to be communicated and leaving the unspoken assumptions to be figured out by the hearer in some way. Underdeterminacy has always been part of language.
>
> (Everett 2017, 3)

Underdeterminacy is a term he borrowed from Pragmatics (for example, Carston 2002, Chapter 1), but he uses it to make the case that language is not about what is said, but about what is meant. Any story about the origins of language has to accommodate the fact that language communication is not a series of unconnected utterances, but a series of ongoing relationships between people; and, as the relationships develop, they become more interpersonal and contextual – and the communication in the relationship becomes more underdetermined. Memory does not just remember the past; it informs the present and directs the future.

What does this tell us about the role of self in language? So far in this book, the case has been made that awareness of self is not a necessary outcome of large or complex brains; and it is not even a necessary outcome of complex social cognition. It is, however, a necessary outcome of the communication of complex social cognition. We don't have a need for self-awareness until we are sharing models of other people's selves, and only then when others are sharing their models of our own self with us. If my self-awareness emerges from my capacity to make a third-person model of myself, and my only need for a capacity to self-model is to incorporate your models of me into my social calculus, and you are only able to present your models of me to me because we share social calculus, then we would expect that the mechanism through which we share social calculus – a communication system that can reliably transmit the complexity of social calculus – will be replete with indicators of that complexity.

It is reasonable to assume, in the absence of a communication system specialised for social calculus, that we share social calculus through language. This is not to say that the sole function of language is the sharing of social calculus, or even that this was the original function of the precursor to language. The sharing of interpersonal information does require both cognitive complexity and a signalling system that can be segmented, differentiated and hierarchical; so social calculus certainly appears to be a strong contender for the origin of complex human language; but that claim is not made here. All we are looking for here is evidence of a close relationship between social calculus and language: the link between social calculus and language needs to be evident in the way the two of them work together.

So is there a relationship between language and the self- and other-modelling of social calculus? Alice's conversation with herself indicates that there does seem to be. She shows a willingness to see herself as both speaker and listener in her monologue ('I advise you to leave off this minute!'); she models herself as both a cultural *she* to advise and a social *herself* to be advised; she further distances these two selves by giving the advised Social self the self-will to ignore the advising Cultural self, and the advising self the right of punishment over the self-willed advised self. Alice's relationship with her models of her selves is simultaneously intensely human and – in the form expressed by Carroll – deeply strange. Her final utterance ('there's hardly enough of me left to make *one* respectable person!') reflects the dilemma of self-modelling: the modelled Cultural self is not a real self, but it is the best approximation we have to the respectable self we hope others believe us to be.

Pronominalisation and selfhood

One of the biggest effects of social modelling on language is likely to be the existence and nature of pronouns – the words that represent the speaker, the listener and anyone and anything else referenced. Dictionaries tell us that pronouns are substitutes for nouns and have very general reference – they are not direct references to things or people, they refer to the communicative roles undertaken by things and people. But as we saw in Chapter 3, they are not merely a simplification of how we name things: they act as ad hoc labels in a discourse, allowing the interlocutors to reduce the utterance load at the cost of increased cognitive load. For instance, when we hear 'you shouldn't do that', we engage in a fast comparison of the possible members of the group *you*, their current activity, the cultural expectation about that activity, and the intention of the speaker themself. Our reaction will be different depending on whether we are likely to be in or out of the group *you*, whether we feel our current action is or is not culturally acceptable, and whether we accept or reject the approbation of the speaker. The two pronouns *you* and *that* indicate people and actions only indirectly, and their underdeterminacy means that the utterance is not just context-specific, it is also listener-specific: different listeners hearing the same utterance will have different objects in mind as *you* and *that*, and thus react to the utterance differently.

This situation is further complicated by the fact that pronouns are not a stable class across languages. If we look at the French version of the utterance, we find an immediate difference. Both '*tu ne devrais pas faire ça*' and '*vous ne devriez pas faire ça*' are valid translations, but they do not mean the same thing: where English 'you' can refer to a single listener or several, French divides the pronoun into singular and plural forms. In Spanish, a different problem arises: '*no deberías hacer eso*' and '*no deberíais hacer eso*' both retain the singular–plural distinction, but the word for 'you' has disappeared. It is only indicated by the ending of the verb 'should'. Spanish is called a pro-drop language because the pronouns are not obligatory, and are usually used only for emphasis ('*tú no deberías hacer eso*', 'you [as a particular individual] shouldn't do that'). However, as an example of underdeterminacy developing out of familiarity, the construct 'shouldn't do that' is also a fully acceptable English form. The term 'pro-drop' does not so much define a language as a way of using the language.

These two examples explore only a fraction of the differences between second-person reference in English, French and Spanish; and other languages add further complications to pronominal reference. Japanese is considered by some linguists to lack full pronouns, using noun phrases instead. For instance, a man often refers to himself in the first person using the word *boku*, which actually means male servant. This removes reference to the speaker from the utterance, turning it into a third-person reference: 'The servant is sorry' rather than 'I am sorry'. *Watashi* is used by both genders, and means something like 'the private self'. This referencing of the self in the third person is not unknown in English, and it is often done using the person's name. For instance, Donald Trump's first-ever tweet in 2009 was 'Be sure to tune in and watch Donald Trump on Late Night with David Letterman as he presents the Top Ten List tonight!' We even have a word, illeism, to describe self-referencing by name; but we tend to view it as either childish (under-4s commonly refer to themselves by name) or as narcissistic and somehow dishonest. In Japanese, it is seen as polite self-effacement.

Malay is another language in which full pronouns seem to be absent, and others are referred to by their social role. A Malay-speaker has no need for *I* or *you*, because they always have a role they can use. For instance, when speaking with a grandparent, the grandparent is *nenda* to both speaker and listener, and the grandchild is *cucunda*. Pirahã, the language documented by Daniel Everett, 'has the simplest pronoun inventory known, and evidence suggests that its entire pronominal inventory may have been borrowed' (Everett 2005, 622). Everett describes it as having only three pronouns, for the three persons, and no differentiation between singular or plural. The pronouns act as prefixes to verbs, although they can be used as stand-alone emphatics, too.

To be more accurate when talking about pronouns, therefore, we should refer not to pronouns but to a process of pronominalisation, which can be defined as reference using communicative roles rather than names or titles. The fact that a language has a mechanism for pronominalisation is more important than how that mechanism works. Nonetheless, I will attempt here to describe pronominalisation through the lens of English. It is not a perfect representation, but it is one that all readers of this version of the text should be able to understand.

Where names come from

Before we start on pronominal replacements for naming, we should perhaps consider how naming itself developed. It seems natural that we all treat ourselves as named individuals, and that somehow our name acts as a proxy for our self in our dealings with others; but that is all evidence after the fact of naming. The truth is that, in important ways, our name is not our own. Most importantly, it is not generated by us but given to us by others. This may not be the case with dolphins, which seem to create their own signature whistles to identify themselves to others. When a dolphin uses another's signature whistle to attract their attention, they use a variant of the whistle – thereby identifying the call as a *you* reference rather than an *I* reference. We cannot know for certain whether this is what is really going on inside the dolphin's head, but it does seem likely that the variations in the signature whistle are there to indicate to other dolphins whether the whistle is self-referring or other-referring (King et al. 2013).

Dolphins, unlike humans, seem to generate their own name-labels: they have the advantage of being born with functional vocal equipment, and usually they have generated their own signature whistle within two months or less of their birth (Tyack 1997). They are also precocious at visual self-recognition, passing the Gallup mirror test at age 7 months (Morrison and Reiss 2018). In contrast, human infants are born with underdeveloped vocal equipment, and the neurological systems controlling vocalisation are rudimentary. By 9 months, they recognise and respond to the name given to them by the adults around them, but it is not until around 18 months that they use it back to the adults (Holinger 2012). Human infants only become recognisably self-aware, and able to pass the self-recognition mirror test, at around 18 months.

Humans do the exact opposite of dolphins. We do not develop our own name; we expect our parents, or the people caring for us, to label us soon after we are born. Recently, the apparatus of the state has also insisted that this name be registered promptly after birth, further emphasising the role of others in naming a human person. This registration requirement remains the case, despite the fact that the state itself now relies on exclusive alpha-numeric combinations, and not our names, to label us – and, of course, these alpha-numeric state labels are also given to us and not chosen by us.

Having been given a name by those around us, we then continue to receive different names throughout our lives. Some are role-specific, such as grandparent and grandchild; some are arbitrary labels, like prisoner KJ4609; and some are comments on our appearance or nature; but they all share the fact that they are given rather than self-selected. Our own attempts to re-label ourselves usually only work if they create a believable new persona for a new audience. For some people, this name-change is a vital part of their self-definition (and may be seen as social recognition of society's definitional error); but in these cases, the old name is abandoned as a legitimate label for the individual. Authors, in contrast, often choose pseudonyms to distance their everyday self from their authorial self: the Reverend Charles Dodgson wrote as Lewis Carroll to preserve the gravitas required by his religious and mathematical work. Sometimes authors choose a pseudonym to differentiate their authorial selves: J.K. Rowling also writes detective books, but as Robert Galbraith. Actors may adopt new names for enduring characterisations they create, such as Barry Humphries's alter ego Dame Edna Everage. Self-selected pseudonyms are also used extensively in selfish deception, which may be why discovered pseudonyms can generate a visceral shock reaction. However, most of the famous criminal pseudonyms are given by the media, not self-selected. Even the words 'pseudonym' or 'alias' show our approach to self-selected names: they are not real names, they are other names.

The human reliance on others to name us may be unique in nature. If selfness comes out of recognition of models of my self offered by others, then the capacity to recognise my self in their offered models is vital; and early acceptance of the social label agreed by others as referring to me – my name – becomes a vital part of self-recognition. Naming itself is not unique in nature, but nominalisation is such a fundamental part of human socialisation and communication that we need to be named at birth; we cannot wait for human individuals to offer their own names.

The internalisation of a group of sounds that others use to identify us, and the understanding that this group of sounds represents us, leaves us open to the idea that our name may be an effective proxy for us as an individual; it can be used to represent all aspects of our self. However, naming is also arbitrary: a name is not a unique way to represent an individual, as we can have many contextual names. This, in turn, allows us to accept alternative labels, both for us and for others, in terms of our roles in group activities – and these include our roles in communicative acts.

We accept general labels (*you*, *they*) as referring to us via our relationship with the speaker; and, as speaker, we offer a general label (*me*) to represent ourself-as-speaker.

The origin of *they*

Pronominalisation allows us to identify the three roles of speaker, listener and talked-about when we make an utterance; so pronouns only have a role in language when it is about sharing social models, social calculus or the relationships between people and objects. When social calculus is cognitive and uncommunicated, stable internal labels (or unshared nicknames) work perfectly well in modelling the individuals involved; and communication that is not about social relationships does not require the sender and receiver of the communication to be identified inside the communication. The only role for pronominalisation in non-social communication is to indicate that a previously referenced thing is still the object of interest; pronominalisation in this form is gestural, verbally pointing to the object of interest, and may well have come directly out of a hybrid sound-and-gesture communication system (for example, McNeill 2012). The language-out-of-gesture debate is complex and still ongoing; but it is peripheral to the discussion here, so we can safely ignore it without taking sides. We can instead appeal to other reasons why the first instance of pronominalisation is likely to have been the third person (in English, *he*, *she*, *it* and the singular and plural *they*).

The first of these reasons is that third-person pronominal reference does not rely on communication, but can be completely cognitive. The simple, linear social calculus model of A-Relationship-B is sufficient to understand the emotions involved in that single pairing; but if I am to build a cognitive model of A as an individual, I have to bring together all the cognitive models of A that I have in my calculus, as in the example set out in Table 6.1.

The emergence of relationship modelling in the primate clade does not require a new neural architecture. Social calculus is, essentially, a networked database with modelled individuals as nodes and relationships as links; and we already know that vertebrate brains work as neural networks (O'Connell and Hofmann 2012). This means that the *Homo* clade already had the cognitive architecture to hold social calculus as a network of nodes and links, rather than as lists. This makes adding or deleting nodes, and establishing, redefining and removing links, easy to do without disturbing the rest of the network. However, maintaining

Table 6.1 List of my social calculus relationships between A and others

A-Relationship(good)-B
A-Relationship(neutral)-C
A-Relationship(poor)-D
A-Relationship(good)-E
A-Relationship(poor)-F
A-Relationship(good)-G
A-Relationship(neutral)-H
A-Relationship(good)-I
A-Relationship(poor)-J
A-Relationship(neutral)-K

a large neural network of relationships would be costly in terms of cognition, so we cannot assume that it was equally available to all members of the *Homo* clade, or that it is equally available to all modern human individuals. There may even have been minimum levels of size and complexity that brains had to reach before they became able to handle social calculus.

Social calculus works both ways: it allows me to understand the relationships between individuals, and it allows me to understand an individual through their relationships with others and with me. However, the more I need to understand A as the container of a complex set of relationships, the more I need a shortcut for the concept 'A' (a nickname), and the more I need to group others into relational hierarchies around A. I can shortcut my list of A's relationships with others by grouping those others in terms of their holistic relationship with A; and I can then modify my personal list of single-argument Relationship-A relationships with others by grouping them in terms of my relationship with A and A's relationship with them. To express this linguistically, I can represent A as a third-person cipher (*he*, *she*, *it* or *they* singular), and a group of individuals sharing a relationship with A becomes a third-person aggregate (*they* plural). Figure 6.1 shows how this could be represented. This process can be repeated for every person with whom I have a single-argument Relationship-A relationship, making the third-person cipher and aggregate representations into reusable non-specific placeholder terms.

Because this process is cognitive and not necessarily communicative, it can precede communicated language; and there does seem to be a precursor for this kind of social calculus in the socio-cognitive modelling of the chacma baboons we met in Chapter 2 (Cheney and Seyfarth 2007).

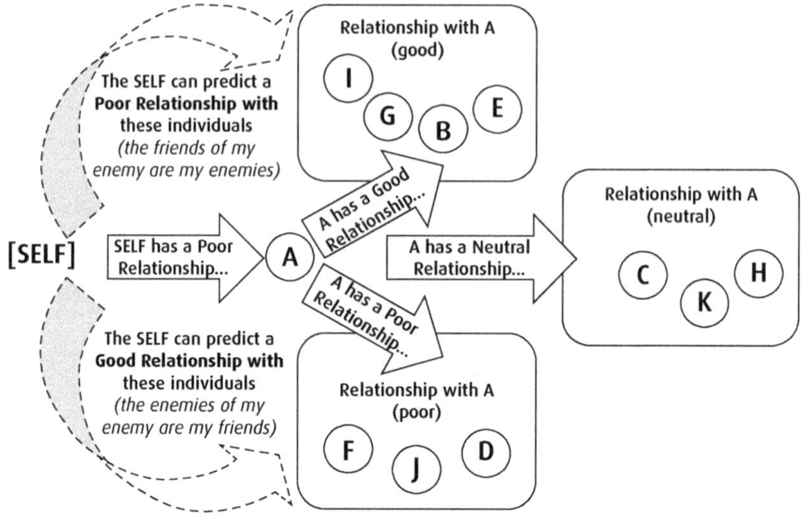

Fig 6.1 Suggested cognitive structure for the self's model of the social calculus relationships

These baboons live in a stable social hierarchy of individuals within families, giving deference to those above them to avoid confrontation, and expecting deference from those below them. The hierarchy is linear, because hierarchy between families takes precedence over hierarchy between individuals; and, by itself, it requires only simple Relationship-A modelling. However, baboons also learn from interactions between others in their group. They can remotely identify callers from their calls, and they pay more attention when, for instance, a threat bark from a subordinate is followed by a fear bark from a dominant. The hierarchy of families overlaying the individual hierarchy is also significant: after a confrontation, reconciliation with another member of the antagonist's family counts as a reconciliation with the antagonist. It seems, therefore, that chacma baboons cognitively maintain a network of relationships between others, albeit filtered through Relationship-A modelling. However, there is no indication that they communicate this network to each other.

The second reason why third-person pronominals are likely to have preceded other pronominals is that this form of reference is not based on the roles of speaker and listener. The first and second person, when used communicatively in a discourse, are in constant flux, depending on who is speaking (because my *me* is your *you* and vice versa). But a third-person reference can remain constant throughout a discourse, regardless of who is speaking: my Alf is the same Alf as your Alf, so my *he* is the same as your *he* while it refers to Alf. Third-person pronouns are meta-referential: they refer to a name or label that has been used previously in the discourse, and that name or label in turn refers to a real person or thing. So, once the name or label has been linked to a pronoun in a conversation, that link remains valid until replaced by a new link.

This also applies to cognition: once a mental place-marker has been created to represent an individual, it can continue to be used in that role. In its basic form, this is nominalisation, as each individual is likely to be represented by a unique label. But in the social calculus form A-Relationship-B, both A and B are meta-referential: they are placeholders that can be filled by any nominalised label, which in turn refers to a cognitive model of a real person or thing. This, once again, indicates that the cognitive modelling of third-person pronominals can precede its communicative usage. This is impossible for first- and second-person pronominals, because they are markers of the communicative act; they identify who is talking and who is being talked to, and have no cognitive meaning outside of communication.

The third reason why the third person is likely to have been the first instance of pronominalisation is that it is object-referring. While it is called 'third person', it is also 'first thing': where *I* and *you* are necessarily communicative, and therefore have an animate and active role in the communication, the third person is only a thing referred to – and, in the third person, people can be treated as inanimate things. The capacity to blur the distinction between animate and inanimate is enshrined in different ways in different languages. While languages like English preserve some form of animate/inanimate distinction (pronouns *he, she, it*), other languages like French do not (pronouns *he, she*). In the Basque language, Euskera, in contrast, the proximity of the object or person is paramount (pronouns are represented by *it* [close], *it* [far] and *it* [between near and far]); like French, there is no animate/inanimate distinction, but where French treats everything as animate, Euskera treats everyone and everything the same.

In cognition, distinguishing between animate, intentional beings and inanimate, passive objects would seem to be a useful capacity. Intentions, however, are only identifiable in terms of outcomes; and 'passive' is an outcome that can be attributed to both animate and inanimate objects. Additionally, inanimate objects do not even need to be persistent, they can be transient events with outcomes; and the nature of those outcomes can even challenge their inanimacy. A lightning flash is just an event, but it can fell trees and kill people, which indicates an apparent intention behind the event, and a possible being behind the intention. Identifying intention as a marker of animacy, and effect as a marker of intention, leads us to fallaciously reverse-link effect with intentionality, and intentionality with animacy. Third-person pronominalisation, like many cognitive capacities, comes with costs as well as benefits.

They is, therefore, a cognitive event, the origin of which may precede the *Homo* lineage, and which may be ancient in the primate clade. Its role in coordinating sets of social calculus pairings makes it cognitively valuable without communication: it contains all the features required for communicative pronominalisation without needing to be communicated – unlike the first- and second-person forms. It seems that, in terms of evolution, we may have long mislabelled our terms here: the first-person form to be used by humans was actually the third-person form.

The origin of *you* and *me*

Social calculus uses third-person pronominalisation to provide meta-reference without any need to communicate it. In contrast, first- and second-person pronominalisation do not have any function before we begin communicating our social calculus (Edwardes 2014). They are not a basic feature of social calculus, but they do simplify the exchange of social calculus models that include the receiver, *you*, or the sender, *me*. They also allow the sender and receiver to recognise the privileged nature of two particular aspects of social calculus: the *they* that is the current receiver of my signal, and the *they* that is the receiver of your signal.

For *they*, the cognitive concept was needed before, and therefore generated before, the communicative representation; but the communicative representation of *you* was needed before its cognitive concept became useful or necessary. Yet it is impossible for a communicative representation to exist without its cognitive concept; so what pre-existing cognitive concept was available to be pressed into service as the cognitive concept *you*? The only clear candidate seems to be the cognitive concept of *they*: *you* is a special case of *they*, a meta-meta-reference derived from the meta-referential value of *they*. The extra meta-level allows the internal short-form reference to an individual to include the communicative role of that individual; *they* is a cognitive reference to a named other, or group of others; and *you* is a cognitive reference to a named other, or group of others, which is the object of a communicative act. *You* is just a privileged form of *they*.

So when, after we began communicating our social calculus, did *you* appear as a communicable representation? If we see *you* as a privileged form of *they*, then the answer has to be: quite soon after social calculus began to be shared, and very soon after the first sharing of an A-Relationship-B construct in which the receiver of the construct is either A or B. When sharing information about third-person others, the relationship construct is not intimate to either the sender or receiver; it is information about things happening 'out there'. But a relationship construct that includes the receiver is only 'out there' for the sender – for the receiver, it is intimate and therefore privileged.

This leaves the problem of *me*, which is at the heart of this book. Just as *you* is a privileged form of *they*, so too is *me*: it is a meta-meta-reference derived from the meta-referential value of *they*. In this case, however, the extra meta-level allows the communicative short-form reference to be recognised as an internal cognitive representation of the individual themself; unlike *you*, what is being recognised is not a pre-existing element in the individual's social calculus. When social calculus is just cognitive, the individual has no need for a model of *me*; the self is the unchanging and undefined centre of the calculus, the base on which the calculus is built. It is only when I am presented with someone else's model of me that I need to acknowledge that there is a *me* to be modelled. This means that my cognitive model of *me* is not a product of perspicacious introspection, it is an amalgam of other people's models of my self, a third-person representation of third-person representations which should not represent me in any sensible way, but which somehow do.

As the appearance of *you* and *me* must have been nearly simultaneous, the question of which came first is difficult to answer. The order of events works either way, because the shared *you* needs to be recognised by the receiver as *me*, and the shared *me* needs to be recognised by the receiver as *you*. Whichever came first, the appearance of the second from the first would have happened very quickly, and quite soon after social calculus constructs were being exchanged. It is possible (and probably best) to treat the exchange of social calculus constructs and the beginnings of *you* and *me* as simultaneous. However, the cognitive consequences of the concepts of *you* and *me* are interrelated but different; and the effects, particularly in the case of *me*, are wide-ranging in defining our species, our self and our selfness.

As we saw in Chapter 3, human cognition distinguishes between two types of human knowledge: etic facts, which are definitionally true but of which we are not necessarily consciously aware; and emic facts, which are true because we agree they are true (Brown 2004). Shared social calculus models are, themselves, emic facts, and their communication generates the emic facts of *you* and *me*. However, the emic fact of *me* relies on an internalised representation of someone else's model of me; it is not me in any self-aware way, it is my awareness of your awareness of my selfhood. This makes it my third-person representation of my self, just another *they* model I can put into future what-if scenarios – including scenarios where my physical self does not survive. Yet the capacity to model my self into the future, and the capacity to model a future in which my model of my self no longer exists, somehow mitigates the very natural and visceral dislike of self-extinction. The ability to project my emic *me* into the future beyond my death is a very strange thing to be able to do. How can I cognitively visualise a world where I have no cognitive existence? And what is the evolutionary advantage of being able to do so? Recognition of the emic *me* may actually be a two-edged sword for the individual, in that the capacity for social self-modelling damps down our primate Machiavellian self-interest.

Self-modelling works backward in time, too: the emic fact of *me* allows me to relate my current model of me to my memories of me, creating the impression of a continuous self that exists through time. I can also receive modelled memories and other stories from other people about times and places in which I have never existed; and I can relate my current model of me to those stories. I can be with Harold at Hastings as he takes one in the eye (an event that probably never happened, and certainly not in my experience); I can be on the steps with Sidney Carton as he does a far, far better thing than he has ever done; I can even be with our early ancestors as they evolved into modern humans. The emic *me* is more than just a placeholder for a cognitive model of the self, but it is less than recognition of the self itself: more than *I think*, but less than *I am*.

This dual deception of the emic *me* (that the modelled self explains the self, and that the modelled self is the self) gives us a more nuanced understanding of self-sacrifice. As we saw in Chapter 5, there is a tendency to dispassionately see the self in our models of self-sacrifice as synonymous with the self that is sacrificed; but this is not the case. It is easy to sacrifice the emic *me* because it 'lives on' (or at least has purported cognitive existence) after death, and 'existed' before birth; it has a timeless quality that death cannot affect. In this cognitive environment, self-sacrifice becomes more than acceptable; it can even be a sought-after, or valued, quality. We do not need to go as far as Martin Luther King Jr when he said, 'if a man has not discovered something that he will die for, he isn't fit to live', but we probably do recognise a personal mental line beyond which death is preferable to living. Yet we also do not recognise the crossing of this mental line in others, treating suicide (especially in the West) as a foolish or bad choice (which, in evolutionary terms, but not in self-modelling terms, it is).

Here we are faced with a conflict between the two different emic *me*'s, the social self-model and the cultural self-model: for the Social self, the emic *me*, it is the costs and benefits to the *is* self-model that need to be assessed; for the Cultural self, it is the costs and benefits to the *should be* self-model that matter. These can be very different things; and there is always the etic subliminal evolutionary drive toward self-survival to be taken into account, too. In self-sacrifice, the social self-model and cultural self-model seem to be working together against the evolutionary drive; in suicide, the social self-model is, by itself, against the cultural self-model and the evolutionary drive (at least, that is the case in cultures where suicide is morally frowned-upon). However, while the outcome of this three-way conflict is not easy to predict, the social self-model wins enough times to make suicide a recognisably human phenomenon.

The origin of possession and the possessive

Pronominalisation in many languages also gives us the power to extend our umbrella of selfhood to include non-self objects: things that are beyond the limits of my self can nonetheless become *my* things. The way this is done varies between languages; there are many different ways of possessing in the world's languages, both in terms of what is possessed and how the possession is expressed.

For instance, several languages differentiate between alienable objects (things that can be possessed by others, like *John's dog*) and inalienable objects (things that can be possessed only by the individual, like *John's dream*). Some languages differentiate between inherent possession (parts of a whole, like *John's finger*) and non-inherent possession (where the two things remain equal and separate objects, like *John's dog*). Some languages treat some things as unpossessable, and some treat the possession of places as different from other forms of possession by using a special locative possessive.

In English, we do not officially differentiate between alienable and non-alienable, or inherent and non-inherent, but there is nonetheless some differentiation. We can use the *of* form of possession with inalienable but not alienable possessions: *the dreams of John* feels acceptable (although it has two very different meanings), but *the dog of John* does not (although *that dog of John's* is acceptable). There is also some differentiation between non-inherent and inherent possession: *John's dog* requires the possessive form (*'s*, as in *Alf's nose*), but *the family's dog* can be reduced to *the family dog*, possibly because the dog is an inherent part of the family in a wider sense. This double-noun formation is very common in English (for example, *history test*, *business contract*, *fly spray*, *bicycle wheel*), and it is unlikely that inherent possession can be invoked to explain all double-noun forms; but it does help with some.

English does not seem to have any restriction on what can be possessed, treating even the ultimate supernatural entity as a personal possession ('My God, my God, why have you forsaken me?' – Psalm 22:1, *Holy Bible, New International Version*). However, we do have an example of a special locative possession form: the ellipsis in *I'm going to John's* indicates a place possessed in some way by John, such as 'house' or 'home'. The way possession is marked in different languages is also variable. English uses: prepositions (*of* and *for* particularly, but not exclusively); a possessive form (*'s*); double nouns; or noun phrases (such as *the dog owned by John* or *the dog John has*). Japanese uses a participle *no* following a noun phrase to indicate the noun is a possessor (*Jon no inu*, John's dog, for instance); Latin uses a genitive case-ending on a noun to indicate it is a possessor (for example, *Pax Romanorum*, the Roman peace); and languages in the South American Cariban group usc a case-form to indicate the possessed thing rather than the possessing thing. To date, however, no language has been identified that does not indicate possession in at least one way.

Possession may be ubiquitous because it is just a particular form of A-Relationship-B social calculus: it is an unequal relationship between a person and a thing, where the person has a dominance relationship over that thing. It possibly comes directly from a social calculus construct that marks a dominance–submission relationship between two people, but replaces the submissive person with a thing. This possessive extension of the A-Relationship-B form is one of many ways the form can be elaborated: it can express other relationships between things and people, or relationships between things and other things. The relationships themselves can also be replaced by actions (existential actions of being, material actions of affecting, relational actions of representing, behavioural actions of performing, verbal actions of describing, and mental actions of ideating) or other links (cultural links like marriage, economic links like debt, service links like employment, social links like group membership, and so on). The expression of possessive relationships is one of many ways in which the simple sentential communicated form of A-Relationship-B can be pressed into new uses: out of this A-Relationship-B social calculus construct can come all the simple grammar we use in modern language.

One common way of expressing possession is to use a pronominal to replace a noun phrase (*mine / ours / yours / his / hers / theirs*). Just as the basic pronominals all trace back to the cognitive meta-referent of *they*, so the possessive pronominals trace back to the use of *they* in an A-Relationship-B construct, where the relationship is one of possession. Social calculus involves sets of paired relationships between known individuals, and the use of *they* allows individuals and groups to be represented by a generic placeholder; possession is just another type of paired relationship, and the same meta-referent pronominal properties apply. So just as the three persons in a communicative act can be represented singularly or plurally by pronominals, so possession can be expressed in all three persons in singular and plural forms.

Possession seems likely to be one of the earliest ways in which the exchange of social calculus was broadened to include other communicable information; and the famous Blombos crayon (Henshilwood et al. 2002) looks like an early exemplar of possessive messages – perhaps the earliest known. A simple cross-hatching on a piece of soft ochre, probably used as a crayon to create red pigment, indicates a relationship between the crayon and at least one human. We cannot know what the cross-hatching means, but we can say with confidence that it is an indicator that, about 75,000 years ago, this particular piece of stone was important enough to be personalised for identification.

Possession is, however, more than just an extension of the human way of seeing the world; its role in communication changes the world. Where first-person possession is expressed (for example, '*my* rock'), it poses a challenge to the worldview of others. It is an assertion about reality, but it is only as real as others allow it to be. Possession plunges us into Karl Popper's *Three Worlds* (1967, Chapter 4), which constructs the human view of knowledge on three levels: what continues to exist even in the absence of humans, such as *rock*, constitutes World 1 (actuality); that which exists only inside human heads, such as *my*, is World 2 (virtuality); and that which has actual existence without humans but has meaning only because of humans, such as *crayon*, is World 3 (reality).[1] It is difficult to represent these three worlds using words, because every word is a negotiation toward meaning – it exists in World 2 and can only represent Worlds 1 and 3, not exist in them. The word *rock* represents an actual rock without being one, and the word *crayon* represents the idea that a particular rock can be described by role as well as by substance. The word *my* is an assertion of possession in World 2, but it represents different things in Worlds 1 and 3: in World 1 it represents actual, physical possession, and in World 3 it represents agreed, or legal, possession. These three meanings together form our understanding of what constitutes 'good' possession: it is asserted, actual and agreed. Without actual possession, it is merely desire, and without agreement it is usurpation; but if all three are present, then our World 2 virtual concept of possession has changed our World 3 real model of how World 1, the actual world, works and is ordered. Language may not have changed the actual world, but it has changed our concept of the world, and therefore our relationship to it.

The origin of recursion and reflexivity

In Chapter 3, we looked very briefly at the topic of recursion in terms of the sharing of the A-Relationship-B constructs we have been offered by others. By attributing the whole construct to the original author, we are able to pass on what may be deceptive information without risking our own reputation. This construct, 'C said A-Relationship-B' is hierarchical in that the basic construct is contained within a larger construct, [[A-Relationship-B] by-C]; and it is recursive in that it can be further nested as [[[A-Relationship-B] by-C] by D]. In English, this makes a sentence like 'Del said that Gemma told him that Alf likes Beth'. In theory, the *by-x* form can be added into the construct an unlimited number of times, but in practice human minds can usually only handle five or six levels of nesting (Dunbar 2004, Chapter 3). The *by-x* form is not the only type of recursion possible in language; but, like self-modelling and first- and second-person pronominalisation, it is probably an early one.

Why should recursion be so significant in terms of language origins? The answer lies in the recent history of linguistic research. For 60 years, linguistics has been strongly influenced by the theories of one man, Noam Chomsky. His theoretical viewpoint, that language is a specialised cognitive computational system (1995b), has been extremely influential and has affected linguistic theory profoundly. It has also encouraged three generations of researchers to adopt four counterintuitive views about language: first, that language is for thought, not communication; second, that language cognition is just for language – it is a specialised system that is not used for other types of thought; third, that we must, if we are to communicate using language, all have the same language engine (Universal Grammar) in our heads; and fourth, that the language engine is exclusively human – no other animals have anything like it (Chomsky 2007). This position has become known as generativism, from the idea that the engine, Universal Grammar, generates all our language capacities and all human languages.

The literature in support of the generativist position is impressive (Chomsky himself has written, or been involved in writing, over 60 linguistics books). But evidence in the last 20 years from psychology (such as Adornetti and Ferretti 2014), neurology (Arbib 2005), physiology (Evans and Levinson 2009), biology (Bickerton 2014), archaeology (Hoffmann et al. 2018), linguistics (Beckner et al. 2009), animal studies (Segerdahl et al. 2005), child studies (Ibbotson and Tomasello 2009), evolutionary theory (Wacewicz 2016) and complexity theory (Kirby et al. 2008) – even economics (Alonso-Cortés 2006, Chapter 4) – is not providing the necessary support for the idea of a genetically specialised and species-exclusive language engine.

The situation is complicated by the fact that not all generativists believe the same things about language, and Chomsky himself has altered his position several times. Most drastically, in 1995 (1995a) he abandoned his previous theoretical suite of Principles & Parameters and Government & Binding (for example, Chomsky 1982) to concentrate on a reduced package involving just two principles: MOVE and MERGE. He has now largely dropped MOVE as a separate principle, concentrating on the single feature of MERGE as the cognitive capacity that separates humans from the rest of nature, and language from other communication systems (Hauser et al. 2002). Another name for MERGE is recursion.

For Chomsky, MERGE is a human-only capacity, the result of a mutation in a single individual sometime between 200,000 and 60,000 years ago (Berwick and Chomsky 2016, Chapter 3). This mutation revolutionised the individual's life, giving them a reproductive advantage that passed down through the generations, out-competing unmutated versions of the affected gene because the cognitive capacity of MERGE provided so many fitness advantages. How a cognitive capacity creates a reproductive advantage has not been fully explored; and how the gene managed to replace the entire unmutated stock of genes has not been examined in a systematic way. Even the wide date range raises some questions. We now know that the single migration out of Africa by *Homo sapiens* 60,000 years ago was probably preceded by an earlier migration about 120,000 years ago (Bae et al. 2017), a date supported by recent discoveries about *Homo sapiens* in China (Liu et al. 2015) and Australia (Clarkson et al. 2017). We also now know that modern *Homo sapiens* was present in Morocco 300,000 years ago (Hublin et al. 2017) and had spread to Omo Kibish in Ethiopia by 195,000 years ago (Sisk and Shea 2008), a distance of over 5,000 km. So, if the new mutation had occurred after 200,000 years ago, it would have needed to spread horizontally into existing populations by interbreeding, as well as vertically down the generations. It would also have needed to coexist with the genetic heritage of other species of humans: we now know that there were signs of interbreeding between *Homo sapiens* and both *Homo neanderthalensis* (Green et al. 2010) and *Homo denisova* (Reich et al. 2010). In Europe, on average, our genome is up to 4 per cent Neanderthal; and in Asia, the human genome includes about 0.2 per cent of Denisovan genetic material as well as the Neanderthal content. African humans have no Neanderthal or Denisovan genetic material, while the Melanesian genome is up to 8 per cent Denisovan and Neanderthal combined (Bustamante and Henn 2010).

This leaves a problem for the generative model of language origins. If Chomsky is right that MERGE is the result of a mutation, then he must be wrong about the timing: the mutation must have happened early enough in the history of *Homo sapiens* to ensure it reached Australia 65,000 years ago, because interbreeding between outsiders and Australian Aboriginal humans was slight-to-non-existent for all but the most recent 300 years. It would also be a better explanation if the mutation happened before 200,000 years ago, to give it a chance to spread through the whole *Homo sapiens* population before *Homo sapiens* started spreading through the world. If, however, the timing is adjusted, then there is the problem of how this mutation changed the fitness profile of the species. If it had a major effect on fitness (as the generativists claim for cognitive recursion), then it should spread quickly, and evidence of what that fitness change did to humans should be evident in the archaeological record; but the technological and social record from archaeology gives no clue as to any cognitive changes before about 100,000 years ago. If it had only a minor effect, then why should it spread quickly through the population? The success of any mutation is measured in terms of relative numbers of offspring, so if it is to spread quickly both vertically through selective inheritance, and horizontally through interbreeding, it has to be quite remarkable in its effects.

There are three ways out of this problem. The first is to treat MERGE (recursion) as non-genetic: it could be a cognitive trick that some humans mastered and then shared; this trick could spread culturally – and, therefore, much more quickly than if it were a mutation. This, however, still leaves the questions of why and how this cognitive trick was first recognised, why it proved so useful, and how it was shared without recursive language already existing. The second way out of the problem is to treat MERGE as an ancient genetic capacity that happened to be communicatively useful when language appeared, but which was available and useful in cognition long before language appeared. However, the question here is: what purpose did recursion in cognition serve? No cognitive cost could survive for long without a countervailing fitness benefit. The third solution is to treat MERGE as a communicative potential already cognitively present in hierarchical social calculus, a potential that was realised only when that calculus was shared. This is the solution offered here: the ability to cognitively model individuals within groups while separately identifying the individual and the group is potentially hierarchical; so when the communication of social calculus actually begins, the recursive tools are already in place. While shared social calculus models are initially linear, they soon require the ability to share one person's model of another person's model of a relationship, indicating the ownership of the information in the model at each level. This sharing of information sources is hierarchical and, within a limited definition of the term, recursive.

Robin Dunbar describes these nested tagged models as 'a hierarchically organised series of belief-states' (2004, 45); and he goes on to show that, while the capacity to nest individuals and groups within groups seems to extend to at least seven levels without diminution in understanding, the nesting of relationship models becomes ineffective and highly error-prone beyond five levels of nesting. Recursion is not, as Wilhelm von Humboldt (1836 [1999], 91) says (and Chomsky is fond of quoting), 'infinite employment of finite means',[2] it is constrained by the capacities of the human brain, which are not as amazing or unusual as we often pretend. Caballero et al. (2018) raise an important issue about infinitely recursive iteration: cognition is about decision points. At some time in the process, the formulation of an idea must result in a formed idea; and this cannot happen without a stop-marker on the iterative recursion formulating the idea. Decision-making does seem to rely on iterative processing, and a large number of those iterative processes are recursive; but that does not make them infinite, or even possibly infinite.

One aspect of recursion that is not often explored using MERGE is reflexivity, the capacity to refer an activity back on itself so that the instigator of the action is also the receiver. In the notation used here, this would be an A_1-Relationship-A_2 construct, a recognition that a *they* has the same ability to model themself as I do. To express reflexivity in English pronouns, we use possessive+self (*myself, ourself, ourselves, yourself, yourselves*) or, in the third-person, object+self (*himself, herself, itself, themself, themselves*). This differentiation of form is neither explicable nor fixed – some dialects allow *meself* or *hisself* or *theyselves*, but never *weselves, youself, youselves* or *sheself*. They do all, however, reflect the fact that A_2 is a model of A_1 made by A_1 – which is itself a model. This is clearer in the semantically complex utterance {name 1}-{has a good relationship with}-{name 1} (*John loves John*). This reflexivity is used to indicate disapproval of the relationship, or surprise that it is possible for anyone to love John; but it is done by intimating that John actually loves John's model of himself, and this is a wrong thing for John to do. In practice, of course, when I utter *John loves John*, I am really saying 'my model of John loves my model of John's model of John'. I leave you to work out what is happening in 'John loves that he loves himself'; but the fact that you are able to extract meaningful information from these six words about my intentions, John's intentions and my relationship with John shows how the sharing of social models, accompanied by recursion, creates a powerful information machine.

Self out of language, language out of self?

This chapter has approached selfhood as a communicative issue, and particularly as a language event. If the story of self this book proposes is close to what actually happened in our prehistory, then the human capacity for language is heavily implicated; and an understanding of what language is becomes necessary. However, we are immediately faced with a definitional problem: what type of communication counts as language? This question is not as easy to answer as it should be. For some linguists, language is how only humans communicate; so, by definition, it is a human-only capacity. For generativists, the key ingredient is recursion; so any human communication system that cannot be used recursively does not count as language. For other linguists, language happens whenever communication is sufficiently complex; so any communicative act could count as language if it is complex enough, whether it is performed by humans or by another species.

In this chapter, the term 'language' has been used cavalierly, with no particular definition attached. This is deliberate, because what counts as language is something of a red herring in the search for selfhood. To begin exchanging social calculus models, there must have been a pre-existing communication system that allowed meaningfully differentiated segments of a signal to be brought together to make a meta-signal. Fortunately, recent evidence shows that this might be an ancient capacity: marmosets, which are in a lineage with which we shared a common ancestor 40 million years ago, appear capable of vocalisations that 'do not consist of one discrete call pattern but are built of many sequentially uttered units, like human speech' (Pomberger et al. 2018). While marmosets are unlikely to have a capacity for social calculus, a call pattern built of sequential units is all that is needed to share social calculus models. Whether we class the exchange of social calculus models as sufficiently linguistic to be called language is immaterial to the fact that all the cognitive resources we needed to share social calculus models were probably already present before *Homo sapiens* appeared.

However, a knowledge of selfhood is not needed to communicate social calculus models. Indeed, if a capacity to model the self as a third person, a dispassionate self, allows in the capacity for self-sacrifice, it can be argued that self-modelling, by itself, makes an individual less fit than an individual who does not self-model. Only if self-modelling is a secondary outcome of something that increases fitness should it become common in a species. Could sharing social models enhance individual fitness sufficiently to counteract the negative effect of self-sacrifice? The answer probably lies in the increased levels of trust that the sharing of models engenders, and the enhanced knowledge of how the individual's group works; but that is not an issue that needs to be pursued here, for we have discovered a viable path from self-serving, self-free Machiavellianism to selfless, self-modelling selfhood.

The journey on from selfhood is of interest in terms of language itself. Sharing second-hand models requires recursion to enter the equation, and this allows human communication to become increasingly complex. This is significant for generativists, because it crosses the Rubicon they believe exists between pre-language communication, or proto-language, and full language. However, whether what happened before communicative recursion counts as language or not is a matter of opinion. We can define language in whichever way we wish, to fit our theory of how humans communicate; it makes no difference to the nature of the communicative act itself. For selfhood, we needed an effective, segmented and differentiated communication system already in place; and we needed a cognitive capacity for social calculus. From selfhood, we gained a complex and iterative communication system that any linguist would be happy to label language.

Notes

1. The terms Actuality, Reality and Virtuality are my own terms for Popper's Three Worlds.
2. What von Humboldt actually said was: 'Sie muss daher von endlichen Mitteln einen unendlichen Gebrauch machen'. So a more literal translation would be: 'It must therefore from limited resources generate unlimited usage'. This is sufficiently different from 'infinite employment of finite means' to argue that von Humboldt and Chomsky may not be talking about the same thing.

7
Metaphors of Self

> 'I'm afraid he'll catch cold with lying on the damp grass,' said Alice, who was a very thoughtful little girl.
>
> 'He's dreaming now,' said Tweedledee: 'and what do you think he's dreaming about?'
>
> Alice said 'Nobody can guess that.'
>
> 'Why, about you!' Tweedledee exclaimed, clapping his hands triumphantly. 'And if he left off dreaming about you, where do you suppose you'd be?'
>
> 'Where I am now, of course,' said Alice.
>
> 'Not you!' Tweedledee retorted contemptuously. 'You'd be nowhere. Why, you're only a sort of thing in his dream!'
>
> 'If that there King was to wake,' added Tweedledum, 'you'd go out – bang! – just like a candle!'
>
> (Lewis Carroll 1872, Chapter 4: 'Tweedledum and Tweedledee')

Dreaming is not an exclusively human capacity. There is some evidence that dogs dream (Walker 1983, 194–236); and, based on body movement during sleep, it seems reasonable to believe that dreaming is common in the mammalian clade. There is currently no way of knowing what dogs dream about and, apart from recollection after waking, we have no way of interrogating our own dreams. Conscious recollection of unconscious dreams is notoriously unreliable: normally, when we wake, our dream goes out – bang! – just like a candle. If we have any recollections at all, they are vague, disjointed and counterintuitive. We cannot know if this is because dreams themselves are vague, disjointed and counterintuitive, or if this is the way our conscious self represents our dreaming self to us.

This chapter looks at some of the ways we represent our self to ourselves, a reflexive trick that is only expressible, and may only be possible, through language. In Chapter 3, we saw that the modelled self can be viewed as a product of the sharing of social calculus through language. So, if language really is the source of awareness of self in humans, then there should be some significant indicators of this within language; and if sharing social calculus is a major cause of language, it should have left some positively megalithic features on the language landscape. Fortunately for the modelling hypothesis, the signs are there, and they are indeed significant.

Metaphor, as George Lakoff and Mark Johnson (1980) argue, is fundamental to language. It is at the heart of linguistic productivity, allowing us to increase the range of meanings in our languages to cover almost every descriptive need we may have. It also allows us to extend our language significantly in terms of grammatical complexity, and even offers an increased range of sounds and gestures we can use to represent our languages. We are able to linguistically model from how language is done now to how it could be done, and then incorporate how it could be done into how it is done. Metaphor puts all our conceptual meaning on a constantly moving conveyor belt, from the possible to the probable to the agreed. For this reason, Lakoff and Johnson label their view of metaphor 'conceptual metaphor', to differentiate it from the older and much more limited definition, 'rhetorical metaphor'. Where rhetorical metaphor involves the conscious and deliberate selection of a metaphorical relationship, conceptual metaphor is a product of an intuitive negotiation toward meaning. For this reason, the term 'metaphor' refers here to conceptual metaphor.

For instance, if we look at a quotation from Winston Churchill, 'If you're going through hell, keep going', a rhetorical approach might consider the use of the word 'hell', a place of suffering, to represent a difficult period in life. This, though, leaves us with a somewhat circular definition, and no clear route into meaning: hell as a place, if it is actually a place, is unknowable to the living; we can only understand it in metaphorical terms, as a place where all the suffering we can imagine happens. Rhetorically, the metaphor devolves to [a place or time of great suffering → hell = a place and time of great suffering], which is not a very productive metaphor. A conceptual approach would take the view that the utterance's key metaphor is LIFE IS A JOURNEY. This is supported by concomitant metaphors like SUFFERING IS A JOURNEY and THE DESTINATION IS NOT THE ROUTE. It is also supported by semantic metaphors like GOING THROUGH IS EXPERIENCING and KEEPING GOING IS CONTINUING; and by the referential metaphor that THE YOU IN *YOU'RE* DOES NOT NECESSARILY REFER TO THE LISTENER. All of these are cognitive concepts we use to negotiate toward Churchill's intended meaning.

One of the strangest features of metaphor is that the receiver is willing to go along with the sender's novel metaphors, negotiating with them toward a shared meaning. If I say 'it's a bullying wind today', your first reaction is probably to interpret the activity of the wind in terms of your knowledge of bullying. You do not seek clarification (at least, not often), even if this is a novel utterance for you; and you do not dismiss the utterance as meaningless just because it is novel. The metaphor allows us to access the unknown through the known: exactly what the sender means by 'bullying wind' may be opaque to us, but we are aware of how humans can bully, and the effect it has on their victims. The wind is not a person, but (as we saw in Chapter 6) we can exchange people and objects in our social calculus, treating people as passive and inanimate, and objects as animate and intentional – equivalences that are, themselves, metaphorical.

It seems that, in many ways, metaphor is deceptive: it works by associating an unknown thing with a known thing, but the association is usually partial and seldom synonymous. A difficult period in life is not a journey through hell, and a bullying wind does not pick its victims. Yet, in both cases, the speaker or writer has conveyed more than just their intended meaning, and has revealed something about themselves. Churchill has given us an insight into his clinical depression, and the weather commentator has told us how they anthropomorphise today's weather. To open our mouths is to reveal our self – or, at least, our model of our self.

This chapter explores five conceptual metaphors defining selfhood: THE MODEL IS THE ACTUAL; THE GROUP IS AN ENTITY; SELF IS OTHER; I AM ME; and ONE AMONG EQUALS. Some of these precede the communication of social models and some of them follow from it. There are many other metaphors involved in our definition of selfhood; but, together, these five metaphors form a basic toolkit for social modelling and self-awareness.

THE MODEL IS THE ACTUAL

This is perhaps the earliest of the selfhood conceptual metaphors to take root in human cognition; indeed, it is possible that the necessary cognitive mechanisms to establish this metaphor were part of our subliminal cognition before the apes and old-world monkeys went off on their different evolutionary paths 25 million years ago. It is certainly needed when social calculus becomes a conscious activity, because understanding the relationships between others means understanding the emotions between individuals; and the only way this can happen is if I am able to represent, or model, those emotions without actually experiencing them myself.

The subliminal mechanisms that enable the metaphor do not produce the metaphor by themselves, however: the modelled A-Relationship-B only becomes a metaphor for the actual relationship between two individuals when we become aware of our social modelling and start to use it in our conscious planning. In terms of Popper's three worlds, social calculus is like language: they both require the individual to be aware that they are using them; and they both exist in World 2, virtuality, and can only represent in Worlds 1 and 3, actuality and reality. I have no way of accessing the actual relationship between the two individuals – I can only use the virtual (World 2) model of the relationship in my social calculus to stand in for the actual (World 1) relationship. But, because it is the only representation I have, it more than represents, it becomes my view of the relationship in both the actual World 1 and my real World 3. My model, no matter how ineffective, must be treated by me as if it were both the actual and the real relationship.

By treating the metaphor, THE MODEL IS THE ACTUAL, as a valid equivalence, I have made it an active component of my conscious cognition: I know that my models of A and B are not the actual people A and B, and I know my model of the relationship between them is not the actual relationship between them – everything is contingent and modal. However, the model, if it is to be of any use to me, has to be treated as a true representation of the actual relationship between A and B; and, when I begin sharing my social calculus, it is my virtual model that I share.

This means that, for the receiver, too, there must be recognition that what I am sharing is a World 2 virtual viewpoint – an opinion rather than a fact. Because language and social calculus both exist in World 2 and only map onto Worlds 1 and 3, language and social calculus form a synchronised system of communication where both are semantically and semiotically collocated: social calculus imposes its structure on language, and the structure is what gives language the capacity to communicate social calculus. THE MODEL IS THE ACTUAL is not just a convenient cognitive methodology, it is at the heart of sharing social calculus through language.

THE GROUP IS AN ENTITY

We have already met this metaphor in another guise in Chapter 6, as part of the discussion of the origin of *they*. If I am to understand individual A as an intentional entity, then I need to be able to understand the relationships of other individuals with A in terms of their grouping around A; in other words, I need to be able to treat those groups of others around A as if they were entities themselves. My social calculus must become hierarchical, recognising both individuals within groups and groups within groups. Like THE MODEL IS THE ACTUAL, the metaphor THE GROUP IS AN ENTITY was at work subliminally long before *Homo sapiens* appeared on the planet.

For the metaphor THE GROUP IS AN ENTITY to become a cognitive reality, the concept of *group* has to be part of an individual's daily experience. This does not mean that being part of a group relies on recognition of the concept *group*: it is not necessary, for instance, that eusocial insects have any concept of group to work together in what appears to be a highly organised way. In fact, the genetic joint enterprise algorithm can be remarkably simple: it only has to promote serial cooperation between pairs of individuals for an apparently highly organised society to emerge. It can even produce the illusion of hierarchy and centralised organisation; this is partly because, as humans, we use our own pseudo-eusocial models as metaphors to explain full eusociality, so we see conscious cooperation where there is none; but it is also because eusocial joint enterprise encourages individual specialisation, which we can then interpret as a grouping mechanism (Lehmann et al. 2008).

However, the concept of group does not come from the whole tribe surrounding the individual; it comes from the recognition of subgroups within a group. My recognition of the subgroups surrounding individual A (based on my models of individual A's common relationship with the individuals in the subgroup) allows me to group my own relationships with others, and to start building productive coalitions with other like-minded individuals; in this way, conscious recognition of ad hoc subgroups in the group emerge from the modelling of individual cooperations. This aggregation of individuals into a subgroup, and the subsequent treatment of the subgroup as a unit, is what creates the metaphor THE GROUP IS AN ENTITY.

This remains a useful subliminal cognitive tool until we begin sharing our social calculus: the sharing of A-Relationship-B uses the same form whether A or B represents an individual or a group – although the joint nature of the group means that the contextually specific meaning of the cognitive shortcut *they* (that is, what it refers to in a particular discourse) also has to be negotiated between the parties to the discourse. The features unifying a set of individuals into a group need to be World 3 real to all members of the discourse (which is what makes the aggregation a useful shortcut), but they do not need to be World 1 actual: 'Alf's friends' may not form a single group; and, with the modern social media culture, they may not even know each other. But they are linked by my belief that a good relationship with Alf somehow makes them all similar; and, if I can persuade you of the value of the aggregation, the contextual *they* becomes a valuable shared tool.

When THE GROUP IS AN ENTITY becomes a shared metaphor, it creates a new world of possibilities. Humans are able to form tribes, nations, chess clubs, academic conferences and so on creating a *we* and a *not-we* out of the negotiated *they*. The separation of in-group and out-group may appear logical and reasonable in all these cases, but it is often based on an evolutionarily inexplicable pretext. Why do individuals who are good at pushing bits of wood across a tessellated board according to arbitrary conventions need to group together? What fitness advantages do they get? To label it a costly signal of group membership somehow misses the point of what that membership represents to the individual.

The arbitrariness of the in-group and out-group division also has a dark side, where the out-group becomes the focus of attention rather than the in-group. This can manifest itself in persecution of the out-group and can lead to prejudice, social exclusion, dehumanisation and even genocide. The in-group is defined solely by not being the out-group. Unlike eusocial species, where wars happen between groups because individuals are not recognised as part of the in-group (usually by scent), human wars are often about punishing the out-group. Where, for eusocial species, the enemy of my enemy is usually my enemy also, for humans, the enemy of my enemy can be my friend. Only humans seem capable of world-straddling alliances defined less by mutual solidarity and more by mutual dislike of an arbitrary subset of *not-we*. Jane Goodall (1990, Chapter 10) has reported that chimpanzees (*Pan troglodytes*) go to war, although it is a very different concept of war from the organised conflicts that even hunter-gatherers are able to mount against each other. And, even though they are territorial, it is very unlikely that any chimpanzee would give cognitive houseroom to the idea, *dulce et decorum est pro patria mori* ('how sweet and fitting it is to die for your country').

Treating the group as an entity can make conformism to the arbitrary rules of the group into a fit strategy, but it also makes membership of multiple groups a fit strategy. Seeing the group as an entity allows a society to consist of not just one group but many subgroups; and it allows individuals to be members of groups that cross what would have been in-group and out-group boundaries. I can be an atheist or theist or deist within the Labour or Liberal or Conservative parties: membership of one group does not automatically preclude or dictate membership of another. The arbitrary meta-rules of a culture determine the nature of the groups available for individuals to join, and the arbitrary rules within the group determine which individuals will join them.

The appearance of THE GROUP IS AN ENTITY metaphor in communication, therefore, creates a very different kind of social structure from what was possible before. Individuals who can manipulate the concept will have an important advantage over those who cannot, being able to create alliances in new ways; and, when the concept becomes more general, the manipulators are better able to negotiate the new and more complex social web that is likely to appear.

SELF IS OTHER

As the metaphor at the heart of this book, so much has been said about it already. It is, however, unlike the other four metaphors examined here, reversible, in that OTHER IS SELF represents a similar cognitive equivalencing to SELF IS OTHER. They both represent the idea that the modelled self and a modelled other are of the same nature: they are both models of individuals where the models represent but do not recreate. This is not that case with THE MODEL IS THE ACTUAL or THE GROUP IS AN ENTITY. The equivalencing of 'model' with 'actual', and 'group' with 'entity', legitimises the model and the group by giving them more significance – and more actuality – than they actually have; the first half of each pair is of a different nature to the second half. (This also applies to the metaphor I AM ME, but the metaphor ONE AMONG EQUALS is of a different type – as we shall see.)

Yet, despite the reversible nature of the SELF IS OTHER metaphor, there is also a difference of emphasis between the two forms. OTHER IS SELF implies that I can take your model of me as a basis for my model of me; it is the realisation that, if you are offering me a model of me, I need to have a model of me in my own social calculus – and the only model of me immediately available is what you have revealed to me about your model of me. Your 'other' model of me has to become my 'self' model if I am to have any model of me. In contrast, SELF IS OTHER implies that my model of me is of the same nature as your model of me. As your model of me is a third-person model, and all the models of other individuals in my social calculus are also third-person models, so my model of me has to be a third-person model.

From the aspectual self of *myself*, through the more holistic selves of *I* and *me*, to the representative selves of *one* and *we*, the self is constantly being linguistically modelled by the self as not the self. Where a chimpanzee, without the capacity to share social calculus, has to present their anger with another chimpanzee as an indexical temper tantrum, humans represent their emotions linguistically, using symbolic models of themselves: the phrase 'You're making me angry' can be spoken with a level, emotionless tone which does not contradict its meaning. Yet the very act of presenting the Actual self's anger through a linguistic model of the self dissipates or mutates the anger that the Actual self actually feels: the modelled self becomes the vehicle through which the Actual self relates to other selves.

We thus find ourselves sharing models of ourselves with utterances such as 'I think I'm not feeling myself today'. In this utterance, I have modelled my self in three ways: as the originator of a thought ('I think'); as the actor in the activity being described ('I'm not feeling'); and as an idealised Cultural self ('myself'), the standard of which the actor in the thought does not currently meet ('myself today'). Strangely, not only do we know what each of the selves represents when we make this utterance, we expect our interlocutors to know, too; and, even stranger, they usually do.

For the metaphor SELF IS OTHER to work, the individual must have a conscious concept of both 'other' and 'self'. A concept of 'other' as an intentional being seems to be present in chimpanzees and orang-utans, but it is a naïve concept that can only handle the idea that others may know or not know things that the self knows, but not that they can believe things that the self knows to be false (Call and Tomasello 1999). The concept that others may believe things that are not true seems beyond them. Residence in Popper's World 1, actuality, is so important to the apes that the possibilities of Worlds 2 and 3 are beyond them. This does not mean that they are impervious to the needs of others, or excluded from cooperation; but it does mean that they do not proactively help – they only reactively help when solicited to do so (Melis et al. 2011).

Bonobos who have been raised with human-language-like communication as part of their experience and repertoire seem to have a more cooperative approach to each other, and to humans, than wild bonobos; and they seem also to have grasped the basics of self-awareness (Savage-Rumbaugh et al. 2005). However, even here their behaviour is less proactively cooperative than that of most human children (Carpenter and Tomasello 1995). Exposure to human culture can make other animals more humanlike by giving them the tools to negotiate toward meaning, but the meanings they negotiate toward are specific to the needs, wants and expectations of their species.

As we have seen, what allowed the concept of 'self' to become a conscious reality was the sharing of social calculus. Somehow a signalling system – which already included segmented meanings, differentiated functions and probably hierarchical structures – was co-opted for the exchange of A-Relationship-B social models. Some examples of this kind of signalling system have been discovered in nature, such as in the calling system of the putty-nosed monkeys (Arnold and Zuberbühler 2006) or the vocal behaviour of marmosets (Pomberger et al. 2018), indicating that the tools for segmented, differentiated and hierarchical communication would have been available before they were needed for sharing social calculus. Scott-Phillips et al. (2009) have also shown that modern humans are ingenious in their efforts to negotiate toward meaning, and they seem able to generate effective rule-based communication systems for specific purposes in very short periods of time. In the circumstance described here, humans would already be using a cognitive grammar of A-Relationship-B constructs to run their internal social calculus, so quickly establishing a communication system that mapped this cognitive grammar onto a signal would be within the realms of possibility.

Once individuals are exchanging A-Relationship-B constructs, it becomes possible to share a construct involving a particular individual with that individual. This poses a problem for the receiver of the signal: to integrate this particular A-Relationship-B construct into their social calculus, they have to be able to model themselves as a node in their social calculus network; but, as we have seen, modelling the self as other entails taking a dispassionate approach to the self, which brings its own disadvantages for the individual. The dispassionate view of the self seems to enhance group selection at the expense of individual fitness: like eusocial insects, we seem ready to sacrifice our selves to ensure the continuation of our 'nest' or 'hive'. Alone among the non-eusocial species, humans are willing to sacrifice themselves for their group, even when there is no relatedness advantage: we are willing to sacrifice ourselves not just for the physical entity of the group but for an abstract concept of 'groupness'. In humans, self-sacrifice has become a powerful mechanism for ensuring the survival of the self's cultural group; but this makes it a terrible tool in the hands of those who exploit the reverse-dominance rules underlying this social system (Boehm 1999). As van Vugt and Ahuja

(2010) show, humans are eager to follow but less eager to lead; which means that we seem genetically predisposed to treat President John F. Kennedy's inaugural speech as stirring rhetoric and not evolutionarily incomprehensible nonsense: 'And so, my fellow Americans: ask not what your country can do for you – ask what you can do for your country'.

The metaphor SELF IS OTHER emerged from the need to accept communicated models of our selves into our personal social calculus; but it seems to have then plugged into an existing social system of reverse dominance to create some very un-Darwinian effects. Clearly, exchanging social calculus constructs is sufficiently advantageous to the individual to outweigh any tendency to self-sacrifice; but how that equation of plusses and minuses plays out is currently still somewhat mysterious. Fortunately for the writer, it is an issue that does not need to be picked-apart here.

I AM ME

Once we have a third-person model of our self, we are faced with the problem of which roles our modelled self can undertake. The models of me offered to me by someone else will be of two types: A in an A-Relationship-B construct (the instigator of a relationship); or B in an A-Relationship-B construct (the recipient of a relationship). These two selves could represent quite different things in our social calculus, but in practice we usually recognise them as the same self behaving in different ways: In terms of social calculus grammar, instigator and recipient are roles that the self undertakes, treating the modelled self as a single representation of the unknowable Actual self, and not as a set of different representations of different selves. The roles of instigator and recipient are interchangeable, while the modelled self is cohesive.

This is odd, because, as we will see in Chapter 8, we do not actually have a cohesive model of our self; instead, we have a series of different models that we use for different purposes in our social interactions. It is, however, also useful to maintain the idea of a cohesive modelled self; and we do this by combining the several models of our self that have been offered by different people and generating an averaged self from them. Our self-modelling involves both separating our selves by function, so that we can model possibilities, and combining our selves to communicate a unified selfhood to others. This may be why inconsistency in self-presentation is treated by others as both valuable and problematic (Laran and Janiszewski 2009): the individual who adjusts their behaviour to meet the expectations of others is likely to be seen as more cooperative.

But if they are caught adjusting their behaviour in contradictory ways for different groups of others, then they will be seen as insincere and untrustworthy.

This is where the metaphor I AM ME becomes useful. It represents the capacity to merge different selves located in the same brain into an apparent amalgam self. Daniel Dennett (1991, 275–81) discusses the possibility of a unified self as a product of episodic memory: we stitch together the events of our life into a narrative to create what he calls a Joycean Machine. This machine adjudicates between different selves, adjusting the self I present to the world to match, as far as possible, the self I wish to present and the self others expect me to present. In this projected model, the self-who-does and the self-who-experiences are merged, so that *I* can also be *me*.

The unified self remains a controversial concept in philosophy. Colin Marshall (2010) shows that Kant's belief in a self unified metaphysically is useful and valid only if there is actually a metaphysical component to the self; if the metaphysical component is actual, then it fully explains the unified self – but it cannot explain why or how we use modelled selves. Paul Katsafanas (2011) looks instead to Nietzsche's concept of unified agency to justify a unified self: selfhood is expressed through activity, and activity is the outcome of an act of decision; decision means that a single, overriding self has made that decision, regardless of the number of selves that contributed to it. This, however, just kicks the problem down the road: is the overriding self actually a unified self, or does the need for an overriding self show that there must be a multiplicity of selves to be overridden, and any one of the multiple selves could have won? David Rosenthal (2004) shows that we believe we are unified selves because of our belief in our freedom of choice: if we can choose freely, then there must be a unified self to make the choices. Our conscious choices, however, are usually dictated by our emotional responses, which are subliminally generated, and over which we have little, if any, control. What appears to be free will is only an explanation we give ourselves after the event of choice, and it cannot be used to support an overriding unified self.

In contrast to the unified self of philosophy, David Lester (2012), from a psychological viewpoint, proposes a multiple self theory of the mind where I AM ME reflects a holistic sub-self that both *does* and *experiences*; a person can have several sub-selves but, unlike the modelled selves hypothesised in this book, Lester's sub-selves do not merge to create amalgam selves, they remain separate and each has their moments of dominance. This, however, creates the counterintuitive idea that every decision is arbitrarily affected by whichever sub-self is dominant at the time; and it raises the question of why we see ourselves as unified individuals.

Allen McConnell (2011) provides a different model for multiple selves, which he calls the multiple self framework. Here, the models of the self that are negotiated with different groups tend to stay separate; so an individual may have, for instance, a family-directed self, a work-directed self, and a different self directed toward each of the individual's social groups; each self has a set of personality aspects that work with the specific group and which will not necessarily work with other groups. In this model, the self making a particular decision is the self that is active in that particular context, so it is also the self that has to live with the decision made. In both the Lester and McConnell models, the I AM ME metaphor reflects the fact that the currently dominant self both *does* and *experiences*, but the different selves switch on and off rather than being merged together on an ad hoc basis.

The I AM ME metaphor, however, also seems to represent more than a simple equivalence of the self-who-does and the self-who-experiences; it represents the fact that these two selves can be merged to create a composite self. Each of our selves consists of a set of aspects or attributes that may, or may not, be shared with other models of our self. In the end, it is not the integrity of a particular self-model that determines the model of our self that we project in a particular context; rather, it is the set of attributes that others believe us to have and which we can convince others we have. If people are expecting a level-headed me, and I have a model of me with a level-headed attribute, I can project the level-headed person I am expected to be; and if people are expecting a self-sacrificing me, and I have a model of me with a self-sacrificing attribute, I can be that self-sacrificing person. I will be that level-headed, dispassionate, self-sacrificing person not because self-sacrifice is a direct evolutionary capacity, but because the modelled me that can experience the idea of self-sacrifice is also the *I* who can do self-sacrifice.

ONE AMONG EQUALS

The last metaphor of self that is reviewed here, ONE AMONG EQUALS, is different from the rest. Where the other metaphors collocate a World 3 real thing (the model, the group, self, *I*) with a representation of a World 1 actual thing (the actual, an entity) or with another real thing (other, me), ONE AMONG EQUALS establishes a social role for the individual, collocating a representation of a World 1 actual thing (one) with a representation of a World 2 virtual thing (equals). The metaphor defines a social role that all individuals share, because every individual is a one, and they are all part of the group of equals. It may look, at first glance, that this is a recent cultural metaphor, a product of modern democracy; but it is actually a modern instantiation of an ancient human attribute that has allowed modern democracy to become a World 2 reality, as studies of human altruism show (Fehr and Fischbacher 2003). Repeated interactions, reputation-formation and strong reciprocity combine to keep the majority compliant with the social compact of sharing fairly, and to facilitate punishment of the non-compliant. Human altruism has been somewhat usurped recently by pre-human alpha instincts, as modern economies of surplus seem to have mitigated the long-established human bias toward social equality (Charlton 1997). The alpha chimpanzees may be temporarily back in charge; but, eventually, robber-baron economies of surplus have a Malthusian tendency to adjust back to economies of scarcity (Malthus 1798). Already we are seeing shortages in basic survival resources (such as potable water; Suweis et al. 2013), demanding a more egalitarian solution to prevent social irruption.

Humans have, for a long time, been willing to demand equalisation in their social transactions; and Erdal and Whiten's model of vigilant sharing (1994) provides an early model for how individuals could have prevented other individuals from dominating resources. By itself, vigilant sharing is not a direct precursor of ONE AMONG EQUALS; instead, it corresponds more closely to Quentin Crisp's aphorism, 'Never keep up with the Joneses. Drag them down to your own level; it's cheaper'. Vigilant sharing is about economic distribution rather than social equalisation; but it does demand a level of cooperation with other members of the group if alphas are to be punished by an altruistic ganging-up of the many against the one.

Boehm's reverse-dominance model (1999) is the next step on the ladder toward ONE AMONG EQUALS. In this model, it is not enough to be fair; you have to be modest as well. Vigilant sharing still allows alpha behaviours to be overtly advertised, which means that alphas can still get preferential advantage from their prowess even if they do not use it to coerce advantage; reverse dominance is aimed at reducing this advantage. Pride, bragging and boastfulness are condemned in the advisory texts of many cultures. The Jewish Torah and the Christian Bible say, 'Pride goes before destruction, a haughty spirit before a fall. Better to be lowly in spirit and among the oppressed than to share plunder with the proud' (*Proverbs* 16: 18–19). The Koran advises, 'Do not treat men with scorn, nor walk proudly on the earth; God does not love the arrogant and the vainglorious. Rather let your stride be modest and your voice low: the most hideous of voices is the braying of the ass' (Koran, 31:18). Mana, or pride, is listed as one of the five poisons in the Mahayana Buddhist tradition and one of the ten fetters in Theravada Buddhism. In the Hindu Gita, 'Hypocrisy, pride, self-conceit, wrath, arrogance and ignorance belong, O Partha, to him who is born to the heritage of the demons' (The Gita, XVI, 4). For those of a more secular mindset, Blaise Pascal advises, 'Do you wish men to speak well of you? Then never speak well of yourself' (Pascal 1846). It seems that un-Darwinian self-effacement is a key component in the process of becoming a Good Human.

What keeps this natural self-effacement as a controlling force in human societies is probably not an un-Darwinian morality, however; it is much more likely to be Dessalles' alpha-suppression through assassination (Dessalles 2014). Unlike chimpanzee politics, where alliances are helpful but not vital, no human alpha can enforce their rule without allies. Modern history tells us that, even with allies and the support of a large part of the local population, no leader is completely safe from assassins. Even leaders who seem well-protected from their opponents can nonetheless succumb to popular uprising if they become unpopular enough (as Louis XVI of France, Nicholas II of Russia, Saddam Hussein of Iraq, and Muammar Gadaffi of Libya, among many others, attest). This vulnerability is a lesson that the more ostentatiously wealthy in modern cultures may wish to take more seriously.

Self-effacement does not mean that individuals need to have a Projected self of which they are aware, and of which they are aware that others are aware; all it needs is a sanctioning of braggers by the group. Braggers will then get fewer genes into the future, and self-effacers will get more. However, both bragging and self-effacement are communicative acts: the first is the simple act of pointing out what you have done; the second is the more complex act of *not* pointing out what you have done, while making sure what you have done is widely known. Reputation becomes important; but this is not the described reputation allowed by the sharing of social models. This is the feeling by others that they like you and want you to like them. This is similar to the way that the fearsome reputation of chimpanzee alpha males prevents challenges, but this human reputation is not about fear. So how could a human individual build a self-effacing reputation? Basically, by demonstrating their value. If a hunter brings home a large kill, drops it in the middle of the group, and walks away, they have demonstrated their relative worth as a provider, and their value to the group; if an individual engages and drives off a predator, they have demonstrated their relative worth as a protector, and their value to the group; and so on. No words are needed. Of course, when social calculus models begin to be shared, reputation can be publicised freely by others. The self-effacers stand out even more, and the braggers really look bad.

In terms of early human culture, self-effacement seems to be sufficient to produce the metaphor ONE AMONG EQUALS, but there remains one final step: the change of self-effacement from a strategy to a real belief. It is not enough to take the view of Groucho Marx when he said, 'The secret of life is honesty and fair dealing. If you can fake that, you've got it made'; the honesty and fair-dealing required by ONE AMONG EQUALS must be sincere. This means that, somehow, an extra layer of cultural self-enforcement has to overlay any still-remaining Darwinian *self-first* prime directive. The selfishness of the gene must be projected through the organism onto the group, and then reflected by the group back onto the individual, creating a group directive toward individual unselfishness (Sober and Wilson 1998). As Alan Barnard (2012, Chapter 4) points out, human story-telling (in the guises of mythmaking, ritual and religion) provides a powerful basis for treating the 'group' as an 'entity', and a reliable way to transmit moral values between generations. It also supplies a ready-built cultural-self-model, providing a template from which a Projected self can be constructed as ONE AMONG EQUALS.

A cultural group directive can operate on the group in the same way as an environmental directive: it can drive the group in a particular evolutionary direction. Adami et al. (2000, 4463) define evolution as 'a simple yet powerful process that requires only a population of reproducing organisms in which each offspring has the potential for a heritable variation from its parent'. This means that, as long as there are genetic variations in a population that favour a particular evolutionary direction, and advantages to the individual in taking that particular direction, the population will, over generations, migrate toward those favoured genetic variations. What makes a particular evolutionary direction advantageous really doesn't matter: where there is a continuing environmental directive of any kind on individuals, genetic conformity is a likely outcome.

Several theories have been proposed about what this environmental directive could have been. For example, Chris Knight et al. (1995) have suggested gendered coalitions as the moral framework promoting self-effacing equality. In this theory, variously called Sex Strike Theory or Female Kin Coalition or Female Cosmetic Coalition, females and males are differentiated by role, with males hunting big game to bring home a cooperative kill (the male hunting group is subject to reverse dominance), which is cooked and shared out by the women. The gendered coalition is maintained by policed access to sex (the female group controls access to fertile females, and therefore reproductive sex, through a coalition of related females). The whole system is driven by a lunar cycle whereby sex is withdrawn at dark moon, the men go hunting at full moon (when the night is bright enough to continue a hunt through the night), the kill is brought back and cooked soon after full moon, and sex happens until dark moon, when the cycle begins again. As a theory, it does explain some aspects of human anatomy and processes: the equivalence of the average human menstrual cycle and the synodic lunar month of 29–30 days; the fact that female cycles may synchronise (McClintock 1971); the significance of red ochre in the archaeological record (Watts 2017); ritualised group hunting (Lewis 2008); and the matrilocal, matrifocal regimes of many hunter-gatherer groups (Jordan et al. 2009). While it is more fully evidenced than other ideas about human evolution and cultural development, Sex Strike Theory remains a theory; but it is a necessary theory. There must have been some form of cultural system similar to that of Sex Strike Theory that focussed the group on individual unselfishness; only with that cultural system in place could ONE AMONG EQUALS become a consciously enforced metaphor.

Mapping metaphor to rhetoric and deception

One major feature of the sharing of social models is that externally referenced truth is not needed. The information in a shared social model is so rich that even deliberate falsehoods reveal important truths about the speaker or sender of the message. As we saw in Chapter 4, deception in childhood is treated equivocally: antisocial deception is discouraged and punished; but shared deception, such as story-telling, and group deception, such as cultural conformity, are encouraged and rewarded. This reward and punishment approach to different truths prepares the child for a nuanced adult relationship with virtual and real truths, which may even contradict unpalatable actual truths.

Language is designed to encourage the right kind of deception and discourage the wrong kind, and metaphor is an important part of that training process. In fact, we have developed a set of skills based around the effective use of metaphoric language to convey the information we want to convey, whether that information is explicitly true, implicitly true or cultural accepted. We call this skill-set 'rhetoric', and whole industries have grown up around the need to inform and (mostly) persuade.

There is not enough room here to do justice to the industry of socialised deception that has become a mainstay of the group choices and individual preferences in our modern culture, so I will provide only one, very small example of how language can subliminally affect our thinking – and how our thinking can subliminally affect our language. A commonly quoted description of rhetoric was given by Deirdre McCloskey, when she wrote:

> Rhetoric is merely a tool, no bad thing in itself. Or rather, it is the box of tools for persuasion taken together, available to persuaders, good and bad.
>
> (McCloskey 1998, 169)

In a discussion between Giles Brandreth and his son, Benet Brandreth, QC (*Giles Brandreth and the Art of Persuasion*, 31 March 2018, BBC Radio 4), Brandreth Senior referred to rhetoric as 'a toolbox or box of tricks'. His son then pointed out the vital difference in meaning between 'box of tools' and 'box of tricks': the first treats rhetoric as a system for persuasion, the second as a system of deception. These, however, are not the only ways that McCloskey's utterance can be varied. Instead of 'box of tools', rhetoric could be described as an *engine* or a *system*, metaphors for something more organised than a box of tools. Or, instead of 'rhetoric … is a box of tools', rhetoric could *offer* a box of tools, converting rhetoric itself from an inanimate to an animate thing, and giving it the power to act; or instead of being 'for persuasion' it could be *to persuade*, implying that there is a person to be persuaded as well as a persuader.

When McCloskey made her linguistic choices, were they choices of which she was aware? Or were they the outcome of subliminal intuitions about how she could best express herself in context? We can probably never know, because we produce language in both of those ways. In every utterance, we make choices about how we say or write things, and we select metaphorical relationships to express ourselves, whether those metaphors are consciously chosen, culturally dictated or subliminally dredged up from deep down in our psyche. Pennebaker et al. (2003) show that word choices reflect our subliminal cognition, both our current emotional state and our deep and unknowable self; and our uttered word choices have similar subliminal effects upon our listeners. We may think we have conscious control over what we are saying and the truths we are giving out; but the truth of what we actually mean is usually there in what we actually say.

The power of metaphor converts a primate communication system, originally designed to mark actualities in the world, into a negotiation toward realities and virtualities. Even if we want them to, honesty and truth don't really come into language.

8
What Is a Self? There and Back Again

> 'What do you mean by that?' said the Caterpillar sternly. 'Explain yourself!'
>
> 'I can't explain *myself*, I'm afraid, sir' said Alice, 'because I'm not myself, you see.'
>
> 'I don't see,' said the Caterpillar.
>
> 'I'm afraid I can't put it more clearly,' Alice replied very politely, 'for I can't understand it myself to begin with; and being so many different sizes in a day is very confusing.'
>
> (Lewis Carroll 1865, Chapter 5: 'Advice from a Caterpillar')

Poor Alice! Not being Alice means that she cannot explain Alice to the Caterpillar; even worse, she cannot understand why she cannot explain Alice, because the Alice she has been since falling down the rabbit-hole has been inconsistent and unanchored. The Caterpillar, on the other hand, has a very firm understanding of the self he is, and cannot understand why Alice is not equally certain about her self; yet, as Alice later points out, the Caterpillar will at some stage undergo his own transformation, much more fundamental than hers, when he chrysalises and transforms into a butterfly. Will the butterfly-self recognise the caterpillar-self? And, if so, will he remember the caterpillar-self as being himself, or just a self? Or will there be a major dislocation of memory and selfhood, so the butterfly does not even remember its life as a caterpillar? There is some evidence that moths can retain aversive behaviours learned as caterpillars (Blackiston et al. 2008), but it is unlikely that a moth or butterfly knows that it used to be a caterpillar. At least Alice has continuity in her selfhood, so that the Alice of today is a product of, and remembers, the Alice of yesterday – even if she cannot explain what it is that defines today's Alice.

However, is there really a continuity of selfhood that humans can use to define their selves? Or is discontinuity actually the way our selves work? Is continuity yet another of the self-illusions (or self-delusions) that humans are so adept at modelling? To examine this debate, we need to look more closely at what kinds of self define us, how they define us and why we let them define us.

Let us start by setting out the types of self we need to talk about. Two of them have been discussed so far in some detail: the Social self and the Cultural self. Two have been mentioned in passing: the Episodic self and the Narrative self. And two have been rather underplayed, considering their importance: the self-model and the Projected self. That leaves the elephant in the room, which has been largely ignored so far: the actual, physical self that continues to sit on the sofa eating peanuts and ignoring all metaphysical attempts to wish it away. It is here that we need to begin our definition of selves.

To help us in our self-definition, we should start in a traditional fantasy-story way, with a map showing the journey 'there and back again'.[1] This does not mean that the story of the selves is a fantasy, but it is, like all good fantasy stories, a metaphor of a reality – and metaphors are both more entertaining and more revealing than gritty reality stories. Figure 8.1 shows us the map of our tour round the selves, and it also shows the relationships between the selves.

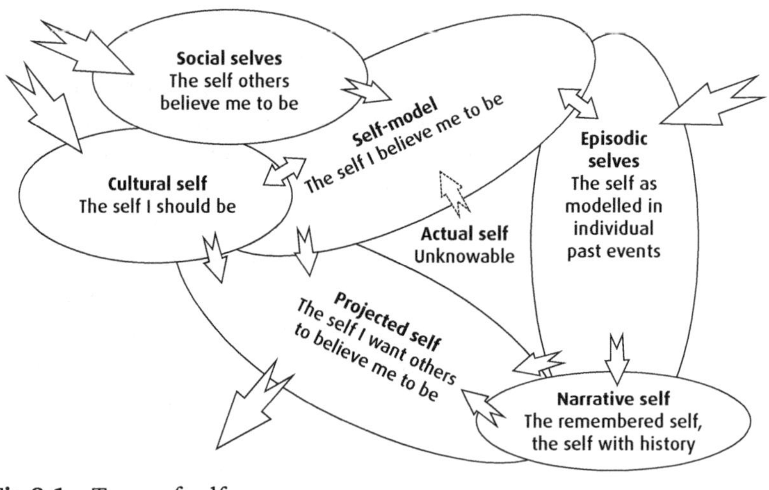

Fig 8.1 Types of self

The arrows indicate information flows. The big ones represent information flows into and out of the individual's cognition, the smaller ones represent information flows within the individual's cognition. The direction of the arrow is the direction of the flow.

The Actual self: unknowable

The fact that we have a physical self is inescapable: all selfhood resides in the brain, which is a component of the physical body; and it is the physical self in the brain that regulates the body. For practical purposes, and ignoring the unprovable non-physical, there is no existent self without the physical self. This makes the physical, or Actual, self a key feature of selfhood. The Actual self is a Darwinian gene-machine – unlike all the other selves, which are cognitive products of a Darwinian gene-machine – which means that the Actual self is directly governed by the twin genetic imperatives to survive and thrive. It has no interest in philosophical positions such as self-sacrifice or generosity, unless they directly lead to enhanced personal survival or enhanced reproductive success. So when William Hamilton said:

> … in the world of our model organisms, whose behaviour is determined strictly by genotype, we expect to find that no one is prepared to sacrifice his life for any single person but that everyone will sacrifice it when he can thereby save more than two brothers, or four half-brothers, or eight first cousins …
>
> (Hamilton 1964, 16)

… he was speaking for his Actual self. Three brothers, five half-brothers or nine first cousins all have more of my genes that I do – that is, if I can be assured of no sexual cheating by my mother, grandmother or aunts. In the actual world, this Hamiltonian kinship calculus is hedged-around with uncertainties, and not just in terms of non-monogamous relatives; so the safest strategy for the Actual self remains, *look out for number one*.

Unlike the other selves, the Actual self is not a conscious representation of the self. Yes, invasions of the self–other boundary cause discomforts or pleasure – injury causes pain, food causes satiation; but these are innate electrochemical reactions generated within the Actual self. They require no conscious attention – the Actual self does not need to be an aware self. An organism can handle pain and pleasure with its autonomic responses (involuntary, innate mechanisms) or its automatic responses (incidentally acquired mechanisms that are non-conscious but which may be subject to contextual override). For the organism to experience pain or pleasure, there is no need for a self that is able to recognise themself as being in pain or being happy.

Also unlike the other selves, the Actual self is not a constructed model. Where the other selves represent, the Actual self just *is*. And where the modelled selves are either differentiated (different selves of the same type) or integrated (the outcome of merging different self-models to create a new modelled self) or both, the Actual self is neither differentiated nor integrated. There is only one Actual self, and it is not the product of modelling or other cognitive manipulation. However, because it is not a conscious representation, it is also rather dull. It may be the elephant in the room, sitting on the couch and eating peanuts, but we have no need to disturb it. It is happy being ignored, although it is not necessarily aware of being happy.

The Social self: the self others believe me to be

The Social self is the first self of which we are consciously aware – the model of my self offered by others as part of the exchange of social calculus. Unlike most of the other selves, therefore, it is provided wholly from outside the self, and is therefore subject to the receiver's dilemma that accompanies any shared information: why should I believe it?

The answer lies in the peculiar nature of social calculus information. First, it is opinion, not knowledge, and it is offered and received as such; it already contains its own veracity warning. Second, it is offered *about* me *to* me: the first time this happens, I have no pre-existing data against which to check the offered model, but at all subsequent times I have a growing database modelling how I am seen by others, so I can accept or reject this new opinion based on that database. Third, if it is offered in a social calculus equation, then I can check the offered information against my own social calculus: does it mesh with the information already in my system or does it produce anomalies or contradictions? Fourth, any social calculus information offered is a World 3 reality, not a World 2 virtuality or a World 1 actuality; all information is subject to negotiation toward meaning – both with the sender and with my models of my self.

These caveats to veracity mean that all models of me offered to me are factually relative: their 'truth' is relative to the social calculus of the sender and to my own social calculus. I should not expect to receive social models of me that give a single group impression of who I am; instead, I will receive a number of different, individual views. Some of these views will differ from each other only slightly, while others will differ markedly; but their multiplicity means that the Social self is differentiated, with more than one model available to the self.

The self-model: the self I believe me to be

Accepting models of my self from others is informative in building a picture of how I am viewed by others; but, more importantly for the story of selfhood, it provides a third-person model of me to sit in my social calculus system – and this model appears to be undifferentiated. So how to collapse the many Social selves into one self-model? The obvious solution is to merge the different social models into an integrated self-model, discarding contradictions; but, because of the wide variation in Social selves offered to me, this is neither possible nor necessary. Instead, we tend to hold cognitive representations of several self-models, although only one at a time (the self-in-context) is treated as the valid self for modelling purposes. Over time, we cycle through a range of self-models depending on our current electrochemical state, the context in which we are self-modelling and the company we are keeping.

Each of my self-models is integrated from sets of social models, but because I have more than one self-model they are also differentiated; and because the currently active model changes over time, the self-model is also protean – like an amoeba, it constantly changes its form. This variable nature of the self can become an important source of self-anxiety: do my inconsistencies represent a failure or fraying of my integrated selfhood? There is only one actual, physical *me*, so why do there seem to be several real *me*'s?

One way out of the dilemma is to ignore the differences and simply believe there is a fully integrated self-model that collocates with the Actual self. This seems to be the solution chosen by narcissists, who usually avoid internalised self-awareness in favour of externalised approbation. Their internal self-models (their egos) are often brittle and easily damaged. Any criticism is not just criticism of the critic's model of the narcissist, it is criticism of the single self-model the narcissist possesses; it is, therefore, criticism of the narcissist in every possible way. Critics are therefore dealt with vindictively and with an overkill out of proportion to the criticism offered (Campbell and Baumeister 2006). However, while this is a description of people who would be clinically diagnosed as narcissists, it is also a description of most of us at one time or another: we all sometimes believe that the currently active self-model is our only self-model, and take criticism badly. What is being described here is a strategy of selfhood, not necessarily an aberrant psychological behaviour (Krajco 2007). What makes it aberrant is if it is an individual's default, or only, strategy.

A second way out of the dilemma is to believe that the differences amount to a negation of an integrated self-model. All I have to inform my self-model are the impressions that others have of me; and these can be manipulated by adopting whatever appearance-model will get me immediate gratification. This seems to be the solution of sociopaths (also called psychopaths), who take the protean aspect of self-modelling to extremes: they will do, say and be whatever they need to in order to manipulate others and satisfy their needs. There is no negotiation toward meaning for sociopaths because there is only one relevant meaning to the universe – that of the undifferentiated self. And criticism does not matter, because there is no self-model to criticise, only a projected model or appearance that can be adjusted to meet current needs. If someone does not like the self you are projecting, project a different self (Gallagher 2013b). To quote Groucho Marx, 'Those are my principles, and if you don't like them ... well, I have others'.

Once again, it must be emphasised that what is described here is not a diagnostic aid for identifying clinical sociopathy. It is a self-modelling behaviour that we all display at one time or another. In fact, the frequency of clinical sociopathy in the general population (about 3 per cent of males and just under 1 per cent of females) makes them unusual but not rare (Mealey 1995). On any London tube train during rush hour, there are likely to be a dozen or more people who would be diagnosed as sociopathic if their behaviour warranted a diagnosis; but, in the vast majority of cases and for most of the time, it does not.

A third way out of the dilemma is not really a way out at all. It is possible to surrender to the multiple selves by losing the capacity to control which single self-model dominates at any one time. This is the problem that schizophrenics face, with the different self-models competing in the conscious mind, rather than being policed by the subconscious mind and presented to the conscious mind one at a time. In this case, my inconsistencies do not represent a failure or fraying of the integrated model of my selfhood, they really are the fraying of my selfhood. This collapsing selfhood causes the boundaries between actuality, reality and virtuality to blur even more than usual, hence typical schizophrenic symptoms include hallucinations and delusions. The lack of a cohesive self-model also affects the self that the person can project, causing breakdowns in their social relationships (Bowes 2014).

Schizophrenia is a particularly interesting 'solution' to the many-selves dilemma, because it seems to be a by-product of having language: the condition has been linked to language in several ways. First, schizophrenia is linked to dysphasia, or the loss of communicative competency; and it also seems to affect phonology, leading to flat-toned speech (Covington et al. 2005). Second, schizophrenia has been shown to be implicated in the language and social-modelling areas of the brain. Radanovic et al. (2013) discovered a link between formal thought disorder (a diagnostic criterion for schizophrenia) and language impairment. The severity of both impairments was correlated with deficits in the left superior temporal gyrus and the left planum temporale, both areas in a Statistically Standard Brain (SSB)[2] implicated in language; and in the orbitofrontal cortex, which is implicated in modelling for decision-making, including social calculus modelling. Pu et al. (2017) identified correlated deficits in the anterior part of the temporal cortex, the ventro-lateral prefrontal cortex, the dorso-lateral prefrontal cortex and frontopolar cortex areas of the brain – all areas implicated in both social cognition (particularly ToM) and language production. It seems that schizophrenia is somehow involved in the neural connections between social cognition and language cognition.

It also seems that there may be a genetic basis to the link between schizophrenia and language. The gene FOXP2 is implicated in both language production and hallucinatory episodes in schizophrenia (Tolosa et al. 2010); there does not seem to be a causal relationship, but there is a strong correlation. Srinivasan et al. (2016) showed that many of the genes implicated in schizophrenia are also involved in general cognitive development, and specifically human versions of the genes seem to have appeared since the split between humans and Neanderthals. These gene-forms seem to be absent from chimpanzee genomes (Srinivasan et al. 2017).

Dissociative Identity Disorder (DID) is another condition in which the individual seems to surrender to the dilemma of multiple selves. This condition has similarities to schizophrenia, and it is often presented in the lay media as schizophrenia. In terms of the SSMH, it poses a slightly different problem for the individual: it is not that the selves are indistinct, it is that there is no concord between them; each self has somehow set itself up as an independent person – sometimes with recognition that there is only one shared body, but sometimes not. Whitehead points out that we all live with multiple modelled personalities when he says, 'Shakespeare can fill a stage with characters, all of whom act and speak convincingly as whole and distinct persons, though all were born within a 'single' mind' (Whitehead 2001, 4). The problem with DID would seem to be that Shakespeare has left the stage, and all that is left are the characters.

Depersonalisation Disorder is yet another condition on the schizophrenia spectrum where SSMH may be relevant. In this condition, individuals feel they are somehow not a real person: the modelling is still working, but the self has gone missing (Baker et al. 2003). It is a state that we are all in at some point in our lives, and it is only a disorder when it becomes prolonged. This condition shows that the metaphor SELF IS OTHER is more than just a cognitive explanation after the fact; it is itself a cognitive fact with consequences.

Between too little modelling, too many selves, and not enough self, the schizophrenia spectrum seems to be a product of self-modelling. However, as with narcissism and sociopathy, it must be emphasised that what is being discussed here is a self-modelling behaviour, and does not necessarily indicate a medical condition. Poor Alice could not explain herself because a very confusing day had exhausted her range of self-models, leaving her with no dominant self to rely on; but she did recover quite spectacularly by the end of the book. In a similar way, we can be left nonplussed and dumbfounded without needing a diagnosis of formal thought disorder and dysphasia. Life may currently be complicated; this, too, shall pass.

Most of us wander around in this triangle of selfhood extremes without particular difficulty, doing what we need to get by as a self-modelling entity; and mostly we do it without being consciously aware of the choices we are making about our self-modelling. The terminology of selfhood modelling often deceptively implies conscious choices are being made in self-modelling; but most self-modelling involves subconscious cognition, implicit knowledge and automatic responses. We first start to build our self-models when we receive our first recognised piece of information about our self from others; and this happens around age 2, when the child becomes aware of the dyadic negotiation toward meaning between them and their caregiver. 'Daddy loves Baby' may sound like a simple idea for adults to comprehend, but it makes huge demands on the social calculus and social modelling of the child, long before the child has conscious knowledge of their social selfhood.

The Episodic self: the self as modelled in individual past events

The Episodic self is a feature that emerges from the combination of self-modelling and conscious memory recall. As an emergent feature, the Episodic self is neither directly learned nor directly innate; it is what becomes possible when there is an interaction between two other features that are, themselves, learned or innate (Pomerantz and Cragin 2015). The emergent feature of the Episodic self seems to be particularly interesting, because one of the interacting features is learned and the other is innate: the combination of the capacity to self-model (learned) and the capacity to remember events in the past (innate) creates the possibility of modelling a self in a remembered past event. Instead of the event being passively visceral – the emotions of the event are remembered as emotions – it becomes actively visceral – the emotions of the event are remembered as *my own* emotions. The Episodic self is, therefore, more than just an episodic memory, and it is equally as real as any self-model.

An Episodic self is not a memory of a past self-model; it is a current representation constructed from the social-self evidence currently available. When we remember our self, we do not remember our self-model as it was when the memory was laid down; rather, we construct a current self-model to represent our previous self. Giorgio Marchetti (2014) says this is because we are prone to three 'sins' of memory: we forget or mitigate the visceral emotions that were actually generated by the event, making our emotional memory of the event unreliable; we distort our memories by remembering the events themselves incorrectly, thus rendering our procedural memory of the event unreliable; and we overemphasise some aspects of the event while under-emphasising others, thus pathologising our memory of the event. To use a von Neumann computer metaphor, recalling a memory is not just accessing a fixed memory-image like a file on a hard drive; it involves copying the memory-image into working memory, adjusting the memory and then writing it back as a new image (Schiller and Phelps 2011). But memory is not just accidentally inherently fallible; it is important that it be so, so that each time I recall the memory I can model the experiences in the past event as *my* experiences in relation to my current self-model.

Yet another feature makes an episodic self-model unreliable as a model of my previous self: it is composed of more than my own memory of the event. The sharing of social models is more effective if the contexts and evidence of those models are also shared; so any memory I have of a past event is overlaid with the memories of others about that event – and every viewpoint of the event is different. What I believe is my memory of the event, seldom is; instead it is, like my models of my self and others, an amalgam of viewpoints and opinions. The Episodic self is a memory of a self-model that was originally generated from the models of me offered by others, and when recalled it is then edited by my current model of me and by more models of me offered by others.

If the Episodic self is just a type of self-model, and self-modelling is an outcome of shared social calculus, and sharing social calculus seems to be limited to humans, then is it possible for non-humans to have Episodic selves? The simple answer would seem to be no; but, because the Episodic self is an emergent feature, the actual answer is more complex. One of the two components of an Episodic self is the capacity to recall past events, which Endel Tulving (2005) calls noetic memory, contrasting it with autonoetic memory (the capacity to recall past events that include the past self's own perspective). Tulving takes the view that autonoetic memory is available only to humans. In his description, autonoetic memory seems similar to episodic memory, having both recall and a self-perspective. Tulving's autonoetic self-perspective is that of a past self; but is that a true self-perspective, and is that past self really available to the current self as a self-model?

Some researchers disagree with Tulving's view. Fabbro et al. (2015) propose that a capacity for autonoetic memory is likely to be present in non-human brains, because the neurologically complex brain areas associated with human selfhood have correlates in those non-human brains. However, it remains to be demonstrated that the correlate areas function in the same capacity in both brains. In contrast, Robert Numan (2015) differentiates non-human from human episodic memory by describing it as 'episodic-like'. This is a more cautious approach that does not necessarily require the generation of an Episodic self. It also gives us a convenient way to label the difference between the autonoetic episodic selfhood of humans and the otherwise episodic memory that many mammals do appear to possess.

If episodic selfhood, like Tulving's autonoetic memory, is an innate capacity in humans, then we have a problem explaining how it evolved. If, however, it emerges from the modelled self plus noetic memory, and the modelled self is an outcome of sharing social calculus, then we can say that episodic selfhood is a synthesis of pre-existing cognitive systems. It is a learned trick, a way of creating a third-person social calculus model that happens to represent the self. Autonoetic memory is not a species-difference requiring its own evolutionary explanation; it is just noetic memory plus a trick.

The Narrative self: the remembered self, the self with history

The concept of Narrative self, or narrative identity, was perhaps first codified by Paul Ricoeur (1990 [1992], Chapter 6) and Jerome Bruner (1990, Chapter 4). Although it had already been discussed by earlier commentators, Ricoeur and Bruner were the first to define what a Narrative self is. Basically, the Narrative self is the model we make of our life experiences as an evolving story – a stitching-together of the various Episodic selves in such a way that they can be viewed as aspects of a single self. Where the Episodic selves, being self-models, are differentiated (a series of models instead of an integrated single model), the Narrative self is an integrated meta-model.

As the Narrative self is a product of the migration of selfhood, from the Social self through the self-model and then the Episodic self, it is more virtual than real; and yet it is the self we most often call on to define our *me*-ness. What is it that makes this self so attractive as a model of me? The answer appears to be that the Narrative self provides the individual with a sense of unity and purpose. It establishes the two cognitive concepts that having a self is supposed to enact: the concept of the single me and the concept of the continuous me. Although we cannot know it from the inside, this is what the Actual self seems to be from the outside: an entity delimited in both space and time; but, within those limits, a single integrated entity.

However, the Narrative self is also the most controversial of the selves. As we saw in Chapter 1, for Thomas Metzinger the Narrative self is an illusion because 'we are not things, but processes' (2003, 325). He is correct in saying this, inasmuch as our cognition is a process; but our brains and our bodies definitely are *things*. Our self can be seen as a system (a set of processes reliant on a particular structure to convert inputs into outputs). And a system contains both structure (a physical organisation which, when activated, converts inputs to outputs in a predictable way) and process (a particular route taken through a structure by an input to become an output). The Narrative self may be a virtuality, but it is also a product of realities that are emplaced in actualities. The Narrative self may not work as a thing; but as a metaphor or representation of a thing, it works just fine.

We have also seen that, for Galen Strawson, a Narrative self is not a prerequisite for being human. He says: 'It is not true that there is only one way in which human beings experience their being in time. There are deeply non-Narrative people and there are good ways to live that are deeply non-Narrative' (Strawson 2004, 13). Non-narrativity is, therefore, likely to be a correct diagnosis for some individuals without it affecting their cognition or socialisation. However, as Drummond et al. (2015) and Grossman et al. (2017) show, deficits in Narrative self do seem, at least in old age, to be associated with deficits in other cognition: the absence of a Narrative self in these cases is a by-product of other cognitive conditions that cause narrativity issues more extensive than just the lack of a Narrative self.

When it comes to efforts to recreate a humanlike experience in machine form, scientists working in artificial intelligence have a clear understanding of the need for a Narrative self. For Pointeau and Dominey (2017), the Narrative self is a necessary tool for sharing plans, and it allows individuals to negotiate toward meaning in joint enterprises. These authors equipped their iCub robot with an AutoBiographical Memory (ABM), which is a simulation of a Narrative self, and showed that, when the ABM is linked to language, plans and activities could be negotiated between the robot and the trainer:

> We previously suggested that shared planning could be developed based on 5 prerequisites: (1) object and agent perception, (2) perception of state changes (allows action perception), (3) ability to distinguish between self and other, (4) emotion/outcome perception, and (5) statistical sequence learning … These mechanisms, plus a specific ABM and methods for operating on the contents of the ABM allow for the capabilities reviewed in this report. As mentioned, we find the need for one additional capability, which is an interface between the language system and the ABM, in the form of a situation model. This is required in order to explicitly represent narrative relations between events that are not accounted for in the ABM.
>
> (Pointeau and Dominey 2017, 16)

The six-feature ABM makes the iCub's interaction with the trainer impressively humanlike. So we can see that, if Strawson is right that the Narrative self is not a necessity for a functioning human, or even if Metzinger is right that the Narrative self is not a thing, there is still a purpose for a Narrative self in the interpersonal negotiation toward meaning and joint enterprise; and a deficit in Narrative self makes that negotiation harder. It may be completely virtual, but there does seem to be some practical use in having a Narrative self.

The Cultural self: the self I should be

A Cultural self, like the Social selves, is a model offered to the individual by others; but, unlike the Social selves, it is a virtual self. It is a model of an ideal individual in this particular culture, explicitly the ideal self that the individual can be. A culture usually has many ideal models, differentiated by gender, role, lineage, age group and any other way that the culture divides up its population. For instance, the Hindu caste system is based largely on gender and lineage, and it delimits not just the range of roles possible for an individual, it dictates how they are treated, whom they can marry, what they can eat and even what or whom they can touch (Pratheesh 2015). There are four main castes: priests, warriors, owning professions and labouring professions – a pattern repeated in internally specialist societies across the world. Unlike most other systems, however, the four Hindu castes are formally subdivided into sub-castes (in other cultures this level of differentiation is usually informal); but, like many other systems, there is also a formal gender-based differentiation, further limiting life choices. The caste system is a powerful engine for ensuring that life goes on regardless of who is in charge; but this also allows one ruling class to be replaced by another relatively seamlessly, without affecting the day-to-day functioning of the society. After seizing power in India, the Delhi Sultanate, the Mughal Empire and the British Raj all re-emphasised the caste system to retain control over the populace. The Hindu caste system is one of several historical systems that modern, global, pluralistic societies are breaking down; but a socially differentiated system nonetheless remains an important feature of most cultures today. The limited mobility between British social classes remains a case in point.

However, even if the range of ideal, or cultural, selves offered by a culture is quite wide, the options offered to each individual usually remain quite limited; and out of the small range offered, each individual often chooses one model as their lifelong Cultural self. This limitation is even observable in perhaps the least class-bound society in the world, that of the USA. Kraus and Park (2014) showed that perceived social class is correlated with self-evaluation: the higher the former, the higher the latter. Yet individuals do not usually change their Cultural self to enhance self-evaluation; the model they have been given is the model they accept. This acquiescence to the group opinion is even more noticeable in another modern culture, which places a high value on conformity to the Cultural self. As Markus and Kitayama (1991) say, 'In America, "the squeaky wheel gets the grease." In Japan, "the nail that stands out gets pounded down"' (224). They describe the American approach as an independent view of the self – the cultural view of the self does not include other individuals; while the Japanese approach is an interdependent view of the self – the Cultural self is projected into the social calculus of the individual. The authors suggest that Western belief in the

Cultural self as independent seems to produce a less happy and healthy human society than the interdependent model.

Toon van Meijl (2008) pursues a similar idea when he describes the need for a 'dialogical self' to counter the limiting idea of a single Cultural self. Nowadays, we are faced not with a single culture to which we must relate, but a multiplicity of cultures we dip into, and aspects of which we incorporate into our Cultural self. The Cultural self is no longer a single target of selfness for which I should aim – the best me I can be – it is a changing and moving target. To keep up with the changes to the Cultural self, we need a dialogical self between the received social models and the received Cultural self. This seems to be missing from the SSMH model presented here, but this is because van Meijl has agglomerated the Cultural self with the Projected self. Where the self-model acts as a buffer between the received Social selves and the Projected self in the SSMH model, van Meijl places the dialogic self between the received Social selves and the Cultural/Projected self.

In the SSMH model, the main route by which the Social selves are incorporated into the Projected self comes around the other side of the 'wheel', through the self-model, the Episodic and the Narrative selves. The Cultural self (the self I should be) stands alone as a separate societal imposition on the self-model and on the Projected self. The best me I can be is a different imposition on my selfhood from the social calculus models of me: it is not how others see me but how others wish me to be. In the SSMH, there is no need to posit a novel mechanism to handle modern differentiated culture, because we could not have developed modern differentiated culture if the mechanisms for it were not already present in some form.

This does not mean, however, that modelling a Cultural self in a modern differentiated culture is simple or even linear. Navarro et al. (2014) showed that, for Mexican American college students, there was an iterative relationship between the Cultural self and the personal self (or self-model), such that retention of cultural heritage increased self-esteem, and higher self-esteem led to greater heritage-culture retention. Nataliya Aristova (2016) showed that changes in the Cultural self can also feed back out to the culture via the Projected self: the Cultural self projected onto the individual by the culture is, in the end, just the sum of the Cultural selves projected onto the culture by the individuals. As Aristova says, 'Self-identification through culture and building up new cultural identities in new socio-cultural environments will always remain very significant factors for the self-determination of nations, countries and regions of the world' (Aristova 2016, 160).

Chien-Ru Sun (2017) looked at a different issue regarding the Cultural self: the number of selves the culture imposes on the individual. Sun identified four types of self in the relationship between the individual and Chinese culture: the individual-oriented self (which collocates with the self-model), and three culturally imposed selves. The Cultural selves are: the models of my ideal self offered to me by individual others in one-to-one exchanges (the relationship-oriented self); the models of my ideal self offered to me by my family (the familistic [group]-oriented self); and the models of my ideal self implicit in my culture (the other-oriented self). Sun describes the other-oriented self as 'the most undeniable' (2017, 14): for an individual in a Chinese culture, the Cultural self plays a significant role in generating self-models, and the cultural-self-models of who I should be, as offered by the society around me, are more significant than for a Western individual.

The Cultural self, like the Narrative self, is a virtual self; it has only as much value as its human society is willing to give it. This can vary from very little (in societies valuing independent selfhood) to very much (in societies valuing interdependent selfhood). However, the Cultural self is also an aspirational self: each individual has an individual relationship with their Cultural self, which varies according to their need or wish to conform, whether they see their Cultural self as attainable and (at the subconscious level) whether the Cultural self is more or less fit for them than other self-models. It is in the Cultural self that dispassionate self-sacrifice begins, so the Cultural self is the key to a large number of our anxieties and self-doubts; the Cultural self supplies both the angel on our right shoulder and the devil on our left. As Aleksandr Solzhenitsyn put it, 'The battleline between good and evil runs through the heart of every person.'

The Projected self: the self I want others to believe me to be

What is the purpose of accepting all the offered models of my self and generating yet more models of my self from them? If the only product of self-modelling is self-sacrifice, then it seems a poor return for a hefty cost in terms of cognition. Two reasons why self-modelling should benefit the individual have been explored so far: first, that a more complete social calculus allows better representation of relationships within my group; and second, that being able to share social models increases the range of cooperative possibilities with other members of my group. In both cases, the fitness of the individual is enhanced by being part of a fitter group. Another reason why self-modelling is so valuable may lie in the fact that, as well as being able to model my self, I can project that model back into the world. I am no longer an *it* modelled by others to manipulate me; I am a *she* or a *he* or a *they*. This makes me a person with an agenda, with whom meanings can be negotiated. Negotiating with others toward meaning about others makes me an active player in communication – a *me* and a *you*; which means that the self-model I present to the world becomes part of the negotiation.

The Projected, or public, self is an emergent feature of the social models I receive, moderated through three routes: first, via self-modelling, Episodic self and Narrative self; second, directly via self-modelling; and third, via Cultural self. Or, to put it another way, the Projected self is an amalgam of my internal representations of myself and the expectations that others put upon me. However, there also seems to be a feedback loop outside of the self that allows the Projected self to affect the Social self: the self I want others to believe me to be can become one of the selves others believe me to be. Dianne Tice (1992) showed that, where a behaviour is performed as a public act (and, therefore, is available to be presented back to me as a Social self), it is more likely to moderate my Projected self than if it is performed as a private act. Where the individual has an ongoing interaction with a group of people, the more pronounced are the adjustments the received Social selves make to the Projected self.

Sedikides and Skowronsi (2000) describe how the public self emerges from the symbolic self (an amalgam of the self-model with the Social, Episodic, Narrative and Cultural selves) to control the presentation of self to others. They see the public self as contributing to private self-knowledge through 'reflected appraisal (i.e., seeing the self as important group members see the self)' (Sedikides and Skowronsi 2000, 100). However, relying on self-appraisal in this way is not an internal process: the only way I can be aware of how others see me is via the social self-models they offer me. For Sedikides and Skowronsi, the symbolic self relies on the opinions we receive, and self-esteem (how much I personally value my self-model as a person) is dictated by the interpersonal evaluations offered by others.

Yet the Projected self is not just an unconscious product of received models of my self; there is conscious input to the model, too. While the relationship between the self-model and the Projected self is largely not under cognitive control – I automatically project a version of my self composed from the models of my self I receive from others – the input from the Cultural self is aspirational. The Cultural self is a virtual model that is not me, but rather what *me* could be; and it opens the way for any virtual self-model to be used in the creation of a Projected self. For instance, Nystedt and Ljungberg (2002), in a series of experiments, found that the public self is on a continuum between style-consciousness (what I am presenting) and appearance-consciousness (how I am presenting); and the private self is on a continuum between self-reflectiveness (knowing I have a self) and internal-state-awareness (knowing I am not invariant). They showed that treating the public and private selves as continua fitted the data from their studies better than treating them as monoliths. The nature of the Projected self seems to be contextual rather than fixed. Nigel Rapport found that we also tend to see our Projected self as aspirational rather than fixed; and, in a biography of the painter Stanley Spencer, he described the artist's Projected self as 'an individual engaged in a life project' (Rapport 2005, 60).

The manipulation of the Projected self by others has become an area of interest recently. For instance, Lambros Malafouris (2008) showed how the Projected self can be socialised via the Social self (self-model) in quite unusual ways, creating selfhood beyond the bounds of the Actual self. He describes how a signet ring from a Mycenean tomb encompasses both a personal concept of *me* within a possessive concept of *mine*, and a sociocultural concept of *him* within a possessive concept of *his*. The fact that this beautiful and valuable artefact was entombed with the corpse means it was treated as part of the individual after death: traditional ownership ceases at death, but tectonoetic ownership (the association of an object with an individual, and only that individual) does not.

Louis Rougier (2014) asked whether, in a modern marketing environment, advertising should be directed toward the consumer's 'real self' (an amalgam of the Actual self and the self-model) or their Projected self. He took the view that both selves need to be addressed, but that 'the product design, packaging and communication must first inspire the projected self' (Rougier 2014, 4). By addressing the *should* factor in the received Cultural self ('the best me I can be'), the aspirations of the 'real self' can be manipulated toward a more conforming Projected self, one that will buy the product because they *should* rather than if they *need to*. The Projected self in this scenario has become a subconscious promise by the Actual self to adjust the self-model to be more like the cultural self-model. This is only a re-emphasis of the group culture's expectations about the individual, conformity to which is a natural result of the individual's gaining fitness from living in the group culture; but it is nonetheless somehow disturbingly coercive.

Recently, Hazem et al. (2018) showed how the manipulation of the Projected self via the inputs of others to the Social self is a subconscious physical process: we create our own automatic self-censorship. When others notice us (by calling our name or by physical touching) it sensitises us to, and primes us for, other bodily inputs; and this priming increases our physical self-awareness and receptivity. Hazem et al. say that, in their experiments, 'the effects of own name, social touch, and eye contact on bodily awareness were subtended by common brain mechanisms' and that 'knowing that the contact is directly created by another human agent is essential to the effect of social contact on bodily self-awareness' (Hazem et al. 2018, 6). They see human self-awareness as being an iterative social process, with the group view of me affecting my own view of me, and my own view of me affecting the group view.

Looking back at Figure 8.1, a simple interpretation would be that the Projected self is the outcome of a process of cognitive self-definition, and provides the route by which I influence the group around me; but it turns out that the group influences me long before I can influence it. In evolutionary terms, this is all rather odd: I need to project my self onto my group to enhance my own agenda and limit those of others; and, for most species, if they do this in a subconscious, no-holds-barred way, using just their Actual self, then they have the best chance of achieving their aims. However, as a human, I am cursed – or advantaged – by sharing social calculus, which requires me to consciously model a different kind of self. This self is, in turn, not one self but many selves, all of which are either real or virtual and not actual. They are not *me* selves but *they* selves, where *they* happens to represent *me*; they are emic selves rather than etic selves, true because the individual and the group agree they are true, not because they are definitionally true; and they can be both differentiated and integrated, generating a continuously changing kaleidoscope of selves as my current Projected self. The self I project to my group as the *real me* is one out of many possibilities: a little bit of the *me* you tell me I am; a little of the *me* I believe I am; a little of the self I was; a little of the self I should, or hope to, be; and all heavily censoring the subconscious *me* I actually am. Yet, after all this, the Projected self is not the final product of the process; instead, it is part of a larger process where my projected model of *me* is further edited in the minds of other individuals in the group, and then offered back to me as a Social self – a self you tell me I am. This larger process is a continuous iteration through a life: it usually starts at about age 2, with a realisation that others are talking to me about me; and it usually only finishes with death.

... And there's more: some other selves

So far, the terminology of selfhood has been shown to be quite diverse. We have seen a multiplicity of terms (the Actual self is also the individual-oriented self, the Narrative self is also a narrative identity, and the Projected self is also the public self). We have seen amalgamation of terms (the symbolic or private self includes everything except the Actual and Projected selves; the autobiographical self is the Episodic and Narrative selves combined; and the real self is an amalgam of the Actual self and the self-model). We have also seen subdivision of terms (the dialogic self recognises that we have more than one cultural-self-model, and those Cultural selves – at least, in terms of Chinese culture – include the relationship-oriented self, the familistic [group]-oriented self and the other-oriented self). And we have seen evidence that the SSMH offered here may not be the whole story (the tectonoetic self includes all the selves plus objects beyond the boundary of the Actual self). Yet there still remain other important subdivisions of selfhood that have not yet been explored here.

One of these is Ulric Neisser's Five Kinds of Self-Knowledge (1988). The significance of his work in the literature on selfhood means that the SSMH needs to be reconciled with the self-knowledge model if it is to be taken seriously. The two models are not that dissimilar, although one important difference is that Neisser discusses knowledge and not models, and he treats his selves as aspects of a single selfhood rather than different ways of being a self. Neisser's five types of self-knowledge map across the SSMH as follows:

- The ecological self is the self as a natural and physical object, a relationship with the actual world. This maps well to the Actual self.
- The interpersonal self is the self in communication with other selves, the self presented for others to communicate with. This maps to the Projected self.
- The extended self is the self that incorporates remembered and planned events involving the self. It maps to an amalgam of the Episodic and Narrative selves.
- The conceptual self 'draws its meaning from a network of socially-based assumptions and theories about human nature in general and ourselves in particular' (Neisser 1988, 35). This is a good description of how the Social self (a network of socially based assumptions) and Cultural self (theories about human nature)

work together, using the inputs of other people as fodder for our cognitively generated self-definitions.

- The private self is the self we create to explain our self to ourself, a conscious representation of our internal, and therefore exclusive, cognition. The first impression is that this maps to the self-model; but, for Neisser, the private self represents a more fundamental and real idea of selfness than the ad hoc and easily changed self-model. To represent Neisser's view in the SSMH, the private self is better represented by an amalgam of everything except the Actual and Projected selves, so it includes the extended self and the conceptual self.

Thus, while there are some differences between the two models regarding what a self actually is, Neisser's kinds of self-knowledge and the SSMH use similar tools to describe how humans generate their selfness. Other models of selfhood are less easy to reconcile to the SSMH. For instance, as we saw in Chapter 1, Baars et al. (2003) introduce the concept of an observing self: if there is conscious perception of sensory inputs, then there must be a mechanism inside the brain that intervenes in the cognition of sensing and inserts that awareness. That mechanism is the observing self. Vast amounts of our sensory inputs are ignored by conscious awareness: our body sends over 10 million bits of information to our brain for processing every second; and, of that, about 40 bits are consciously processed (Nørretranders 1991, 125–6). We are probably perfectly capable of operating without an observing self to generate conscious intervention; so the fact it needs to be posited to explain conscious awareness is significant.

The observing self poses problems for the SSMH. First, the selection of what is given attention must be a subconscious choice, but the giving of attention itself must be conscious; but how can something be both subliminal and intentional at the same time? Second, the difference between the Actual self and the other selves is that the Actual self is unmodelled. Modelling is a matter of attention; so where in the SSMH would an observing self be able to provide that needed attention? Third, how does the observing self interface between the Actual self and the other selves? These are questions that the SSMH perhaps should, but does not at present, address.

On the other hand, a different question may indicate that the observing self is not without its own problems: where in the act of observing is a self useful? Surely selfhood comes into the interpretation of observation, not into the act of observing? If this is the case, then the observing self is an aspect of the unknowable Actual self, and thus not a self that can be modelled; it is beyond the ambit of the SSMH. Krauzlis et al. (2014) argue from neurological evidence that attention is not a cause of decision-making but an outcome; it is not a part of the interpretation of observation, just a conscious recognition of the decision made by a subliminal interpreting mechanism. Domenico Guarino (2018) argues that this provides neurological evidence for Daniel Dennett's (2009) 'strange inversion of reasoning', thus linking together cognitive attention as an evolutionary outcome with most other evolutionary outcomes: attention and evolution occur because an event produces an outcome that becomes significant, not because the event itself is significant.

Another approach is the patterned self, proposed by Shaun Gallagher (2013a). This model of the self is more deeply differentiated than the SSMH, but the SSMH largely corresponds with the patterned self in terms of form. What differs is that, where the patterned self is a single, coherent self that can present different patterns generated from a set of innate and personal psychological aspects, the SSMH treats the Actual self as singular but subliminal (and therefore consciously unknowable), and the consciously modelled selves are disparate products of received models of the self. The aspects of the patterned self include: minimal embodied and minimal experiential aspects; affective and psychological aspects; intersubjective, narrative and extended aspects; and situated aspects. However, within these aspects, it is not clear how much is under conscious control and how much is subliminal; and this matters, because humans are both slaves to our genes and controllers of our cognitive destiny. Any theory of selfhood has to address the fact that we have both selfness and awareness of selfness (Edwardes 2014).

Of the two models, the patterned self seems to be intuitively closer to how we believe our selves to work: we think of our self as unitary and integrated, with every social projection of our self being in some way honest and faithful to that integrated self. However, we also recognise that our single, integrated self is mutable, so the projection we make today need not be the same as the projection we made yesterday; but we also intuitively believe that today's and yesterday's projections remain faithful representations of the integrated self. In addition, we recognise that we have the capacity to deceive (both others and our own self) when we socially project our self. This is a lot of things to simultaneously expect from our unitary and integrated self, which indicates that treating the self as unitary may be intuitive, but it may not match the way selves actually work.

Another self is the culturally evolved self, proposed by Lloyd Hawkeye Robertson (2017). He takes the view that free will is an emergent outcome of being immersed in a complex cultural environment, and self-awareness is an emergent feature of free will. He does not address the question of how a complex cultural environment could emerge or evolve, or why it should emerge or evolve in the particular case of human socialisation; and he does not convincingly explore why complex cultural environments should be exclusive to humans, although he assumes them to be so. There is also a hint of circularity in his argument: our culture gave us free will, and our free will gave us self-awareness. However, he also says that 'Free will originates from the first person experience of the world and one's self-constructed understanding of his or her agency in the course of action' (Robertson 2017, 4). So, if self-awareness comes from free will, and free will comes from first-person experience, what is the difference between self-awareness and first-person experience? And, if there is no difference, where does free will come in? Robertson raises important questions about the relationship between free will, culture and selfhood, but he may not have them correctly sequenced to provide answers.

Robertson also says that, 'Questions of free will could not have been asked by beings unable to visualize the concept' (2017, 6). This reminds me of the exchange between Alice and the Red Queen:

> Alice laughed. 'There's no use trying,' she said: 'one can't believe impossible things.'
>
> 'I daresay you haven't had much practice,' said the Queen. 'When I was your age, I always did it for half-an-hour a day. Why, sometimes I've believed as many as six impossible things before breakfast.'
>
> (Lewis Carroll 1872, Chapter 5: 'Wool and Water')

Indeed, the capacity to believe impossible things would seem a much more reliable definition of humanity than either free will or self-awareness. We live in a world of solutions that were, at one time, impossible (metal ships, aircraft, cybernetic limbs, nanobots – the list is long and growing); but the problems were worried-at and debated until solutions were finally visualised and shared with others.

Another type of self that is not properly explored in the SSMH is what we can call the e-self. This is a version of my Projected self that is not subject to the knowledge others already have about me; it can therefore be more exploratory and less constrained than other Projected selves. The e-self is not really a new phenomenon, and it has been described as an authorial self or authorial persona when discussed in relation to printed publications (Hyland 2001). However, the rise of electronic media and the appearance of the 'casual' (rather than 'packaged') author has meant that many more people are producing Projected selves directed at people who do not know the projecting individual except through the media. The Projected self in these cases is unverifiable, so one downside of the increasing technical sophistication that has made electronic media possible is the appearance of blocks of code complex enough to imitate a human e-self. They are often treated as actual humans, and they can be used to manipulate the gullible and cause havoc in a modern electronic democracy (Deb et al. 2017). This aspect of e-selves will not be further explored here, but the significance for the study of human selfhood is extensive.

The e-self is mostly unverifiable and uncensored. This means the individual has the potential to be brutally honest in their projected e-self, putting forward an image that they would never dream of presenting in face-to-face contact with longer-term acquaintances. Hu et al. (2017) show that, in all forms of communication where the individual's identity is known and their reputation is at stake, the individual projects a positive self, which agrees with their positive self-model (the *ought self*) and their Cultural self (the *ideal self*). By contrast, in cases where the individual believes they are anonymous, they project more of their socially negative self-model and mostly ignore their Cultural self. For some people, this can have the effect of making communication in the anonymised online environment more attractive than in the actual reputation-driven world: some individuals seem to derive greater satisfaction from online anonymous communication than from any other form of human contact.

On the other side, Gil-Or et al. (2015) showed that e-communication makes it easier to project a deceptive self-image. This deception involves not just the daily white lies of normal, reputation-driven communication; it allows the individual to alter major features of their Projected self – age, gender, beliefs – anything, really. This creates what Gil-Or et al. call a false Facebook self, which can become a pathology in itself, or can license other psychopathologies the individual may have. Because of this, the creation of a false Facebook self is not just a personal choice, it can be a social problem; and the authors recommend that steps be taken to identify and suppress these pathological false Facebook selves. We are only now beginning to address the serious social issues that the projected e-self creates.

The final approach to human selfhood examined here was provided by George Lakoff (1992) with his multiple selves. Lakoff approached the question in a very similar way to this book, giving a series of conceptual metaphors to show how human selfhood works; and I must acknowledge Lakoff's inspiration for many of the ideas I have presented. He proposed a binary approach, with the Subject consisting of consciousness, will and judgement, and the Self being the rest of the person. However, there is no single way in which the Subject interfaces with the Self, creating different types of self-models within the individual's Subject+Self cognition. The first of these is the Projectible Self Model, which is not the same as the Projected self; instead it is the capacity to produce a Projected self, using tools like pronominalisation. The second is the Objective Subject Model, which allows the Self to perceive the Subject as an object – somewhat like a self-model, but once again more about the capacity to produce a self-model than the self-model itself.

The Objective Subject Model gives Lakoff his first conceptual metaphor: KNOWING IS VIEWING allows us to treat our subject-model as if it were a thing, because we are consciously aware of ourselves as subjects. Two other conceptual metaphors Lakoff presents in relation to the Objective-Subject Model – ENHANCED CONSCIOUSNESS IS THE ABILITY OF THE SUBJECT TO SEE THE SELF FROM THE OUTSIDE and OBJECTIVITY IS THE SEPARATION OF THE SUBJECT FROM THE SUBJECT'S VALUES AND PRESUPPOSITIONS – are more definitions than metaphors, so will not be considered here.

The third way the Subject interfaces with the Self is the Separable Subject Model, which reverses the Objective Subject Model, allowing the Subject to perceive the Self as an object. Lakoff sees this as generating a series of metaphors, such as LACK OF NORMAL CONSCIOUSNESS AND CONTROL IS BEING OUTSIDE THE SELF, RETURNING TO NORMAL CONSCIOUSNESS IS COMING BACK and EUPHORIC STATES ARE UP. This leads on to the Scattered Self Model, which reflects the fact that the Subject can maintain several different selves (or several different loci of self) at the same time – for instance 'I'm all over the place today, I don't know whether I'm coming or going'; and the Scattered Self Model leads to Loss of Self models, where the self is separated from the Subject and even from other selves.

Lakoff and Johnson (1999, Chapter 13) revised the model, proposing six selves: the Physical-Object Self, a self we can manipulate; the Locational Self, the self situated as an object in space; the Scattered Self, the result of trying to maintain several different self-models simultaneously; the Social Self, the self as a product of, and link to, other selves;

the Projecting Self, the self we present to other selves; and the Essential Self, a conscious representation of the unconscious Actual self. Lakoff and Johnson's six selves have some correspondences with the SSMH, but there is one important difference: Lakoff's Multiple Selves are all conscious selves, whereas the SSMH includes the subliminal Actual self. This difference gives the SSMH, an origins model, a physical base on which the other aspects of selfhood can be anchored and from which they can be built; the Multiple Selves model, an embodied model, does not need this.

Why self defines us

What defines a self? Thagard and Wood (2015) produced a list of 80 self-phenomena, grouping them into six main classes: self-representing (oneself to oneself, oneself to others, and evaluation); self-effecting (facilitating and limiting); and self-changing. This list of phenomena shows that, whatever a self is, it is a widespread feature of human cognition, being involved in sub-phenomena such as compassion, forgiveness, reliance, effacement, deception and realisation. The widespread effects of selfhood in cognition mean that a simple, one-line definition of self is probably impossible, and very likely deceptive.

Significantly, Thagard and Wood place *consciousness* under the *experience* of *self-representing oneself to oneself*: in other words, they see awareness as a cause or outcome of selfhood. In this book, we have separated other-awareness and self-awareness, meaning that awareness can be treated as both a cause (other awareness) and an outcome (self-awareness) of shared selfhood: selfness and awareness of selfness emerge from the sharing of awareness of others through language. Thagard and Wood show that having a self, with its concomitant self-phenomena, is a defining feature of humans – both in terms of its source (social calculus shared through language) and in terms of its outcome (the enhanced cooperation of joint enterprise).

A self is a useful thing to have: it allows us to show the persona we wish to show to the people around us. However, what makes it really useful is if other people have a self, too: when humans relate together through their Projected selves or personae, rather than their personalities, they create a pragmatic layer in their communication. This pragmatic layer acts as a lubricant between personalities, allowing them to cooperate efficiently enough to engage in complex joint enterprises. Human language is full of expressions that represent this pragmatic layer at work; for instance, 'don't take this the wrong way, but …' (a way of criticising a persona without involving the personality) or 'let's do this' (a depersonalised way of generating provisional agreement between personae) or 'so what do we do now?' (an invitation to the other persona to offer a solution for consideration, not action). Our Projected selves are able to work together in ways that our personalities cannot.

Personality is not a human-only characteristic; many other animals display identifiable differences between individuals. Daniel Nettle (2006) reviewed several very different species, including birds, fish and insects, and found evidence of personality in all of them. Seyfarth et al. (2014) show that, while kinship is a major feature in determining rank for baboons, having a less aggressive, more conciliatory personality also has an effect on the individual's rank. Baan et al. (2014) found the same was true for wolves. However, to date, there has been no evidence for persona in any other species. To select a persona to project, an individual needs to be aware of themself as a self – which we humans can do only because we share our social calculus using language. So language, shared social calculus and modelling a Projected self all seem to be markers of being human. Having selves is what makes human culture what it is: the reality of each individual self, both for others and for the individual, makes our self-driven society (as compared to the ego-driven society of chimpanzees) an actuality.

However, while the existence of a human self-driven society is an actuality, that society is composed of self-aware selves. Self-awareness is a modelling process; so, while the process of modelling can be an actual thing, the models themselves are mental constructs, which are virtual. We can agree to treat them as if they were real, but we cannot give them actuality with just our belief. This is where the link between the personality (an aspect of the Actual self) and the persona (the Projected self) comes in: inasmuch as the Projected self is treated as a personality by others, it is a proxy, or a metaphor, for an actual thing. This still leaves a dilemma: is the reality of selfness enough to prove that the aware self is not an illusion or delusion? The answer relies on how we define selfness, and what we want selfness to say about us. If selfness is a way of explaining how humans are able to work together, then the fact that we engage in actual joint enterprises is enough to justify selfness as a necessary part of that process. If, however, I am looking for my self as a concrete example of selfness, then I am on a fool's errand.

One feature of the SSMH still needs to be addressed: the hypothesis relies on an ability to take models of my self offered by others and treat them as if they were third-person models of me. This means we would expect that modelling others and modelling me would be similar cognitive experiences, using many of the same cognitive processes. Fortunately, this is just what Francesca Happé (2003) has found. She looked at nine brain-imaging studies conducted by seven teams to assess brain usage in ToM tasks, and found that the same areas were active in both self- and other-modelling. In her conclusion she says, 'neuroimaging findings to date appear to suggest a network of regions involved in attribution of mental states to others which largely overlaps with areas of activity in self-reflection tasks' (Happé 2003, 141). It seems that, as the SSMH predicts, modelling others and modelling me are treated by the brain as similar processes.

In summary, therefore, we can say that having selfness is being human; and that is why self defines each of us – both from the outside, with others' models of me, and from the inside, with my models of me.

Notes

1. *There and Back again* is the second half of the title *The Hobbit, or There and Back again* by J.R.R. Tolkien – which starts with a map of the journey. *There and Back again* was missed off the cover of the first edition (George Allen & Unwin, UK, 1937), but has been reinstated in some subsequent printings.
2. The Standard Statistical Brain (SSB) is a convenient model of language in the brain, which corresponds quite well to about 95% of actual brains; the other 5% can differ quite markedly from the SSB without the language capacity being affected. The SSB is a useful tool; problems only arise when it is seen as a real standard brain, an actual standard brain or, worst of all, an ideal standard brain.

9

Epilogue: Snarks or Boojums?

> 'Now, Kitty, let's consider who it was that dreamed it all. This is a serious question, my dear, and you should not go on licking your paw like that—as if Dinah hadn't washed you this morning! You see, Kitty, it must have been either me or the Red King. He was part of my dream, of course—but then I was part of his dream, too! Was it the Red King, Kitty? You were his wife, my dear, so you ought to know—Oh, Kitty, do help to settle it! I'm sure your paw can wait!'
>
> But the provoking kitten only began on the other paw, and pretended it hadn't heard the question.
>
> (Lewis Carroll 1865, Chapter 12: 'Which Dreamed It?')

Kittens are not good at sharing their social calculus, if they do indeed have any; and, as far as we have currently discovered, they do not indulge in speculation about their dreams, as Alice does about hers. For Kitty, a firm follower of etic facts, the idea that a dream-thought could somehow be part of actuality is probably beyond the limits of its cognition; and the idea that a dreamed-up person could be part of the dream of a person dreamed up by the dreamed-up person is, in all likelihood, incomprehensible to the kitten. Yet we emic thinkers accept that, for Alice, this is a conundrum worth pursuing. It is almost as if we were able to treat a modelled person as if it were a real person, even if there is no actual person in our experience with whom we can associate our model. For us, Alice is both our model of Alice and a real person in an actual book; and the same goes for the Red King. If real people can create real dreams, then Alice can dream of the Red King and the Red King can dream of Alice; but, in the story, the two dreams form a single dream. So which dreamed it? We may, if we are in a particularly etic frame of mind, wash our paws of the whole nonsense; but, even then, there will be a faint voice telling us that this remains, for humans, a logical reality.

Language does not help us out of this conundrum, because it lives in the same world as the social calculus we use to model Alice, Kitty, the Red King, Lewis Carroll as the writer, and ourself as the reader. The modelling of others in our social calculus provides the basic structure of language, and the sharing of social calculus through language provides us with the tools to begin modelling our self as another. But all of this is happening in Popper's World 3 of reality, where actual and virtual things can only be represented, not exist. We cannot use a World 3 system to anchor another World 3 system into Worlds 1 and 2.

It also does not really help to appeal to the idea that I have a self because others believe me to have a self. The model of me that others carry around in their heads is just another World 3 object – and it is not even in the reality of my World 3. We may treat our models as if they were the same as the actual things they represent, but a model is still just a representation – and, in uncommunicated social calculus, your model of me represents no more than what you need it to represent about me. Your model of me may be the only guide you have to me, but that does not mean it has to be an accurate representation of me. So when you share your model of me with me, you are not sharing an etic model of my self, you are sharing an emic model of your belief about my self; and that belief may well be arbitrary and partisan.

This inability to fix the nature of the objects in our real World 3 means that we cannot be completely sure whether our social calculus self-model refers to a real interpretation of an actual object out there in World 1 (as words and cognitive models are traditionally believed to do), whether it refers to a real interpretation of a virtual World 2 item with no actual World 1 object (as words like *unicorn* and cognitive models like *Alice* can do) or whether it refers to a World 3 real concept (as words like *nothing* and *empty* are supposed, but usually fail, to do; they are supposed to refer to absence, but they are usually used to represent the presence of absence).

There is one final representation of a self that could actually refer to my self, and that is myself: the personal feeling that my self-reflection represents self-reflexion. 'I am what I am,' the song says, 'I am my own special creation' (Herman 1983); it's rather like a modern version of Descartes' *Dubito ergo cogito, cogito ergo sum*, but it suffers the same logical fate. When Descartes wrote his *dubito* construct, he was unaware that Augustine of Hippo (426 [1871]) had preceded him with a similar argument by twelve centuries: *Si fallor, sum* ('If I am mistaken, I am'). This idea fails, however, in one particular – but fundamental – case of being mistaken: *Si fallor ut sum, non possum esse* ('If I am mistaken that I am, I cannot be'); it may be only one case, but it is the case that disproves the rule. *Myself* cannot prove my self, because they are both World 3 concepts, and neither has the actuality to prove the etic existence of the other.

The route to self-modelling

How did we become the socially calculating, self-aware species we are? This book has looked at some of the mechanisms, but it has not indicated a timescale or a developmental map. Our study of our selves is still too basic to set out our cognitive and cultural capacities in a developmental calendar, but at least the capacities enabling social calculus to be shared, and self-modelling to begin, can be reasonably described.

The sharing of social calculus models would have required the pre-existence of several things. Foremost is the cognitive existence of social calculus itself: we must have been consciously using the mechanics of social calculus in our interpersonal relationship cognition if they were to be available for voluntary communication. This cognitive social calculus relies on the pre-existence of at least three capacities, the first of which is the capacity to live in large social groups. Large social groups do not necessarily rely on large brains – eusocial insect societies work fine with tens of thousands of small-brained individuals – but, in social groups of volitional individuals, the individuals with a wider range of interpersonal strategies will fare better than those with a narrower range. In primates, therefore, large social groups generate a genetic trend toward larger brains to handle the interpersonal strategies involved in the larger group. This is convenient because cognitive social calculus is, itself, an interpersonal strategy, which both relies on, and generates, greater cognitive sophistication. This was set out in Chapter 3.

The second capacity needed for social calculus is a willingness to work together in joint enterprises. These joint enterprises do not need to be the complex organisations we see today; they would have been simpler groupings in which specialisations could begin to appear and begin to be valued. For instance, an individual who could make good throwing-stones had to work together with an individual good at throwing if they were to maximise the fitness of their individual skills. Of course, this willingness to share skills had to be accompanied by a willingness to share the products of the joint enterprise; it would require a mutual altruism policed by reputation, as discussed in Chapter 5.

The third pre-existent capacity required for sharing social calculus would have been a system of voluntary communication: we must have been able to exchange practical (non-interpersonal) information in some way for early socialisation and enculturation to spread through a population. This intentional communication system would have emerged from an earlier attentional signalling system; but where the signalling system involved the production of vocal responses to environmental cues, which others could then treat as equivalent to the environmental cues, the communication system involved the intentional sharing of information between individuals. The signalling system relied on pre-established and indexical links between the signal form and the signal meaning; but the communication system allowed both sender and receiver to negotiate toward a shared meaning, by letting them establish ad hoc symbolic links between form and meaning.

What early humans were communicating about did not have to be social knowledge – in fact, it was probably environmental knowledge, as we see in the signalling systems of modern primates: warning signals, food indicators, locative vocalisations, attention-getting signals and emotional displays. The main difference between a signalling system based on environmental knowledge and a communication system based on the same knowledge is not complexity of form but complexity of meaning. Indexes are simple one-to-one correspondences between actual-world events and cognitive meaning; symbols, in contrast, have many-to-many correspondences with cognitive meaning. For instance, the sound-symbol *serpent* may refer to an animal of the order *Serpentes* or any long and legless animal, or a treacherous colleague of the speaker – or even Alice, when her neck grows instead of her whole body, causing a pigeon she encounters to scream 'Serpent!' and attack her (*Alice's Adventures in Wonderland*, Chapter 5). And all of these objects can equally well be represented by the sound-symbol *snake*.

What environmental knowledge signalling and environmental knowledge communication share in common is that they are both about events extrinsic to the communicating parties: the sender and the receiver do not signify in the meaning of the utterance. No structural or grammatical complexity is required, therefore, in either the signalling or communication system: whether signal or communication, the snake warning used by vervets is just a chutter (Seyfarth et al. 1980); the chimpanzee's food call is just a grunt (Schel et al. 2013); and the gibbon's 'I am here' call is just a hoo (Clarke et al. 2015). In each of these cases, the call can often be modulated to more particularly reference the type of snake or food, or the individual calling, which is impressively subtle. But the sounds all rely on extrinsic meaning (the meaning is out there in the world, whether it be an actual snake or Alice); they have no context-free generalised reference, or intrinsic meaning, as words like *this* and *look* have. This was discussed in Chapter 6.

Fortunately, the sharing of social calculus carries us over this divide between extrinsic and intrinsic reference. The A-Relationship-B social calculus construct requires A, B and the relationship to be individually meaningful: the particular grunts that represent A and B must mean A and B to the sender and receiver, and the relationship grunt must mean that particular relationship. But the form A-Relationship-B is a context-free framework into which any number of individual-representing grunts can be inserted, and any number of relationships can link them. In addition, sharing of social calculus requires an open-ended communication system: as new individuals join the group, new representing grunts need to be generated and negotiated into meaning. And as new types of relationship develop, new grunts to represent the relationships must be agreed. The language of social calculus, therefore, is in a constant state of renewal and negotiation toward meaning; and tools such as metaphor, as discussed in Chapter 7, facilitate this constant renewal and meaning-negotiation.

This leaves only the topic of Chapter 8, the appearance of self-modelling. It may only be a side-effect of shared social calculus, but it is a big factor in the life of almost every human on the planet. Our self-model feeds back into our social calculus, changing the social calculus we have,

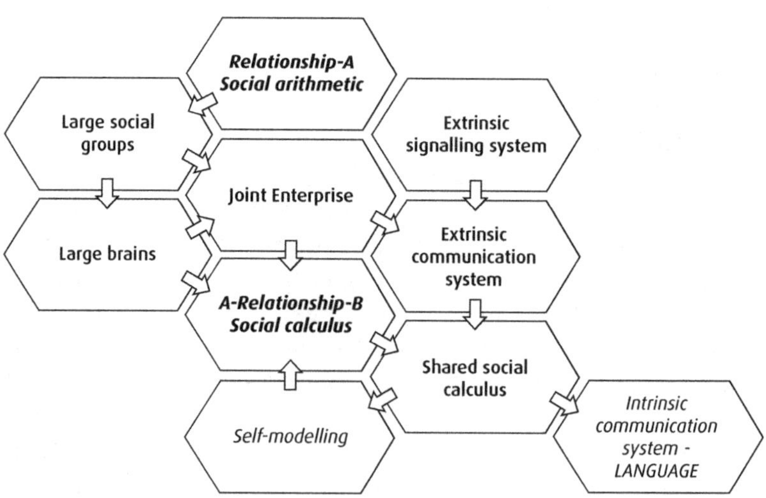

Fig 9.1 The route to self-modelling

changing the social calculus we share, and changing the way we share. The self-model, and the other generated selves in the SSMH, give us that particularly human feeling of believing we know who we are. We think we can have objective knowledge about ourselves because we can see ourselves from outside ourselves. Yet there is something clearly wrong with this assumption: our senses, and the interpretation of them, are clearly 'inside'; how would a mechanism for putting our senses 'outside' work?

Yes, but ... who am I?

So, at the end of this book, the final – and perhaps biggest – question of selfhood remains unanswered: are Hume, Metzinger, Wegner, Nørretranders and Hood (and many others) correct when they say that we do not have an Actual self? Is every self I believe myself to be just a product of my social modelling of self as other? If we accept the absence of an Actual self, then we can treat the whole of selfhood as a World 3 problem of reality; but this still leaves us with a serious definitional problem. Even if all conscious knowledge of selfhood were stripped away, I would nonetheless be different from you, because there is an individually differentiated core genetic being that is dictated by an actual World 1 chemical code that I carry around in every cell of my body. Even without personae, I still have personality. Yet is this chemically driven personality sufficient to claim there is an Actual self in every human? Where would that self be located?

If we accept that having a World 3 real core self is sufficient, the question of what counts as the core self has not been answered. As was discussed in Chapter 8, we have access to many different types of self, and we can generate more than one version of each type of self. So which, if any, of those selves is the core World 3 real self? We have already dismissed the Actual self as unknowable; and we can dismiss the Cultural self, the Social selves and the Episodic selves as candidates – the first because it is an internalised target rather than an internal self, and the others because there is no dominant Social or Episodic self. But that still leaves three candidates for the core self.

So, is my self-model my core self, or is it just the self of which I am currently aware? Can it be the core self merely because I am currently thinking of it, and is my current commitment to it sufficient? Or is my Narrative self my core self because it has historical continuity with my self-model, and is therefore much more detailed than my current self-model? Or Was Richard O'Brien (1973) right when he wrote, 'Don't dream it – be it', and is my Projected self my core self because it is what I present to the world? Or does awareness of selfness mean that self-awareness is always a cognitive concept with no existence in actuality or reality – a mere metaphor? It is a choice between a Snark and a Boojum: choose carefully, because choosing wrongly means your self may softly and suddenly vanish away:

> They hunted till darkness came on, but they found
> Not a button, or feather, or mark,
> By which they could tell that they stood on the ground
> Where the Baker had met with the Snark.
>
> In the midst of the word he was trying to say,
> In the midst of his laughter and glee,
> He had softly and suddenly vanished away –
> For the Snark *was* a Boojum, you see.
>
> (Lewis Carroll 1876, Fit the Eighth: 'The Vanishing')

Glossary

Actual self	The incontrovertible, physical self. The Actual self is a Darwinian gene-machine, unlike all the other selves, which are cognitive products of the Darwinian gene-machine; and this means that the Actual self is directly governed by the twin genetic imperatives to survive and thrive.
Actuality	What continues to exist even in the absence of humans, such as 'rock'. Also referred to as World 1 in Karl Popper's terminology.
Affect	Noun: An emotion. Verb: To change.
Altruistic Self-sacrifice	Reducing your own capacities to survive and thrive, to increase those capacities for others. The extreme end of altruism, the maximal version of the small, everyday sacrifices that are a frequent and commonplace expectation in our human social systems. Altruistic self-sacrifice is viewed as an honourable thing to display in most human cultures.
A-Relationship-B modelling	The capacity to model relationships between other individuals in the group. The reverse-dominance cultural environment means that my relationships are contingent and variable, so the binding of the relationship to the imaged individuals is weak. Segmented A-Relationship-B models are more adaptable to change than holistic models.
A-Relationship-B-by-C modelling	By tagging a received A-Relationship-B model with its source, I can measure it against my existing knowledge to identify C's stance toward A and B. This enhances my knowledge of the group social relationships, and allows me to extract useful empirical data from an utterance that is, essentially, opinion.

Autobiographical self	With the Protoself and the Core self, this is one of the components of selfhood in Damasio's (2010) model. It corresponds to an amalgam of the Episodic self and the Narrative self in the SSMH.
Automatic response	Responses that are under a level of control by the organism, but which require no conscious attention from the organism to make them happen. Conscious attention can, however, suppress a response.
Autonoetic memory	One of the two components of an Episodic self: the capacity to recall past events that include the past self's own perspective.
Autonomic response	An electrochemical response that does not involve choice; it is the inevitable response to a particular stimulus.
Awareness	Conscious knowledge, the capacity to gather conscious knowledge, and the conscious manipulation of knowledge. Awareness is all about attention.
Awareness of other	Explicit knowledge that the other individuals in the group are intentional beings who have relationships with each other; and I am able to consciously make and manipulate models of those relationships.
Awareness of self	Explicit knowledge that I am able to make models of my self. I am a third party in the modelling of others, so A-Relationship-B constructs offered to me may include me as A or B. To incorporate these offered constructs into my cognitive social modelling, I have to be able to model myself as a third party.
Awareness of selfness	Explicit knowledge that my modelled self is simultaneously a special first-person case and a mundane third-person case in my cognitive social modelling. By modelling myself as a third party, I am able to see my self from an external perspective. This carries with it all the concomitant advantages and disadvantages of Machiavellian Intelligence, but applied reflexively.
Clade	Any logically consistent group of species. For instance, the several *Homo* species form a clade; the human lineage since the last common ancestor with the *Pan* clade is a clade; the *Pan* clade and the human clade are a clade; and so on. It is a very useful term to describe any non-arbitrary group of species.

Code model of communication	The idea that communication involves the production and apprehension of a signal, and it is the signal that carries the meaning. For comparison, see Ostensive-inferential model of communication.
Cogitant ut sum, ergo sum	They think I am, therefore I am – the key argument in this book.
Cogito cogito, ergo cogito sum	Ambrose Bierce's response to Descartes' *Dubito*: I think I think, therefore I think I am.
Cogito ergo sum	See *Dubito* ...
Cognitive social modelling	The capacity to maintain a cognitive database of relationships in one's social group. There are two types of social model possible: relationships with others, where the self is an unmodelled constant; and relationships between others, where the self is not needed. See Relationship-A modelling and A-Relationship-B modelling. Cognitive social modelling can be conscious and attentional, or it can be subliminal.
Conscious knowledge	See Explicit knowledge
Core self	With the Protoself and the Autobiographical self, this is one of the components of selfhood in Damasio's (2010) model. It corresponds to an amalgam of the Social self and Projected self in the SSMH.
Conspecific	An animal of the same species. Perhaps the earliest in-group (conspecific) versus out-group (heterospecific) distinction.
Costly signalling	If it is important to the receiver that a signal be true, then it is worth paying attention to the cost of the signal (Zahavi and Zahavi 1997).
Cultural self	A model of an ideal individual in a particular culture, particularly the ideal self that the individual can be. It is a virtual self.
Delusional Misidentification Syndrome	A failure to reliably identify self and others.
Differentiation	The second of the four features of language. The 'atoms' of cognition can have different roles in the construction of thoughts. In the minimal case of language (as conceived here), 'words' can represent entities or relationships between entities. See also Segmentation, Hierarchy and Recursion.

Dispassionate self	By modelling myself as a third party, I can treat my self as I treat other third parties.
Dubito ergo cogito, cogito ergo sum	The formula used by Descartes to prove his existence: I doubt, therefore I think; I think, therefore I am.
Effect	Noun: An outcome or result. Verb: To make or do.
Ego	In Freudian psychology, the ego acts as a referee and arbiter between the subconscious id (what the physical person wants) and the super-ego (what the intellectual person believes is best).
Emic facts	Emic facts are true because we agree they are true. They do not need to be based on evidence; they can be based on beliefs. Most cultural facts are emic facts. See Chapter 3, Language, culture and the self.
Episodic self	The combination of the capacity to self-model (learned) and the capacity to remember events in the past (innate) creates the possibility of modelling a self in a remembered past event. This is the Episodic self.
Etic facts	Etic facts are definitionally true, or verifiably true, regardless of human opinion. They have to be based on evidence; they cannot be based on beliefs. Etic facts are common throughout nature and, if they enhance individual fitness, can become genetic facts. See Chapter 3, Language, culture and the self.
Eusociality	The social organisation of animals that live in large colonies of mostly sterile individuals, such as many species of ant, wasp, bee and termite, and naked mole rats. There is usually only one fertile female, with most of the offspring being infertile. The only way they can get their genes into the future is to protect their queen.
Explicable production	Communication that is intended by the sender and can be explained by the sender. Produced from explicit knowledge only.
Explication	The process of converting Implicit knowledge into Explicit knowledge. The Explicit knowledge represents the Implicit knowledge – it does not reveal it.
Explicit knowledge	Explicit knowledge is conscious awareness of 'facts' about the universe (the facts do not need to be ontologically true, just culturally plausible). We must also be able to explain not just the facts but how and why we know or believe them. Because this type of knowledge is essentially cognitive, it is also known as 'head knowledge'.

First person	Probably the last of the language 'voices' to emerge. It allows me to represent my self in utterances made to others.
Group cooperation	The capacity of members of a species to work together against common enemies or for common purposes. Group cooperation is difficult for either predator or prey to counter. Coordinated action against predators and prey is not an unusual capacity in nature, and is not limited to socially clever species. It does not take a high level of cognitive sophistication to produce the social cohesion needed for tactical defensive or offensive cooperation.
Hierarchy	The third of the four features of language. The 'atoms' of cognition can be combined to make composite units that behave in many ways like 'atoms'. See also Segmentation, Differentiation and Recursion.
Id	In Freudian psychology, the emotional, primal and largely subliminal expression of the self.
Implicit knowledge	Implicit knowledge is knowledge we have because we have inherited it genetically or we have acquired it subconsciously. It seems to be distributed through the body, even though the brain may be acting as a control node, so it is often referred to as 'body knowledge'.
Inarticulate knowledge	See Implicit knowledge
Incidental learning	Learning that does not require attention, so we cannot explain what we learned, or how or when we learned it.
Individual-oriented self	See Actual self
Inherent knowledge	See Implicit knowledge
Innate knowledge	Knowledge we have inherited genetically. It can be fundamental, needed to keep a person alive even when they are unconscious, such as breathing; it can be affective, used to handle emotional events; or it can be performative, controlling our locomotion and kinaesthetics. It cannot be learned.
Inner speech	The ability to converse with our own self inside our heads, as if we were two (or more) selves.
Intentional learning	Knowledge that we set out to acquire, which we may have used particular strategies to learn, and where we can explain not just the knowledge but the process of acquiring it. Intentional learning requires attention.

Irreality	A version of the world that is real because some people agree it is real, even though they have no evidence of (or consensus about) its reality – like the value of Bitcoin.
Joint enterprise	If we can work together to achieve something we cannot each achieve alone, then it is worthwhile sharing information honestly (Melis and Semmann, 2010).
Kin selection	I should share information with individuals who share my genes because their survival is also, in part, my own genetic survival. People with whom I have a familial relationship are more likely to share genes with me than unrelated individuals (Hamilton, 1964).
Machiavellian Intelligence	First described by Whiten and Byrne (1988), Machiavellian Intelligence is the capacity to model others as intentional beings, and use that intentionality to increase one's fitness at the expense of the other individual. It is the main obstacle to sharing social models, creating the Sender's and Receiver's dilemmas.
MERGE	See Recursion
Metaphysical self	The idea that we have a component of our self that is not detectable.
Mirror test	The idea that, if an animal can recognise its reflection in a mirror as itself, it must have a level of self-awareness (Gallup 1970).
Modality	Utterances can have conditionality (they are true if ...); they can have perspective (they are true to some individuals and not others); and they can have fictionality (they are true only within a non-existent scenario). If one type of modality is possible for a species, all types are possible.
Monomyth	The idea, instigated by Claude Lévi-Strauss but named by Joseph Campbell, that there is a single mythic structure that reflects the structure of early human society.
Narrative self	The model we have of our life experiences as an evolving story – a stitching-together of the various Episodic selves in such a way that they can be viewed as aspects of a single self.
Negotiation toward meaning	A feature of Ostensive-inferential communication, in that the sender anticipates possible misunderstanding by the receiver, and the receiver checks particular meanings with the sender. It is *not* a feature of Code-model communication, where the signal by itself is the carrier of meaning, not the signal–sender combination.

Nested functionality	Being able to nest a function inside another function is a necessary precursor to recursion. Arithmetic is the process of nesting quantities inside another quantity (e.g. 1+2=3), and therefore has nested functionality. The capacity to nest numbers inside each other (simple addition) has now been demonstrated in rhesus monkeys (Livingstone et al. 2014).
Noetic memory	One of the two components of an Episodic self: the capacity to recall past events that do not include the past self's own perspective.
Observing self	The cognitive mechanism that allows us to see ourselves as if we were observers outside our selves. Composed of the parietal component, which places the self within a sensory context, and the frontal component, which places the self in a socio-cultural context. Proposed by Baars et al. (2003).
Ostensive-inferential model of communication	The idea that human communication is contractual, based on the provision and interpretation of evidence for meaning. Ostensive-inferential communication is an immediate negotiation toward meaning between two people, not a slow, evolutionary negotiation of signal and response.
Persona	A modelled self. It can be a cognitively internal self-model or an externalised Projected self. When humans relate together through their Projected selves or personae, rather than their personalities, they create a pragmatic layer in their communication.
Personality	The particular set of species-variable traits that an individual has. Unlike aspects of a persona, personality traits are not modelled – they are affective identifiers of the individual and are difficult to hide. Many non-humans have personalities, but modelling a persona may be a human-only capacity.
Physical culture	A species that is able to transmit physical survival skills between individuals by teaching and learning has a physical culture. The transmission of termite-fishing skills between female chimpanzees and their offspring is an example of this.
Process	A particular route taken through a structure by an input, to become an output. See also Structure, System.

Projected self	An emergent feature of the social models I receive, moderated through two routes: first via self-modelling, Episodic self and Narrative self; and second via Cultural self. To put it another way, the Projected self is an amalgam of my internal representation of myself and the expectations others put upon me.
Protoself	With the Core self and the Autobiographical self, this is one of the components of selfhood in Damasio's (2010) model. It corresponds to the Actual self in the SSMH.
Pseudo-eusociality	A social organisation that is not completely eusocial. A fully eusocial species has high levels of socialisation and an extremely limited number of fertile individuals. There are two ways of being pseudo-eusocial: limited fertility with lower levels of socialisation (e.g. meerkats), and widespread fertility with high levels of socialisation (humans).
Psyche	In Freudian psychology, the combination of the Ego,Super-ego and Id. The whole psychological self.
Public self	See Projected self
Reality	That which has actual existence without humans, but has meaning only because of humans, such as 'crayon'. Also referred to as World 3 in Karl Popper's terminology.
Receiver's dilemma	If the sender is disadvantaged by giving me true information, but advantaged by giving me false information, why should I believe the information shared?
Reciprocal altruism	I should help you today because you will help me tomorrow; and you will help me tomorrow because you will need my help the next day (Trivers 1971).
Recursion	The fourth of the four features of language. Hierarchy can occur at multiple levels: composite units can contain composite units. Hauser et al. (2002) see recursion as a language-related evolutionary event; this book treats it as emergent from hierarchy and attribution of received utterances, with a genetic explanation outside of language. See also Segmentation, Differentiation and Hierarchy.

Relationship-A modelling	I have models in my mind of my relationships with other individuals in the group. The reverse-dominance cultural environment means that my relationships are contingent and variable, so the binding between the imaged individual and my relationship to them is weak.
Second person	Probably the second of the language 'voices' to emerge. It allows me to represent the receiver as a special class of 'they'. This permits referential dialogue, and 'talking to' as an enhancement to 'talking about'.
Segmentation	The first of the four features of language. Utterances are composed of 'atoms' of cognition; they are not monolithic correspondences between thought and signal. See also Differentiation, Hierarchy and Recursion.
Self	1. The physical body, including the conceptualising organ, the brain. 2. The concept of the physical body as held in the brain. 3. The concept of a non-physical self that transcends the body. The first two types of self do not require selfness. The third type does.
Self-as-knower	A meta-knowledge about the self's knowledge. Generated from the Core self and the Autobiographical self. See Antonio Damasio's (2010) model, Chapter 1.
Self-as-object	A meta-knowledge about the self's knowledge of itself. Generated from the Core self and the Autobiographical self. See Antonio Damasio's (2010) model, Chapter 1.
Selfhood	Having a self.
Self-model	A composite picture of my self as presented to me by others, providing a third-person model of me to locate in my social calculus system.
Selfness	Believing you have a self, or being aware of the self you have.
Self-sacrifice	See Altruistic self-sacrifice
Sender's dilemma	Why give away valuable information? If having the information advantages me and not having it disadvantages you, why should I share it?
Sense of almost-self	Electrochemical recognition by cells of their clonal relatives, allowing different reactions to clones and to alien cells.

Sense of not-self	Things outside a cell's membrane are qualitatively different from things inside the membrane. It is therefore useful to be able to detect and react differently to items outside the cell membrane. For all practical purposes, this is a sense of not-self.
Sense of other	An enhanced sense of not-self that can distinguish between different types of not-self. It operates at the level of the multi-cellular organism rather than the level of the cell.
Sense of self	Not a conscious representation of the self, it is more akin to feelings of satisfaction when things are going well for the organism, and a sense of unease when they are not. It operates at the level of the multi-cellular organism.
Seven-Selves Modelling Hypothesis (SSMH)	The model of selfhood set out in Chapter 8. It consists of the Actual self, the Social self, the self-model, the Episodic self, the Narrative self, the Cultural self and the Projected self.
Shared Social Calculus	The capacity to share modelled relationships between others, thus enhancing the receiving individual's social calculus and the sending individual's reputation.
Signature whistle	The identity signal of dolphin (*Tursiops truncatus*), which seems to be used in the same way humans use names.
Social arithmetic	The cognitive systems that allow an individual to maintain a social map of their relationships with others, and to use these models to manipulate those others. It is the mechanism behind Machiavellian Intelligence and it relies on Relationship-A modelling.
Social calculus	The cognitive systems that allow an individual to maintain models of others and the relationships between others, and to use these models to accommodate the intentions of those others. It requires an Awareness of Other and a Theory of Mind, and it relies on A-Relationship-B modelling.
Social self	The Social self is the first self of which we are consciously aware. It is the model of my self offered by others as part of the exchange of social calculus.
Soul	See Metaphysical self
Structure	A physical organisation that, when activated, converts inputs to outputs in a predictable way. See also Process, System.

Subconscious knowledge	See Implicit knowledge
Sublimation	The process of converting explicitly learned knowledge into implicit knowledge, which does not require attentional awareness to be used.
Subliminal knowledge	See Implicit knowledge
Super-ego	In Freudian psychology, the internalisation of externally enforced, cultural rules.
Survival of the fittest	Herbert Spencer's (1864) phrase to describe Darwin's Descent through modification. Individuals in a species must have strategies to overcome challenges to their survival, and the individuals with a wider range of strategies can overcome more challenges.
Symbolic culture	A species that is able to transmit social conventions between individuals has a symbolic culture. The social conventions do not directly enhance individual fitness, but they create social inclusion for the individual, which indirectly enhances their fitness. Burial practices provide an example of this.
System	A set of processes reliant on a particular structure to convert inputs into outputs. See also Structure, Process.
Tacit knowledge	See Implicit knowledge
Tectonoetic self	All the selves in the SSMH plus objects beyond the boundary of the actual self that are intimately associated with the self.
Theory of Mind (ToM)	The way humans model others as intentional beings. ToM is two things: a theory that others have minds, so they cannot be manipulated simply by using stimulus–response sequences; and a theory about the kind of minds they have, and how those minds can be manipulated by belief and expectation.
Third person	Probably the first of the language 'voices' to emerge. Allows me to represent others as entities, initially in my cognition and later in my signalling.
Unaware knowledge	See Implicit knowledge
Unconsciousness	A cognitive state in which we are not aware of our self, e.g. deep sleep, general anaesthesia, vegetative state, or epileptic loss of consciousness.
Unmodelled self	See Actual self

Virtuality	That which exists only inside human heads, such as 'my'. Also referred to as World 2 in Karl Popper's terminology.
Will to survive	The genetic imperative to take advantage of things that enhance survival and avoid things that reduce survival. The will to survive involves biological imperatives that support surviving and thriving, such as territoriality, competition, reproduction and cooperation.

Bibliography

Adami, Christoph, Ofria, Charles and Collier, Travis C. 2000. 'Evolution of Biological Complexity', *PNAS* 97.9: 4463–8.

Adler, Alfred. 1927. Colin Brett (tr.), *Understanding Human Nature*. Oxford: Oneworld Publications.

Adornetti, Ines and Ferretti, Francesco. 2014. 'The Pragmatic Foundations of Communication: An Action-Oriented Model of the Origin of Language', *Theoria et Historia Scientiarum* XI: 63–80.

Allemand, Mathias, Steiger, Andrea E. and Fend, Helmut A. 2015. 'Empathy Development in Adolescence Predicts Social Competencies in Adulthood', *Journal of Personality* 83.2: 229–41.

Alonso-Cortés, Ángel. 2006. 'From Signals to Symbols: Grounding Language Origins in Communication Games'. In *Game Theory and Linguistic Meaning*, edited by Ahti-Veikko Pietarinen, Chapter 4, 21–32. Oxford: Elsevier.

Amsterdam, Beulah. 1972. 'Mirror Self-Image Reactions Before Age Two', *Developmental Psychobiology* 5.4: 297–305.

Arain, Mariam, Haque, Maliha, Johal, Lina, Mathur, Puja, Nel, Wynand, Rais, Afsha, Sandhu, Ranbir and Sharma, Sushil. 2013. 'Maturation of the Adolescent Brain', *Neuropsychiatric Disease and Treatment* 9: 449–61.

Arbib, Michael A. 2005. 'From Monkey-Like Action Recognition to Human Language: An Evolutionary Framework for Neurolinguistics', *Behavioral and Brain Sciences* 28: 105–67.

Aristotle. 350 BCE [1908]. Book V. In W.D. Ross (tr.), *Nichomachean Ethics*. Adelaide: University of Adelaide.

Aristotle. 330 BCE? [1915]. Magna Moralia, Book 2. In W.D. Ross (tr.), *The Works of Aristotle*. Oxford: Clarendon Press.

Aristova, Nataliya. 2016. 'Rethinking Cultural Identities in the Context of Globalization: Linguistic Landscape of Kazan, Russia, as an Emerging Global City', *Procedia – Social and Behavioral Sciences* 236: 153–60.

Arnold, Kate and Zuberbühler, Klaus. 2006. 'The Alarm-Calling System of Adult Male Putty-Nosed Monkeys, *Cercopithecus Nictitans Martini*', *Animal Behaviour* 72: 643–53.

Arp, Robert. 2007. 'Consciousness and Awareness – Switched-On Rheostats: A Response to de Quincey', *Journal of Consciousness Studies* 14.3: 101–6.

Artinger, Florian, Exadaktylos, Filippos, Koppel, Hannes and Sääksvuori, Lauri. 2014. 'In Others' Shoes: Do Individual Differences in Empathy and Theory of Mind Shape Social Preferences?' *PLoS ONE* 9.4: e92844.

Atran, Scott and Ginges, Jeremy. 2012. 'Religious and Sacred Imperatives in Human Conflict', *Science* 336: 855–7.

Augustine of Hippo. 426 [1871]. *The Works of Aurelius Augustine, Bishop of Hippo. A New Translation by Rev. Marcus Dods, The City of God, volume 1*. Edinburgh: T. & T. Clark.

Avilés, Leticia. 2002. 'Solving the Freeloaders Paradox: Genetic Associations and Frequency-Dependent Selection in the Evolution of Cooperation among Nonrelatives,' *PNAS* 99.22: 14268–73.

Baan, Candice, Bergmüller, Ralph, Smith, Douglas W. and Molnar, Barbara. 2014. 'Conflict Management in Free-Ranging Wolves, *Canis Lupus*', *Animal Behaviour* 90: 327–34.

Baars, Bernard J., Ramsøy, Thomas Z. and Laureys, Steven. 2003. 'Brain, Conscious Experience and the Observing Self', *Trends in Neurosciences* 26.12: 671–5.

Bae, Christopher J., Douka, Katerina and Petraglia, Michael D. 2017. 'On the Origin of Modern Humans: Asian Perspectives', *Science* 358.6368: eaai9067.

Baker, Dawn, Hunter, Elaine, Lawrence, Emma, Medford, Nicholas, Patel, Maxine, Senior, Carl, Sierra, Mauricio, Lambert, Michelle V., Phillips, Mary L. and David, Anthony S. 2003. 'Depersonalisation Disorder: Clinical Features of 204 Cases', *British Journal of Psychiatry* 182: 428–33.

Barnard, Alan. 2012. *Genesis of Symbolic Thought*. Cambridge: Cambridge University Press.

Baron-Cohen, Simon. 1995. *Mindblindness: An Essay on Autism and Theory of Mind*. Cambridge, MA: MIT Press.

Baron-Cohen, Simon, Leslie, Alan M. and Frith, Uta. 1985. 'Does the Autistic Child Have a "Theory of Mind"?' *Cognition* 21: 37–46.

Bault, Nadège, Fahrenfort, Johannes J., Pelloux, Benjamin, Ridderinkhof, K. Richard and van Winden, Frans. 2017. 'An Affective Social Tie Mechanism: Theory, Evidence, and Implications', *Journal of Economic Psychology* 61: 152–75.

Becchetti, Andrea and Amadeo, Alida. 2016. 'Why We Forget Our Dreams: Acetylcholine and Norepinephrine in Wakefulness and REM Sleep', *Behavioral and Brain Sciences* 39: e202.

Beckner, Clay, Ellis, Nick C., Blythe, Richard, Holland, John, Bybee, Joan, Ke, Jinyun, Christiansen, Morten H., Larsen-Freeman, Diane, Croft, William and Schoenemann, Tom. 2009. 'Language Is a Complex Adaptive System: Position Paper', *Language Learning* 59, suppl: 1–26.

Bens, Martin, Szafranski, Karol, Holtze, Susanne, Sahm, Arne, Groth, Marco, Kestler, Hans A., Hildebrandt, Thomas B. and Platzer, Matthias. 2018. 'Naked Mole-Rat Transcriptome Signatures of Socially Suppressed Sexual Maturation and Links of Reproduction to Aging', *BMC Biology* 16: 77.

Benson, Margaret S. 1993. 'The Structure of Four- and Five-Year-Olds' Narratives in Pretend Play and Storytelling', *First Language* 13: 203–23.

Benveniste, Émile. 1958 [1971]. 'Subjectivity in Language'. In *Problems in General Linguistics*, edited by M.E. Meek. Coral Gables, FL: University of Miami Press.

Benveniste, Émile. 1970 [1996]. 'The Nature of Pronouns'. In *The Communication Theory Reader*, edited by Paul Cobley. London: Routledge.

Berwick, Robert C. and Chomsky, Noam. 2016. *Why Only Us: Language and Evolution*. Cambridge, MA: MIT Press.

Bianchi, Serena, Stimpson, Cheryl D., Duka, Tetyana, Larsen, Michael D., Janssen, William G.M., Collins, Zachary, Bauernfeind, Amy L., Schapiro, Steven J., Baze, Wallace B., McArthur, Mark J., Hopkin, William D., Wildman Derek E., Lipovich, Leonard, Kuzawa, Christopher W., Jacobs, Bob, Hof, Patrick R. and Sherwood, Chet C. 2013. 'Synaptogenesis and Development of Pyramidal Neuron Dendritic Morphology in the Chimpanzee Neocortex Resembles Humans', *PNAS* 110.s2: 10395–401.

Bickerton, Derek. 2002. 'How Protolanguage Became Language'. In *The Evolutionary Emergence of Language*, edited by Chris Knight, Michael Studdert-Kennedy and James. R. Hurford, 264–84. Cambridge: Cambridge University Press.

Bickerton, Derek. 2014. 'Some Problems for Biolinguistics', *Biolinguistics* 8: 73–96.

Bierce, Ambrose. 1911 [1999]. Cartesian, adj. In *The Devil's Dictionary*. Oxford: Oxford University Press.

Blackiston, Douglas J., Silva Casey, Elena and Weiss, Martha R. 2008. 'Retention of Memory through Metamorphosis: Can a Moth Remember What It Learned as a Caterpillar?' *PLoS ONE* 3.3: e1736.

Blechschmidt, Erich. 1977. *The Beginnings of Human Life*. Berlin: Springer-Verlag.

Boehm, Christopher. 1993. 'Egalitarian Behavior and Reverse Dominance Hierarchy', *Current Anthropology* 34.3: 227–54.

Boehm, Christopher. 1999. *Hierarchy in the Forest: The Evolution of Egalitarian Behaviour*. Cambridge, MA: Harvard University Press.

Borrego, Natalia and Gaines, Michael. 2016. 'Social Carnivores Outperform Asocial Carnivores on an Innovative Problem', *Animal Behaviour* 114: 21–6.

Bourdieu, Pierre. 2008. Richard Nice (tr.), *Sketch for a Self-Analysis*. Chicago: University of Chicago Press.

Bowes, Eleanor. 2014. *Understanding Schizophrenia*. London: Mind (National Association for Mental Health).

Boyd, Robert, Gintis, Herbert and Bowles, Samuel. 2010. 'Coordinated Punishment of Defectors Sustains Cooperation and Can Proliferate When Rare', *Science* 328: 617–620.

Bradbury, Jack W. and Vehrencamp, Sandra L. 1998. *Principles of Animal Communication*. Sunderland, MA: Sinauer Assocs. Inc.

Brewer, Sarah and Cutting, Alex. 2001. *A Child's World: A Unique Insight into How Children Think*. London: Headline.

Brosnan, Sarah F., Talbot, Catherine, Ahlgren, Megan, Lambeth, Susan P. and Schapiro, Steven J. 2010. 'Mechanisms Underlying Responses to Inequitable Outcomes in Chimpanzees, *Pan Troglodytes*', *Animal Behaviour* 79.6: 1229–37.

Brown, Donald E. 2004. 'Human Universals, Human Nature and Human Culture', *Daedalus*, 133.4: 47–54.

Bruner, Jerome. 1986. *Actual Minds, Possible Worlds*. Cambridge, MA: Harvard University Press.

Bruner, Jerome. 1990. *Acts of Meaning*. Cambridge, MA: Harvard University Press.

Bruner, Jerome. 1991. 'The Narrative Construction of Reality', *Critical Inquiry* 18: 1–21.

Bustamante, Carlos D. and Henn, Brenna M. 2010. 'Shadows of Early Migrations', *Nature* 468: 1044–5.

Byard, Roger W. 2016. 'Traditional Medicines and Species Extinction: Another Side to Forensic Wildlife Investigation', *Forensic Science Medicine and Pathology* 12: 125–7.

Byrne, Richard. 1995. *The Thinking Ape: Evolutionary Origins of Intelligence*. Oxford: Oxford University Press.

Caballero, Javier A., Humphries, Mark D. and Gurney, Kevin N. 2018. 'A Probabilistic, Distributed, Recursive Mechanism for Decision-Making in the Brain', *PLoS Computational Biology* 14.4: e1006033.

Call, Josep, Hare, Brian, Carpenter, Malinda and Tomasello, Michael. 2004. '"Unwilling" Versus "Unable": Chimpanzees' Understanding of Human Intentional Action', *Developmental Science* 7.4: 488–98.

Call, Josep and Tomasello, Michael. 1999. 'A Nonverbal False Belief Task: The Performance of Children and Great Apes', *Child Development* 70.2: 381–95.

Call, Josep and Tomasello, Michael. 2008. 'Does the Chimpanzee Have a Theory of Mind? 30 Years Later', *Trends in Cognitive Sciences* 12.5: 187–197.

Callaway, Ewen. 2015. 'Monkeys Seem to Recognize Their Reflections', *Nature*. 16692.

Campbell, Joseph. 1949. *The Hero With a Thousand Faces*. London: Fontana Press.

Campbell, Keith W. and Baumeister, Roy F. 2006. 'Narcissistic Personality Disorder'. In *Practitioner's Guide to Evidence-Based Psychotherapy*, edited by J.E. Fisher and W.T. O'Donohue, Chapter 42. New York: Springer.

Carbon, Claus-Christian. 2014. 'Understanding Human Perception by Human-Made Illusions', *Frontiers in Human Neuroscience* 8: 566.

Carpenter, Malinda and Tomasello, Michael. 1995. 'Joint Attention and Imitative Learning in Children, Chimpanzees, and Enculturated Chimpanzees', *Social Development* 4.3: 217–37.

Carroll, Lewis. 1865 [1982]. 'Alice's Adventures in Wonderland'. In *The Complete Illustrated Works of Lewis Carroll*. London: Chancellor Press.

Carroll, Lewis. 1872 [1982]. 'Through the Looking Glass, and What Alice Found There'. In *The Complete Illustrated Works of Lewis Carroll*. London: Chancellor Press.

Carroll, Lewis. 1876 [1982]. 'The Hunting of the Snark, An Agony in Eight Fits'. In *The Complete Illustrated Works of Lewis Carroll*. London: Chancellor Press.

Carston, Robyn. 2002. 'Pragmatics and Linguistic Underdeterminacy'. In *Thoughts and Utterances*, edited by Robyn Carston, 15–93. Malden: Blackwell Publishing.

Casey, B.J., Somerville, Leah H., Gotlib, Ian H., Ayduk, Ozlem, Franklin, Nicholas T., Askren, Mary K., Jonides, John, Berman, Marc G., Wilson, Nicole L., Teslovich, Theresa, Glover, Gary, Zayas, Vivian, Mischel, Walter and Shoda, Yuichi. 2011. 'Behavioral and Neural Correlates of Delay of Gratification 40 Years Later', *PNAS* 108.36: 14998–15003.

CDC (Centers for Disease Control and Prevention). 2018. *Community Report from the Autism and Developmental Disabilities Monitoring (ADDM) Network*. Washington DC: CDC.

Chang, Liangtang, Fang, Qin, Zhang, Shikun, Poo, Mu-ming and Gong, Neng. 2015. 'Mirror-Induced Self-Directed Behaviors in Rhesus Monkeys after Visual-Somatosensory Training', *Current Biology* 25: 212–17.

Chao, S. 1987. 'The Effect of Lactation on Ovulation and Fertility', *Clinics in Perinatology* 14.1: 39–50.

Charlton, Bruce G. 1997. 'The Inequity of Inequality: Egalitarian Instincts and Evolutionary Psychology', *Journal of Health Psychology* 2: 413–25.

Cheney, Dorothy L. and Seyfarth, Robert M. 1990. *How Monkeys See the World: Inside the Mind of Another Species*. Chicago: University of Chicago Press.

Cheney, Dorothy L. and Seyfarth, Robert M. 2007. *Baboon Metaphysics: The Evolution of a Social Mind*. Chicago: University of Chicago Press.

Chomsky, Noam. 1982. *Some Concepts and Consequences of the Theory of Government and Binding*. Cambridge, MA: MIT Press.

Chomsky, Noam. 1995a. *The Minimalist Program*. Cambridge, MA: MIT Press.

Chomsky, Noam. 1995b. 'Language and Nature', *Mind* 104.413: 1–61.

Chomsky, Noam. 2007. 'Of Minds and Language', *Biolinguistics* 1: 9–27.

Christiansen, Morten H. and Chater, Nick. 2008. 'Language as Shaped by the Brain', *Behavioral and Brain Sciences* 31: 489–558.

Clarke, Esther, Reichard, Ulrich H. and Zuberbühler, Klaus. 2015. 'Context-Specific Close-Range "Hoo" Calls in Wild Gibbons (*Hylobates Lar*)', *BMC Evolutionary Biology* 15: 56.

Clarkson, Chris, Jacobs, Zenobia, Marwick, Ben, Fullagar, Richard, Wallis, Lynley, Smith, Mike, Roberts, Richard G., Hayes, Elspeth, Lowe, Kelsey, Carah, Xavier, Florin, S. Anna, McNeil, Jessica, Cox, Delyth, Arnold, Lee J., Hua, Quan, Huntley, Jillian, Brand, Helen E.A., Manne, Tiina, Fairbairn, Andrew, Shulmeister, James, Lyle, Lindsey, Salinas, Makiah, Page, Mara, Connell, Kate, Park, Gayoung, Norman, Kasih, Murphy, Tessa and Pardoe, Colin. 2017. 'Human Occupation of Northern Australia by 65,000 Years Ago', *Nature* 547: 306–10.

Collias, Nicholas E. and Collias, Elsie C. 1984. *Nest Building and Bird Behavior*. Princeton: Princeton University Press.

Connor, Richard C. 2007. 'Dolphin Social Intelligence: Complex Alliance Relationships in Bottlenose Dolphins and a Consideration of Selective Environments for Extreme Brain Size Evolution In Mammals', *Philosophical Transactions of the Royal Society B* 362: 587–602.

Connor, Richard C., Smolker, Rachel and Bejder, Lars. 2006. 'Synchrony, Social Behaviour and Alliance Affiliation in Indian Ocean Bottlenose Dolphins, *Tursiops Aduncus*', *Animal Behaviour* 72: 1371–8.

Cook, Mandy L.H., Sayigh, Laela S., Blum, James E., and Wells, Randall S. 2004. 'Signature-Whistle Production in Undisturbed Free-Ranging Bottlenose Dolphins (*Tursiops Truncatus*)', *Proceedings of the Royal Society B* 271: 1043–9.

Copernicus, Nicolaus. 1543. *De Revolutionibus Orbium Coelestium*. Nuremberg: Johannes Petreium.

Cordingley, John S. and Trzyna, Wendy C. 2008. 'Multiple Factors Affecting Growth and Encystment of *Acanthamoeba Castellanii* in Axenic Culture', *Acta Protozoologica* 47: 307–16.

Covington, Michael A., He, Congzhou, Brown, Cati, Naçi, Lorina, McClain, Jonathan T., Sirmon Fjordbak, Bess, Semple, James and Brown, John. 2005. 'Schizophrenia and the Structure of Language: The Linguist's View', *Schizophrenia Research* 77: 85–98.

Crockford, Catherine, Herbinger, Ilka, Vigilant, Linda and Boesch, Christophe. 2004. 'Wild Chimpanzees Produce Group-Specific Calls: A Case for Vocal Learning?' *Ethology* 110: 221–43.

Csordas, Thomas J. 1990. 'Embodiment as a Paradigm for Anthropology', *Ethos* 18.1. 5–47.

Damasio, Antonio. 2010. *Self Comes to Mind: Constructing the Conscious Brain*. London: Vintage Books.

Darwin, Charles. 1859 [2001]. *On the Origin of Species: A Facsimile of the First Edition*. Cambridge, MA: Harvard University Press.

Darwin, Charles. 1874. *The Descent of Man, and Selection in Relation to Sex* (2nd edition). New York: Prometheus Books.

Darwin, Charles. 1897. *The Expression of the Emotions in Man and Animals* (2nd edition). New York: D. Appleton.

Davila-Ross, Marina, Allcock, Bethan, Thomas, Chris and Bard, Kim A. 2011. 'Aping Expressions? Chimpanzees Produce Distinct Laugh Types When Responding to Laughter of Others', *Emotion* 11.5: 1013–20.

Dawkins, Richard. 1989. *The Selfish Gene* (2nd edition). Oxford: Oxford University Press.

Deacon, Terrence, Haag, James and Ogilvy, Jay. 2011. 'The Emergence of Self'. In *In Search of Self: Interdisciplinary Perspectives on Personhood*, edited by J. Wentzel van Huyssteen and Erik P. Wiebe. Grand Rapids, MI: Wm. B. Eerdmans Publishing Co.

Deb, Anamitra, Donohue, Stacy and Glaisyer, Tom. 2017. *Is Social Media a Threat to Democracy?* Redwood City, CA: The Omidyar Group.

de Balzac, Honoré. 1835 [1991]. *Père Goriot (La Comédie Humaine #23)*. Oxford: Oxford University Press.

Delfour, Fabienne and Marten, Ken. 2001. 'Mirror Image Processing in Three Marine Mammal Species: Killer Whales (*Orcinus Orca*), False Killer Whales (*Pseudorca Crassidens*) and California Sea Lions (*Zalophus Californianus*)', *Behavioural Processes* 53: 181–90.

Dennett, Daniel C. 1991. *Consciousness Explained*. London: Penguin.

Dennett, Daniel C. 2009. 'Darwin's "Strange Inversion of Reasoning"', *Proceedings of the National Academy of Science* 106.suppl: 10061–5.

Derrida, Jacques. 1998. Patrick Mensah (tr.), *Monolingualism of the Other*. Redwood City, CA: Stanford University Press.

Descartes, René. 1641 [1998]. 'Meditations on First Philosophy'. *Meditations and Other Metaphysical Writings*. London: Penguin.

Descartes, René. 1649 [1998]. Letter to Henry More, 5 February 1649, part 5. *Meditations and Other Metaphysical Writings*. London: Penguin, 173–5.

Dessalles, Jean-Louis. 2014. 'The Role of the Human Political Singularity in the Emergence of Language'. In *The Evolution of Language: Proceedings of the 10th International Conference (Evolang-X, Vienna)*, edited by E.A. Cartmill, S. Roberts, H. Lyn and H. Cornish, 423–4. Singapore: World Scientific.

de Waal, Frans B.M., Dindo, Marietta, Freeman, Cassiopeia A. and Hall, Marisa J. 2005. 'The Monkey in the Mirror: Hardly a Stranger', *PNAS* 102.32: 11140–7.

Diamond, Jared. 2005. *Guns, Germs, and Steel: The Fates of Human Societies (revised)*. New York: W.W. Norton and Co., Inc.

Dickens, Charles. 1859 [2000]. *A Tale of Two Cities*. London: Penguin.

Dienes, Zoltan and Perner, Josef. 1999. 'A Theory of Implicit and Explicit Knowledge', *Behavioral and Brain Sciences* 22: 735–808.

Diogo, Rui, Molnar, Julia L. and Wood, Bernard. 2017. 'Bonobo Anatomy Reveals Stasis and Mosaicism in Chimpanzee Evolution, and Supports Bonobos as the Most Appropriate Extant Model for the Common Ancestor of Chimpanzees and Humans', *Nature Scientific Reports* 7: 608.

Drummond, Cláudia, Coutinho, Gabriel, Paz Fonseca, Rochele, Assunção, Naima, Teldeschi, Alina, de Oliveira-Souza, Ricardo, Moll, Jorge, Tovar-Moll, Fernanda and Mattos, Paulo. 2015. 'Deficits in Narrative Discourse Elicited by Visual Stimuli Are Already Present in Patients with Mild Cognitive Impairment', *Frontiers in Aging Neuroscience* 7: 96.

Dugas, Michelle, Bélanger, Jocelyn J., Moyano, Manuel, Schumpe, Birga M., Kruglanski, Arie W., Gelfand, Michele J., Touchton-Leonard, Kate and Nociti, Noëmie. 2016. 'The Quest for Significance Motivates Self-Sacrifice', *Motivation Science* 2.1: 15–32.

Dunbar, Robin I.M. 1996. *Grooming, Gossip and the Evolution of Language*. London: Faber & Faber Ltd.

Dunbar, Robin I.M. 2004. *The Human Story: A New History of Mankind's Evolution*. London: Faber & Faber Ltd.

Dunbar, Robin I.M. 2010. *How Many Friends Does One Person Need? Dunbar's Number and Other Evolutionary Quirks*. London: Faber & Faber Ltd.

Durkheim, Émile. 1895 [1982]. W.D. Halls (tr.), *The Rules of Sociological Method* (8th edition). New York: The Free Press.

Durkheim, Émile. 1912. *The Elementary Forms of Religious Life*. Oxford: Oxford University Press.

Edwardes, Martin. 2003. 'I Like Both Myself and Me'. In *Camling 2003: Proceedings of the University of Cambridge First Postgraduate Conference in Language Research,* edited by Damien Hall, Theodore Markopoulos, Angeliki Salamoura and Sophia Skoufaki. Cambridge: CILR.

Edwardes, Martin. 2010. *The Origins of Grammar: An Anthropological Perspective*. London: Continuum.

Edwardes, Martin. 2014. 'Awareness of Self and Awareness of Selfness: Why the Capacity to Self-Model Represents a Novel Level of Cognition in Humans'. In *Selected Papers from the 4th UK Cognitive Linguistics Conference*, edited by G. Rundblad, A. Tytus, O. Knapton and C. Tang, 68–83. London: UK Cognitive Linguistics Association.

Emery, Nathan. 2016. *Bird Brain: An Exploration of Avian Intelligence*. Lewes, East Sussex: Ivy Press.

Erdal, David and Whiten, Andrew. 1994. 'On Human Egalitarianism: An Evolutionary Product of Machiavellian Status Escalation?' *Current Anthropology* 35.2: 175–83.

Evans, Nicholas and Levinson, Stephen C. 2009. 'The Myth of Language Universals: Language Diversity and Its Importance for Cognitive Science', *Behavioral and Brain Sciences* 32: 429–92.

Everett, Daniel L. 2005. 'Cultural Constraints on Grammar and Cognition in Pirahã: Another Look at the Design Features of Human Language', *Current Anthropology* 46.4: 621–46.

Everett, Daniel L. 2016. *Dark Matter of the Mind: The Culturally Articulated Unconscious*. Chicago: University of Chicago Press.

Everett, Daniel L. 2017. *How Language Began: The Story of Humanity's Greatest Invention*. London: Profile Books.

Fabbro, Franco, Aglioti, Salvatore M., Bergamasco, Massimo, Clarici, Andrea and Panksepp, Jaak. 2015. 'Evolutionary Aspects of Self- and World Consciousness in Vertebrates', *Frontiers in Human Neuroscience* 9: 157.

Fehr, Ernst and Fischbacher, Urs. 2003. 'The Nature of Human Altruism', *Nature* 425: 785–91.

Fehr, Ernst and Gächter, Simon. 2002. 'Altruistic Punishment in Humans', *Nature* 415: 137–40.

Feinberg, Todd E. and Keenan, Julian P. 2005. 'Where in the Brain is the Self?' *Consciousness and Cognition* 14.4: 661–78.

Fingelkurts, Andrew A. and Fingelkurts, Alexander A. 2015. 'Present Moment, Past, and Future: Mental Kaleidoscope'. In *The Long and Short of Mental Time Travel: Self-Projection over Time-Scales Large and Small*, edited by James M. Broadway, Claire M. Zedelius, Jonathan W. Schooler and Simon Grondin, 32–5. Lausanne: Frontiers Media.

Flower, Tom P., Gribble, Matthew and Ridley, Amanda R. 2014. 'Deception by Flexible Alarm Mimicry in an African Bird', *Science* 344.6183: 513–16.

Foer, Joshua. 2015. 'Dolphin Intelligence', *National Geographic* 227.5: 30–55.

Fouts, Roger and Mills, Stephen Tukel. 1997. *Next of Kin: My Conversations with Chimpanzees*. New York: Avon Books Inc.

Fowler, Andrew, Koutsioni, Yianna and Sommer, Volker. 2007. 'Leaf-Swallowing in Nigerian Chimpanzees: Evidence for Assumed Self-Medication', *Primates* 48: 73–6.

Fowler, James H. 2005. 'Altruistic Punishment and the Origin of Cooperation', *PNAS* 102.19: 7047–9.

Freud, Sigmund. 1923 [2010]. *The Ego and the Id*. Seattle: Pacific Publishing Studio.

Frith, John. 2012. 'Syphilis: Its Early History and Treatment Until Penicillin and the Debate on its Origins', *Journal of Military and Veterans' Health* 20.4: 49–58.

Fromm, Erich. 1964. *The Heart of Man: Its Genius for Good and Evil*. New York: Harper & Row.

Futuyma, Douglas J. 2015. 'Can Modern Evolutionary Theory Explain Macroevolution?' *Interdisciplinary Evolution Research 2 (Macroevolution)*, 29–85.

Gage, Fred H. 2002. 'Neurogenesis in the Adult Brain', *Journal of Neuroscience* 22.3: 612–13.

Gallagher, Shaun. 2013a. 'A Pattern Theory of Self', *Frontiers in Human Neuroscience* 7: 443.

Gallagher, Shaun. 2013b. 'Intersubjectivity and Psychopathology'. In *Oxford Handbook of Philosophy of Psychiatry*, edited by B. Fulford, M. Davies, B. Graham, J. Sadler and G. Stanghellini, 257–74. Oxford: Oxford University Press.

Gallup, Gordon G., Jr. 1970. 'Chimpanzees: Self-Recognition', *Science* 167.3194: 86–7.

Gardner, Andy and West, Stuart A. 2004. 'Cooperation and Punishment, Especially in Humans', *American Naturalist* 164.6: 753–64.

Genty, Emilie, Breuer, Thomas, Hobaiter, Catherine and Byrne, Richard W. 2009. 'Gestural Communication of the Gorilla (*Gorilla Gorilla*): Repertoire, Intentionality and Possible Origins', *Animal Cognition* 12: 527–46.

Gil-Or, Oren, Levi-Belz, Yossi and Turel, Ofir. 2015. 'The "Facebook-Self": Characteristics and Psychological Predictors of False Self-Presentation on Facebook', *Frontiers in Psychology* 6: 99.

Giummarra, Melita J. and Moseley, G. Lorimer. 2011. 'Phantom Limb Pain and Bodily Awareness: Current Concepts and Future Directions', *Current Opinion in Anesthesiology* 24: 524–31.

Godfrey-Smith, Peter. 2016. *Other Minds: The Octopus and the Evolution of Intelligent Life*. London: William Collins.

Goodall, Jane. 1990. *Through a Window: Thirty Years with the Chimpanzees of Gombe*. London: Phoenix.

Graziano, Michael S.A. 2013. *Consciousness and the Social Brain*. Oxford: Oxford University Press.

Graziano, Michael S.A. 2016. 'Consciousness Engineered', *Journal of Consciousness Studies* 23.11/12: 98–115.

Graziano, Michael S.A. and Kastner, Sabine. 2011. 'Human Consciousness and Its Relationship To Social Neuroscience: A Novel Hypothesis', *Cognitive Neuroscience* 2.2: 98–113.

Graziano, Michael S.A., Taylor, Charlotte S.R., Moore, Tirin and Cooke, Dylan F. 2002. 'The Cortical Control of Movement Revisited', *Neuron* 36: 1–20.

Green, Richard E., Krause, Johannes, Briggs, Adrian W., Maricic, Tomislav, Stenzel, Udo, Martin, Kircher, Patterson, Nick, Li, Heng, Zhai, Weiwei, Hsi-Yang Fritz, Markus, Hansen, Nancy F., Durand, Eric Y., Malaspinas, Anna-Sapfo, Jensen, Jeffrey D., Marques-Bonet, Tomas, Alkan, Can, Prüfer, Kay, Meyer, Matthias, Burbano, Hernán A., Good, Jeffrey M., Schultz, Rigo, Aximu-Petri, Ayinuer, Butthof, Anne, Höber, Barbara, Höffner, Barbara, Siegemund, Madlen, Weihmann, Antje, Nusbaum, Chad, Lander, Eric S., Russ, Carsten, Novod, Nathaniel, Affourtit, Jason, Egholm, Michael, Verna, Christine, Rudan, Pavao, Brajkovic, Dejana, Kucan, Željko,

Gušic, Ivan, Doronichev, Vladimir B., Golovanova, Liubov V., Lalueza-Fox, Carles, de la Rasilla, Marco, Fortea, Javier, Rosas, Antonio, Schmitz, Ralf W., Johnson, Philip L.F., Eichler, Evan E., Falush, Daniel, Birney, Ewan, Mullikin, James C., Slatkin, Montgomery, Nielsen, Rasmus, Kelso, Janet, Lachmann, Michael, Reich, David and Pääbo, Svante. 2010. 'A Draft Sequence of the Neandertal Genome', *Science* 328: 710–22.

Grossman, Murray, Irwin, David J., Jester, Charles, Halpin, Amy, Ash, Sharon, Rascovsky, Katya, Weintraub, Daniel and McMillan, Corey T. 2017. 'Narrative Organization Deficit in Lewy Body Disorders Is Related to Alzheimer Pathology', *Frontiers in Neuroscience* 11: 53.

Guarino, Domenico. 2018. 'Krauzlis' Strange Inversion of Reasoning', *Frontiers in Systems Neuroscience* 12: 34.

Gutiérrez-Ibáñez, Cristián, Iwaniuk, Andrew N. and Wylie, Douglas R. 2018. 'Parrots Have Evolved a Primate-Like Telencephalic-Midbrain-Cerebellar Circuit', *Nature Scientific Reports* 8: 9960.

Haeckel, Ernst. 1866. *Generelle Morphologie der Organismen*. Berlin: G. Reimer.

Hamilton, William D. 1964. 'The Genetical Evolution of Social Behaviour I and The Genetical Evolution of Social Behaviour II', *Journal of Theoretical Biology* 7.1: 1–52.

Happé, Francesca. 2003. 'Theory of Mind and the Self', *Annals of the New York Academy of Sciences* 1001: 134–44.

Hardin, Garrett. 1968. 'The Tragedy of the Commons', *Science* 162.3859: 1243–8.

Hauser, Marc D., Chomsky, Noam and Fitch, W. Tecumseh. 2002. 'The Faculty of Language: What Is It, Who Has It, and How Did It Evolve?' *Science* 298: 1569–79.

Hayes, Catherine. 1951. *The Ape in Our House*. New York: Harper and Brothers.

Hazem, Nesrine, Beaurenaut, Morgan, George, Nathalie and Conty, Laurence. 2018. 'Social Contact Enhances Bodily Self-Awareness', *Nature Scientific Reports* 8: 4195.

Heidegger, Martin. 1933 [1993]. 'German Students', 3 November 1933; 'German Men and Women!' 10 November 1933; 'Declaration of Support for Adolf Hitler and the National Socialist State', 11 November 1933. In *The Heidegger Controversy: A Critical Reader*, edited by Richard Wolin, Chapter 2. Cambridge, MA: MIT Press.

Henshilwood, Christopher S. and Dubreuil, Benoît. 2011. 'The Still Bay and Howiesons Poort, 77–59 ka: Symbolic Material Culture and the Evolution of the Mind During the African Middle Stone Age', *Current Anthropology* 52.3: 361–400.

Henshilwood, Christopher S., d'Errico, Francesco, Yates, Royden, Jacobs, Zenobia, Tribolo, Chantal, Duller, Geoff A.T., Mercier, Norbert, Sealy, Judith C., Valladas, Helene, Watts, Ian and Wintle, Ann G. 2002. 'Emergence of Modern Human Behavior: Middle Stone Age Engravings from South Africa', *Science* 295: 1278–80.

Herman, Jerry. 1983. *I Am What I Am*. Milwaukee, WI: Hal-Leonard.

Herman, Louis M. and Uyeyama, Robert K. 1999. 'The Dolphin's Grammatical Competency: Comments on Kako', *Animal Learning & Behavior* 27.1: 18–23.

Hockett, Charles F. 1960. 'The Origin of Speech', *Scientific American* 203: 88–111.

Hockett, Charles F. 1963. 'The Problem of Universals in Language'. In *Universals of Language*, edited by J.H. Greenberg, 1–29. Cambridge, MA: MIT Press.

Hoffmann, Dirk L., Standish, Chris D., García-Diez, Marcos, Pettitt, Paul B., Milton, James A., Zilhão, João, Alcolea-González, José Javier, Cantalejo-Duarte, Pedro, Collado, Hipólito, de Balbín, Rodrigo, Lorblanchet, Michel, Ramos-Muñoz, José, Weniger, Gerd-Christian and Pike, Alistair W.G. 2018. 'U-Th Dating of Carbonate Crusts Reveals Neandertal Origin of Iberian Cave Art', *Science* 359: 912–15.

Holinger, Paul C. 2012. 'Self-Awareness: Transition from Infant to Toddler', *Psychology Today: Great Kids, Great Parents*, at www.psychologytoday.com/blog/great-kids-great-parents/201211/self-awareness (accessed 21 March 2019).

Hood, Bruce. 2012. *The Self Illusion: Why There Is No 'You' Inside Your Head*. London: Constable & Robinson Ltd.

Horner, Victoria, Whiten, Andrew, Flynn, Emma and de Waal, Frans B.M. 2006. 'Faithful Replication of Foraging Techniques Along Cultural Transmission Chains By Chimpanzees and Children', *PNAS* 103.37: 13878–83.

Hrdy, Sarah Blaffer. 2009. *Mothers and Others: The Evolutionary Origins of Mutual Understanding*. Cambridge, MA: Belknap Press.

Hu, Chuan, Kumar, Sameer, Huang, Jiao and Ratnavelu, Kurunathan. 2017. 'Disinhibition of Negative True Self for Identity Reconstructions in Cyberspace: Advancing Self-Discrepancy Theory for Virtual Setting', *PLoS ONE* 12.4: e0175623.

Hublin, Jean-Jacques, Ben-Ncer, Abdelouahed, Bailey, Shara E., Freidline, Sarah E., Neubauer, Simon, Skinner, Matthew M., Bergmann, Inga, Le Cabec, Adeline, Benazzi, Stefano, Harvati, Katerina and Gunz, Philipp. 2017. 'New Fossils from Jebel Irhoud, Morocco and the Pan-African Origin of *Homo Sapiens*', *Nature* 546: 289–92.

Hudson, Richard Ellis, Aukema, Juliann Eve, Rispe, Claude and Roze, Denis. 2002. 'Altruism, Cheating, and Anticheater Adaptations in Cellular Slime Molds', *American Naturalist* 160.1: 31–43.

Huebner, Bryce and Hauser, Marc D. 2011. 'Moral Judgments About Altruistic Self-Sacrifice: When Philosophical and Folk Intuitions Clash', *Philosophical Psychology* 24.1: 73–94.

Hume, David. 1739 [1896]. *A Treatise on Human Nature*. Oxford: Clarendon Press.

Hyland, Ken. 2001. 'Humble Servants of the Discipline? Self-Mention in Research Articles', *English for Specific Purposes* 20.3: 207–26.

Ibbotson, Paul and Tomasello, Michael. 2009. 'Prototype Constructions in Early Language Acquisition', *Language and Cognition* 1.1: 59–85.

Ingram, Catherine J.E., Mulcare, Charlotte A., Itan, Yuval, Thomas, Mark G. and Swallow, Dallas M. 2009. 'Lactose Digestion and the Evolutionary Genetics of Lactase Persistence', *Human Genetics* 124: 579–91.

Jackson, Mark. 2010. '"Divine Stramonium": The Rise and Fall of Smoking for Asthma', *Medical History* 54.2: 171–94.

Jarvis, Jennifer U.M. and Sherman, Paul W. 2002. 'Mammalian Species No. 706: *Heterocephalus Glaber*', *Mammalian Species* 706: 1–9.

Jensen, Keith, Call, Josep and Tomasello, Michael. 2007. 'Chimpanzees Are Vengeful But Not Spiteful', *PNAS* 104.32: 13046–50.

Jespersen, Otto. 1922. *Language: Its Nature, Development and Origin*. London: George Allen & Unwin Ltd.

Jordan, Fiona M., Gray, Russell D., Greenhill, Simon J. and Mace, Ruth. 2009. 'Matrilocal Residence Is Ancestral in Austronesian Societies', *Proceedings of the Royal Society B* 276: 1957–64.

Jung, Carl Gustav. 1958 [2014]. *The Undiscovered Self*. Oxford: Routledge.

Kaminski, Juliane, Call, Josep and Fischer, Julia. 2004. 'Word Learning in a Domestic Dog: Evidence for "Fast Mapping"', *Science* 304: 1682–3.

Kant, Immanuel. 1798 [1974]. Mary Gregor (tr.), *Anthropology from a Pragmatic Point of View*. The Hague: Martinus Nijhoff.

Katsafanas, Paul. 2011. 'The Concept of Unified Agency in Nietzsche, Plato, and Schiller', *Journal of the History of Philosophy* 49.1: 87–113.

Kellogg, W.N. and Kellogg, L.A. 1933. *The Ape and the Child: A Study of Environmental Influence upon Early Behavior*. New York: Hafner Publishing Company.

King, Stephanie L., Friedman, Whitney R., Allen, Simon J., Gerber, Livia, Jensen, Frants H., Wittwer, Samuel, Connor, Richard C. and Krützen, Michael. 2018. 'Bottlenose Dolphins Retain Individual Vocal Labels in Multi-Level Alliances', *Cell Biology* 28: 1993–9.

King, Stephanie L., Sayigh, Laela S., Wells, Randall S., Fellner, Wendi and Janik, Vincent M. 2013. 'Vocal Copying of Individually Distinctive Signature Whistles in Bottlenose Dolphins', *Proceedings of the Royal Society B* 280: 2013.0053.

Kirby, Simon, Cornish, Hannah and Smith, Kenny. 2008. 'Cumulative Cultural Evolution in the Laboratory: An Experimental Approach to the Origins of Structure in Human Language', *PNAS* 105.31: 10681–6.

Kirkpatrick, Casey. 2011. 'Tactical Deception and the Great Apes: Insight into the Question of Theory of Mind', *Totem: The University of Western Ontario Journal of Anthropology* 15.1.4: 31–7.

Knight, Chris. 1991. *Blood Relations: Menstruation and the Origins of Culture*. New Haven, CT: Yale University Press.

Knight, Chris, Power, Camilla and Watts, Ian. 1995. 'The Human Symbolic Revolution: A Darwinian Account', *Cambridge Archaeological Journal* 5.1: 75–114.

Kondo, Dorinne. 1986. 'Dissolution and Reconstitution of Self: Implications for Anthropological Epistemology', *Cultural Anthropology* 1.1: 74–88.

Kotowicz, Zbigniew. 2007. 'The Strange Case of Phineas Gage', *History of the Human Sciences* 20.1: 115–31.

Krajco, Kathleen. 2007. *What Makes Narcissists Tick? Understanding Narcissistic Personality Disorder* (3rd edition). Janesville, WI: OperationDoubles.

Kraus, Michael W. and Park, Jun W. 2014. 'The Undervalued Self: Social Class and Self-Evaluation', *Frontiers in Psychology* 5: 1404.

Krauzlis, Richard J., Bollimunta, Anil, Arcizet, Fabrice and Wang, Lupeng. 2014. 'Attention as an Effect Not a Cause', *Trends in Cognitive Sciences* 18.9: 457–64.

Kuzawa, Christopher W., Chugani, Harry T., Grossman, Lawrence I., Lipovich, Leonard, Muzik, Otto, Hof, Patrick R., Wildman, Derek E., Sherwood, Chet C., Leonard, William R. and Lange, Nicholas. 2014. 'Metabolic Costs and Evolutionary Implications of Human Brain Development', *PNAS* 111.36: 13010–15.

Lahr, Marta Mirazón and Foley, Robert A. 2016. 'Human Evolution in Late Quaternary Eastern Africa'. In *Africa from MIS 6–2: Population Dynamics and Paleoenvironments*, edited by S.C. Jones and B.A. Stewart, Chapter 12, 215–31. Dordrecht: Springer.

Lakoff, George. 1992. 'Multiple Selves: Metaphorical Models of Self Inherent in Our Conceptual System'. Presentation at The Conceptual Self in Context: A Conference of the Mellon Colloquium on the Self. Emorey University, Atlanta, Georgia, 1–2 May.

Lakoff, George and Johnson, Mark. 1980. *Metaphors We Live By*. Chicago: University of Chicago Press.

Lakoff, George and Johnson, Mark. 1999. *Philosophy in the Flesh: The Embodied Mind and its Challenge to Western Thought*. New York: Basic Books.

Laran, Juliano and Janiszewski, Chris. 2009. 'Behavioral Consistency and Inconsistency in the Resolution of Goal Conflict', *Journal of Consumer Research* 35: 967–84.

La Rocca, Cristian E., Braunstein, Lidia A. and Vazquez, Federico. 2014. 'The Influence of Persuasion in Opinion Formation and Polarization', *EPL Journal* 106.40004.

LeDoux, Joseph. 2002. *Synaptic Self: How Our Brains Become Who We Are*. London: Penguin.

Le Guin, Ursula K. 1969. *The Left Hand of Darkness*. New York: Ace Books.

Lehmann, Laurent, Ravigné, Virginie and Keller, Laurent. 2008. 'Population Viscosity Can Promote the Evolution of Altruistic Sterile Helpers and Eusociality', *Proceedings of the Royal Society B* 275: 1887–95.

Lester, David. 2012. 'A Multiple Self Theory of the Mind', *Comprehensive Psychology* 1: 5.

Lévi-Strauss, Claude. 1955 [1963]. J. Russell (tr.), *Tristes Tropiques*. New York: Atheneum.

Lévi-Strauss, Claude. 1962. *La pensée sauvage*. Paris: Librairie Plon.

Lewis, Jerome. 2008. 'Ekila: Blood, Bodies, and Egalitarian Societies', *Journal of the Royal Anthropological Institute* 14: 297–315.

Libet, Benjamin. 2004. *Mind Time: The Temporal Factor in Consciousness*. Cambridge, MA: Harvard University Press.

Liu, Wu, Martinón-Torres, María, Cai, Yan-jun, Xing, Song, Tong, Hao-wen, Pei, Shu-wen, Jan Sier, Mark, Wu, Xiao-hong, Edwards, R. Lawrence, Cheng, Hai, Li, Yi-yuan, Yang, Xiong-xin, Bermúdez de Castro, José María and Wu, Xiu-jie. 2015. 'The Earliest Unequivocally Modern Humans in Southern China', *Nature* 526: 696–9.

Livingstone, Margaret S., Pettine, Warren W., Srihasam, Krishna, Moore, Brandon, Morocz, Istvan A. and Lee, Daeyeol. 2014. 'Symbol Addition by Monkeys Provides Evidence for Normalized Quantity Coding', *PNAS* 111.18: 6822–7.

Locke, John. 1689 [1836]. *Essay Concerning Human Understanding*. London: T. Tegg & Son.

Lonsdorf, Elizabeth V., Eberly, Lynn E. and Pusey, Anne E. 2004. 'Sex Differences in Learning in Chimpanzees', *Nature* 428: 715–16.

Lorimer, Doug. 1997. *The Collapse of 'Communism' in the USSR: Its Causes and Significance* (2nd edition). Chippendale, NSW Australia: Resistance Books.

Løvtrup, Søren. 1987. *Darwinism: The Refutation of a Myth*. Beckenham: Croom Helm Ltd.

Lucas, Molly V., Anderson, Laura C., Bolling, Danielle Z., Pelphrey, Kevin A. and Kaiser, Martha D. 2015. 'Dissociating the Neural Correlates of Experiencing and Imagining Affective Touch', *Cerebral Cortex* 25.9: 2623–30.

Lumsden, Charles J. and Wilson, Edward O. 1980. 'Gene-Culture Translation in the Avoidance of Sibling Incest', *PNAS* 77.10: 6248–50.

Malafouris, Lambros. 2008. 'Between Brains, Bodies and Things: Tectonoetic Awareness and the Extended Self', *Philosophical Transactions of the Royal Society B* 363: 1993–2002.

Malthus, Thomas Robert. 1798. *An Essay on the Principle of Population*. London: John Murray.

Marchetti, Giorgio. 2014. 'Attention and Working Memory: Two Basic Mechanisms for Constructing Temporal Experiences'. In *The Long and Short of Mental Time Travel: Self-Projection over Time-Scales Large and Small*, edited by James M. Broadway, Claire M. Zedelius, Jonathan W. Schooler and Simon Grondin, 64–78. Lausanne: Frontiers Media.

Markus, Hazel Rose and Kitayama, Shinobu. 1991. 'Culture and the Self. Implications for Cognition, Emotion, and Motivation', *Psychological Review* 98.2: 224–53.

Marshall, Colin. 2010. 'Kant's Metaphysics of the Self', *Philosopher's Imprint* 10: 8.

Martin, Luther H., Gutman, Huck and Hutton, Patricia H. 1988. *Technologies of the Self: A Seminar with Michel Foucault*. Amherst: University of Massachusetts Press.

Marx, Karl. 1844 [1959]. Martin Milligan (tr.), *Economic & Philosophic Manuscripts of 1844*. Moscow: Progress Publishers.

Mauss, Marcel. 1950. *The Gift: The Form and Reason for Exchange in Archaic Societies*. London: Routledge.

McClintock, Martha K. 1971. 'Menstrual Synchrony and Suppression', *Nature* 299: 244–5.

McCloskey, Deirdre N. 1998. *The Rhetoric of Economics*. Madison: University of Wisconsin Press.

McConnell, Allen R. 2011. 'The Multiple Self-Aspects Framework: Self-Concept Representation and Its Implications', *Personality and Social Psychology Review* 15.1: 3–27.

McNeill, David. 2012. *How Language Began: Gesture and Speech in Human Evolution*. Cambridge: Cambridge University Press.

Mealey, Linda. 1995. 'The Sociobiology of Sociopathy: An Integrated Evolutionary Model', *Behavioral and Brain Sciences* 18.3: 523–99.

Melis, Alicia P. and Semmann, Dirk. 2010. 'How is Human Cooperation Different?' *Philosophical Transactions of the Royal Society B* 365: 2663–74.

Melis, Alicia P., Warneken, Felix, Jensen, Keith, Schneider, Anna-Claire, Call, Josep and Tomasello, Michael. 2011. 'Chimpanzees Help Conspecifics Obtain Food and Non-Food Items', *Proceedings of the Royal Society B* 278: 1405–13.

Mercader, Julio, Barton, Huw, Gillespie, Jason, Harris, Jack, Kuhn, Steven, Tyler, Robert and Boesch, Christophe. 2007. '4,300-Year-Old Chimpanzee Sites and the Origins of Percussive Stone Technology', *PNAS* 104.9: 3043–8.

Metzinger, Thomas. 2003. *Being No One: The Self-model Theory of Subjectivity*. Cambridge, MA: MIT Press.

Miles, H. Lyn White. 2011. 'Language and the Intellectual Abilities of Orangutans'. In *Cultural Anthropology: The Human Challenge*, edited by William A. Haviland, Harald E.L. Prins, Bunny Mcbride and Dana Walrath, 107–8. Belmont, CA: Wadsworth Cengage Learning.

Mischel, Walter. 2014. *The Marshmallow Test: Understanding Self-Control and How to Master It*. London: Corgi Books.

Mischel, Walter and Ebbesen, Ebbe B. 1970. 'Attention in Delay of Gratification', *Journal of Personality and Social Psychology* 16.2: 329–37.

Mittelbrunn, Maria and Sánchez-Madrid, Francisco. 2013. 'Intercellular Communication: Diverse Structures for Exchange of Genetic Information', *Nature Reviews, Molecular Cell Biology* 13.5: 328–35.

Moody Blues. 1969. *In the Beginning* (author: Graeme Edge). Track 1 of 'On the Threshold of a Dream'. London: Deram Records.

Moor, Argo and Luks, Leo. 2015. 'Networks and Hierarchies: Two Ways of Thinking', *Problemos* 88: 114–29.

Morin, Alain. 2005. 'Possible Links Between Self-Awareness and Inner Speech: Theoretical Background, Underlying Mechanisms, and Empirical Evidence', *Journal of Consciousness Studies* 12.4/5: 115–34.

Morrison, Rachel and Reiss, Diana. 2018. 'Precocious Development of Self-Awareness in Dolphins', *PLoS ONE* 13.1: e0189813.

Morsella, Ezequiel, Godwin, Christine A., Jantz, Tiffany K., Krieger, Stephen C. and Gazzaley, Adam. 2016. 'Homing In on Consciousness in the Nervous System: An Action-Based Synthesis', *Behavioral and Brain Sciences* e168: 1–70.

Navarro, Rachel L., Ojeda, Lizette, Schwartz, Seth J., Piña-Watson, Brandy and Luna, Laura L. 2014. 'Cultural Self, Personal Self: Links with Life Satisfaction among Mexican American College Students', *Journal of Latina/o Psychology* 2.1: 1–20.

Neisser, Ulric. 1988. 'Five Kinds of Self-Knowledge', *Philosophical Psychology* 1.1: 35–59.

Nettle, Daniel. 2006. 'The Evolution of Personality Variation in Humans and Other Animals', *American Psychologist* 61.6: 622–31.

Nietzsche, Friedrich. 1899 [1909]. Thomas Common (tr.), *Thus Spake Zarathustra: A Book for All and None*. London: T.N. Foulis.

Nowak, Martin and Sigmund, Karl. 2005. 'Evolution of Indirect Reciprocity', *Nature* 437: 1291–8.

Nørretranders, Tor. 1991. *The User Illusion: Cutting Consciousness Down to Size*. London: Penguin.

Numan, Robert. 2015. 'A Prefrontal-Hippocampal Comparator for Goal-Directed Behavior: The Intentional Self and Episodic Memory', *Frontiers in Behavioral Neuroscience* 9: 323.

Nystedt, Lars and Ljungberg, Anneli. 2002. 'Facets of Private and Public Self-Consciousness: Construct and Discriminant Validity', *European Journal of Personality* 16: 143–59.
O'Brien, Richard. 1973. *Don't Dream It, Be It*. Scene 10, 'The Rocky Horror Show'. London: Rocky Music.
O'Connell, Lauren A. and Hofmann, Hans A. 2012. 'Evolution of a Vertebrate Social Decision-Making Network', *Science* 336.6085: 1154–7.
Olson, Eric T. 2015. 'Life After Death and the Devastation of the Grave'. In *The Myth of an Afterlife: The Case Against Life After Death*, edited by Michael Martin and Keith Augustine. Lanham, MD: Rowman & Littlefield.
Osbon, Diane K. (ed.). 1991. *A Joseph Campbell Companion: Reflections on the Art of Living*. New York: Harper Collins.
Ouattara, Karim, Lemasson, Alban and Zuberbühler, Klaus. 2009. 'Campbell's Monkeys Use Affixation to Alter Call Meaning', *PLoS ONE* 4.11: e7808.
Pack, Adam A. and Herman, Louis M. 2006. 'Dolphin Social Cognition and Joint Attention: Our Current Understanding', *Aquatic Mammals* 32.4: 443–60.
Parker, David. 2007. *The Best Me I Can Be*. Witney: Scholastic.
Pascal, Blaise. 1846. *Thoughts of Blaise Pascal*. Andover: Allen, Morrill & Wardwell.
Patterson, Eric M. and Mann, Janet. 2011. 'The Ecological Conditions that Favor Tool Use and Innovation in Wild Bottlenose Dolphins (*Tursiops Sp.*)', *PLoS ONE* 6.7: e22243.
Patterson, Francine. 1987. *Koko's Kitten*. Danbury, CT: Scholastic Inc.
Patterson, Francine and Gordon, Wendy. 1993. 'The Case for the Personhood of Gorillas'. In *The Great Ape Project*, edited by Paola Cavalieri and Peter Singer, 58–77. New York: St. Martin's Griffin.
Penfield, Wilder and Boldrey, Edwin. 1937. 'Somatic Motor and Sensory Representation in the Cerebral Cortex of Man as Studied by Electrical Stimulation', *Brain* 60.4: 389–443.
Pennebaker, James W. 2011. *The Secret Life of Pronouns: What Our Words Say About Us*, Chapter 4. London: Bloomsbury Press.
Pennebaker, James W., Mehl, Matthias R. and Niederhoffer, Kate G. 2003. 'Psychological Aspects of Natural Language Use: Our Words, Our Selves', *Annual Review of Psychology* 54: 547–77.
Pepperberg, Irene Maxine. 1999. *The Alex Studies: Cognitive and Communicative Abilities of Grey Parrots*. Cambridge, MA: Harvard University Press.
Perner, Josef, Leekam, Susan R. and Wimmer, Heinz. 1987. 'Three-Year-Olds' Difficulty with False Belief: The Case for a Conceptual Deficit', *British Journal of Developmental Psychology* 5: 125–37.
Piaget, Jean. 1959. *The Language and Thought of the Child*. London: Routledge.
Pilley, John W. and Reid, Alliston K. 2011. 'Border Collie Comprehends Object Names as Verbal Referents', *Behavioural Processes* 86: 184–95.
Plato. ~370 BCE [1871]. Phaedrus. In Benjamin Jowett (tr.), *The Essential Plato*. London: The Softback Preview.
Plotnik, Joshua M., de Waal, Frans B.M. and Reiss, Diana. 2006. 'Self-Recognition in an Asian Elephant', *PNAS* 103.45: 17053–7.
Pointeau, Gregoire and Dominey, Peter F. 2017. 'The Role of Autobiographical Memory in the Development of a Robot Self', *Frontiers in Neurorobotics* 11: 27.
Pomberger, Thomas, Risueno-Segovia, Cristina, Löschner, Julia and Hage, Steffen R. 2018. 'Precise Motor Control Enables Rapid Flexibility in Vocal Behavior of Marmoset Monkeys', *Current Biology* 28: 1–7.
Pomerantz, James R. and Cragin, Anna I. 2015. 'Emergent Features and Feature Combination'. In *The Oxford Handbook of Perceptual Organization*, edited by Johan Wageman. Oxford: Oxford University Press.
Popper, Karl. 1967 [1985]. 'Knowledge: Subjective versus Objective'. In *Popper Selections*, edited by David Miller. Princeton: Princeton University Press.
Power, Camilla. 1998. 'Old Wives' Tales: The Gossip Hypothesis and the Reliability of Cheap Signals'. In *Approaches to the Evolution of Language*, edited by James R. Hurford, Michael Studdert-Kennedy and Chris Knight. Cambridge: Cambridge University Press.
Power, Camilla and Aiello, Leslie. 1997. 'Female Proto-Symbolic Strategies'. In *Women in Human Evolution*, edited by Lori D. Hager. London: Routledge.
Power, Camilla, Sommer, Volker and Watts, Ian. 2013. 'The Seasonality Thermostat: Female Reproductive Synchrony and Male Behavior in Monkeys, Neanderthals, and Modern Humans', *PaleoAnthropology* 2013: 33–60.

Pratheesh, P. 2015. 'The History and Structure of the Caste System in India', *Contemporary Research in India* 5.3: 105–10.

Premack, David and Premack, Ann James. 1983. *The Mind of an Ape*. London: W.W. Norton.

Premack, David and Woodruff, Guy. 1978. 'Does the Chimpanzee Have a "Theory of Mind"?' *Behavioral and Brain Sciences* 4: 515–26.

Prinz, Jesse. 2006. 'The Emotional Basis of Moral Judgments', *Philosophical Explorations* 9.1: 29–43.

Prior, Helmut, Schwarz, Ariane and Güntürkün, Onur. 2008. 'Mirror-Induced Behavior in the Magpie (*Pica Pica*): Evidence of Self-Recognition', *PLoS Biology* 6.8: e202.

Prüfer, Kay, Munch, Kasper, Hellmann, Ines, Akagi, Keiko, Miller, Jason R., Walenz, Brian, Koren, Sergey, Sutton, Granger, Kodira, Chinnappa, Winer, Roger, Knight, James R., Mullikin, James C., Meader, Stephen J., Ponting, Chris P., Lunter, Gerton, Higashino, Saneyuki, Hobolth, Asger, Dutheil, Julien, Karakoç, Emre, Alkan, Can, Sajjadian, Saba, Catacchio, Claudia Rita, Ventura, Mario, Marques-Bonet, Tomas, Eichler, Evan E., André, Claudine, Atencia, Rebeca, Mugisha, Lawrence, Junhold, Jörg, Patterson, Nick, Siebauer, Michael, Good, Jeffrey M., Fischer, Anne, Ptak, Susan E., Lachmann, Michael, Symer, David E., Mailund, Thomas, Schierup, Mikkel H., Andrés, Aida M., Kelso, Janet and Pääbo, Svante. 2012. 'The Bonobo Genome Compared with the Chimpanzee and Human Genomes', *Nature* 486: 527–31.

Pu, Shenghong, Nakagome, Kazuyuki, Itakura, Masashi, Iwata, Masaaki, Nagata, Izumi and Kaneko, Koichi. 2017. 'Association of Fronto-Temporal Function with Cognitive Ability in Schizophrenia', *Nature Scientific Reports* 7: 42858.

Radanovic, Marcia, de Sousa, Rafael T., Valiengo, Leandro L., Gattaz, Wagner F. and Forlenza, Orestes V. 2013. 'Formal Thought Disorder and Language Impairment in Schizophrenia', *Arquivos de Neuro-Psiquiatria* 71.1: 55–60.

Raichle, Marcus E. and Gusnard, Debra A. 2002. 'Appraising the Brain's Energy Budget', *PNAS* 99.16: 10237–9.

Rapport, Nigel. 2005. 'The Power of the Projected Self: A Case Study in Self Artistry', *Journal of Medical Ethics. Medical Humanities Edition* 31: 60–6.

Reich, David, Green, Richard E., Kircher, Martin, Krause, Johannes, Patterson, Nick, Durand, Eric Y., Viola, Bence, Briggs, Adrian W., Stenzel, Udo, Johnson, Philip L.F., Maricic, Tomislav, Good, Jeffrey M., Marques-Bonet, Tomas, Alkan, Can, Fu, Qiaomei, Mallick, Swapan, Li, Heng, Meyer, Matthias, Eichler, Evan E., Stoneking, Mark, Richards, Michael, Talamo, Sahra, Shunkov, Michael V., Derevianko, Anatoli P., Hublin, Jean-Jacques, Kelso, Janet, Slatkin, Montgomery and Pääbo, Svante. 2010. 'Genetic History of an Archaic Hominin Group from Denisova Cave in Siberia', *Nature* 468, 1053–60.

Reiss, Diana and Marino, Lori. 2001. 'Mirror Self-Recognition in the Bottlenose Dolphin: A Case of Cognitive Convergence', *PNAS* 98.10: 5937–42.

Ricoeur, Paul. 1990 [1992]. *Oneself as Another*. Chicago: University of Chicago Press.

Ridley, Matt. 1993. *The Red Queen: Sex and the Evolution of Human Nature*. London: Penguin.

Riedl, Katrin, Jensen, Keith, Call, Josep and Tomasello, Michael. 2012. 'No Third-Party Punishment in Chimpanzees', *PNAS* 109.37: 14824–9.

Riehl, Christina and Frederickson, Megan E. 2016. 'Cheating and Punishment in Cooperative Animal Societies', *Philosophical Transactions of the Royal Society B* 371: 2015.0090.

Roberts, Sam G.B. and Roberts, Anna I. 2016. 'Social Brain Hypothesis: Vocal and Gesture Networks of Wild Chimpanzees', *Frontiers in Psychology* 7: 1756.

Robertson, Lloyd Hawkeye. 2017. 'Implications of a Culturally Evolved Self for Notions of Free Will', *Frontiers in Psychology* 8: 1889.

Roellig, Kathleen, Drews, Barbara, Goeritz, Frank and Hildebrandt, Thomas B. 2011. 'The Long Gestation of the Small Naked Mole-Rat (*Heterocephalus Glaber* RÜPPELL, 1842) Studied with Ultrasound Biomicroscopy and 3D-Ultrasonography', *PLoS ONE* 6.3: e17744.

Rohde, Marieke, Di Luca, Massimiliano and Ernst, Marc O. 2011. 'The Rubber Hand Illusion: Feeling of Ownership and Proprioceptive Drift Do Not Go Hand in Hand', *PLoS ONE* 6.6: e21659.

Rosenthal, David M. 2004. 'Unity of Consciousness and the Self', *Proceedings of the Aristotelian Society* 103.1: 325–52.

Rougier, Louis. 2014. *Real Self or Projected Self: Who Should Brands Talk To?* New York: Ipsos UU.

Ryabov, Vyacheslav A. 2016. 'The Study of Acoustic Signals and the Supposed Spoken Language of the Dolphins', *St. Petersburg Polytechnical University Journal: Physics and Mathematics* 2.3: 231–9.

Sachdeva, Sonya, Iliev, Rumen, Ekhtiari, Hamed and Dehghani, Morteza. 2015. 'The Role of Self-Sacrifice in Moral Dilemmas', *PLoS ONE* 10.6: e0127409.

Sahlins, Marshall. 1963. 'Poor Man, Rich Man, Big Man, Chief: Political Types in Melanesia and Polynesia', *Comparative Studies in Society and History* 5.3: 285–303.

Santos, Rachel M., Zanette, Sarah, Kwok, Shiu M., Heyman, Gail D. and Lee, Kang. 2017. 'Exposure to Parenting by Lying in Childhood: Associations with Negative Outcomes in Adulthood', *Frontiers in Psychology* 8: 1240.

Savage-Rumbaugh, Sue E., Fields, William M., Segerdahl, Pär and Rumbaugh, Duane. 2005. 'Culture Prefigures Cognition in *Pan/Homo* Bonobos', *Theoria* 54: 311–28.

Savage-Rumbaugh, Sue E. and Lewin, Roger. 1994. *Kanzi: The Ape at the Brink of the Human Mind*. New York: John Wiley & Sons Inc.

Savage-Rumbaugh, Sue E., McDonald, Kelly, Sevcik, Rose A., Hopkins, William D. and Rubert, Elizabeth. 1986. 'Spontaneous Symbol Acquisition and Communicative Use by Pygmy Chimpanzees (*Pan Paniscus*)', *Journal of Experimental Psychology: General* 115.3: 211–35.

Savage-Rumbaugh, Sue E., Murphy, Jeannine, Sevcik, Rose A., Brakke, Karen E., Williams, Shelly L., Rumbaugh, Duane M. and Bates, Elizabeth. 1993. 'Language Comprehension in Ape and Child', *Monographs of the Society for Research in Child Development* 58.3/4. New York: Wiley.

Schel, Anne Marijke, Machanda, Zarin, Townsend, Simon W., Zuberbühler, Klaus and Slocombe, Katie E. 2013. 'Chimpanzee Food Calls are Directed at Specific Individuals', *Animal Behaviour* 86.5: 955–65.

Schiller, Daniela and Phelps, Elizabeth A. 2011. 'Does Reconsolidation Occur in Humans?' *Frontiers in Behavioral Neuroscience* 5: 24.

Scott-Phillips, Thomas C. 2010. 'The Evolution of Communication: Humans May be Exceptional', *Evolution Studies* 11.1: 78–9.

Scott-Phillips, Thomas C. 2015. *Speaking Our Minds: Why Human Communication is Different, and How Language Evolved to Make it Special*. Basingstoke: Palgrave Macmillan.

Scott-Phillips, Thomas C., Kirby, Simon and Ritchie, Graham R.S. 2009. 'Signalling Signalhood and the Emergence of Communication', *Cognition* 113: 226–33.

Sedikides, Constantine and Skowronsi, John J. 2000. 'On the Evolutionary Functions of the Symbolic Self: The Emergence of Self-Evaluation Motives'. In *Psychological Perspectives on Self and Identity*, edited by A. Tesser, R.B. Felson and J.M. Suls, 91–117. Washington DC: American Psychological Association.

Segerdahl, Pär, Fields, William and Savage-Rumbaugh, Sue. 2005. *Kanzi's Primal Language: The Cultural Initiation of Primates into Language*. Basingstoke: Palgrave Macmillan.

Sellar, Walter C. and Yeatman, Robert J. 1930. *1066 and All That: A Memorable History of England, Comprising All the Parts You Can Remember, Including 103 Good Things, 5 Bad Kings and 2 Genuine Dates*. London: Methuen & Co., Ltd.

Sewall, Kendra B., Young, Anna M. and Wright, Timothy F. 2016. 'Social Calls Provide Novel Insights into the Evolution of Vocal Learning', *Animal Behaviour* 120: 163–72.

Seyfarth, Robert M. and Cheney, Dorothy L. 2013. 'Affiliation, Empathy, and the Origins of Theory of Mind', *PNAS Early Edition*, pnas.1301223110.

Seyfarth, Robert M., Cheney, Dorothy L. and Marler, Peter. 1980. 'Vervet Monkey Alarm Calls: Semantic Communication in a Free-Ranging Primate', *Animal Behaviour* 28: 1070–94.

Seyfarth, Robert M., Silk, Joan B. and Cheney, Dorothy L. 2014. 'Social Bonds in Female Baboons: The Interaction Between Personality, Kinship and Rank', *Animal Behaviour* 87: 23–9.

Sisk, Cheryl L. and Zehr, Julia L. 2005. 'Pubertal Hormones Organize the Adolescent Brain and Behaviour', *Frontiers in Neuroendocrinology* 26: 163–74.

Sisk, Matthew L. and Shea, John J. 2008. 'Intrasite Spatial Variation of the Omo Kibish Middle Stone Age Assemblages: Artifact Refitting and Distribution Patterns', *Journal of Human Evolution* 55: 486–500.

Slobodchikoff, Con N. 2002. 'Cognition and Communication in Prairie Dogs'. In *The Cognitive Animal: Empirical and Theoretical Perspectives on Animal Cognition*, edited by Marc Bekoff, Colin Allen and Gordon M. Berghardt, 257–64. Cambridge, MA: MIT Press.

Slocombe, Katie E. and Zuberbühler, Klaus. 2005. 'Functionally Referential Communication in a Chimpanzee', *Current Biology* 15: 1779–84.

Smith, John Maynard and Szathmáry, Eörs. 1995. *The Major Transitions in Evolution*. Oxford: Oxford University Press.

Smith, John Maynard and Szathmáry, Eörs. 1999. *The Origins of Life*. Oxford: Oxford University Press.

Sober, Elliott and Wilson, David S. 1998. *Unto Others: The Evolution and Psychology of Unselfish Behaviour*. Cambridge, MA: Harvard University Press.

Spencer, Herbert. 1864. *Principles of Biology, Volume I, Part III: The Evolution of Life*. London: Williams & Norgate.

Srinivasan, Saurabh, Bettella, Francesco, Hassani, Sahar, Wang, Yunpeng, Witoelar, Aree, Schork, Andrew J., Thompson, Wesley K., Collier, David A., Desikan, Rahul S., Melle, Ingrid, Dale, Anders M., Djurovic, Srdjan and Andreassen, Ole A. 2017. 'Probing the Association between Early Evolutionary Markers and Schizophrenia', *PLoS ONE* 12.1: e0169227.

Srinivasan, Saurabh, Bettella, Francesco, Mattingsdal, Morten, Wang, Yunpeng, Witoelar, Aree, Schork, Andrew J., Thompson, Wesley K., Zuber, Verena, The Schizophrenia Working Group of the Psychiatric Genomics Consortium, The International Headache Genetics Consortium, Winsvold, Bendik S., Zwart, John-Anker, Collier, David A., Desikan, Rahul S., Melle, Ingrid, Werge, Thomas, Dale, Anders M., Djurovic, Srdjan and Andreassen, Ole A. 2016. 'Genetic Markers of Human Evolution Are Enriched in Schizophrenia', *Biological Psychiatry* 80: 284–92.

Steger, Michael F., Frazier, Patricia, Oishi, Shigehiro and Kaler, Matthew. 2006. 'The Meaning in Life Questionnaire: Assessing the Presence of and Search for Meaning', *Journal of Counseling Psychology* 53: 80–93.

Stevens, Jeffrey R. and King, Andrew J. 2012. 'The Lives of Others: Social Rationality in Animals'. In *Simple Heuristics in a Social World*, edited by R. Hertwig, U. Hoffrage and the ABC Research Group, 409–31. Oxford: Oxford University Press.

Stiles, Joan. 2000. 'Neural Plasticity and Cognitive Development', *Developmental Neuropsychology* 18.2: 237–72.

Strawson, Galen. 2004. 'Not Every Life is a Narrative: A Fallacy of Our Age', *The Times Literary Supplement* 15 October, 13–15.

Strawson, Galen. 2009. *Selves*. Oxford: Oxford University Press.

Sun, Chien-Ru. 2017. 'An Examination of the Four-Part Theory of the Chinese Self: The Differentiation and Relative Importance of the Different Types of Social-Oriented Self', *Frontiers in Psychology* 8: 1106.

Suweis, Samir, Rinaldo, Andrea, Maritan, Amos and D'Odorico, Paolo. 2013. 'Water-Controlled Wealth of Nations', *PNAS* 110.11: 4230–3.

Thagard, Paul and Wood, Joanne V. 2015. 'Eighty Phenomena about the Self: Representation, Evaluation, Regulation, and Change', *Frontiers in Psychology* 6: 334.

Thompson, Melissa Emery, Jones, James H., Pusey, Anne E., Brewer-Marsden, Stella, Goodall, Jane, Marsden, David, Matsuzawa, Tetsuro, Nishida, Toshisada, Reynolds, Vernon, Sugiyama, Yukimaru and Wrangham, Richard W. 2007. 'Aging and Fertility Patterns in Wild Chimpanzees Provide Insights into the Evolution of Menopause', *Current Biology* 17: 2150–6.

Thornton, Alex. 2008. 'Early Body Condition, Time Budgets and the Acquisition of Foraging Skills in Meerkats', *Animal Behaviour* 75: 951–62.

Tibbetts, Elizabeth A., Sheehan, Michael J. and Dale, James. 2008. 'A Testable Definition of Individual Recognition', *Trends in Ecology and Evolution* 23.7: 356.

Tice, Dianne M. 1992. 'Self-Concept Change and Self-Presentation: The Looking Glass Self Is Also a Magnifying Glass', *Journal of Personality and Social Psychology* 63.3: 435–51.

Tolosa, Amparo, Sanjuán, Julio, Dagnall, Adam M., Moltó, María D., Herrero, Neus and de Frutos, Rosa. 2010. 'FOXP2 Gene and Language Impairment in Schizophrenia: Association and Epigenetic Studies', *BMC Medical Genetics* 11: 114.

Tormala, Zakary L. 2016. 'The Role of Certainty (and Uncertainty) in Attitudes and Persuasion', *Current Opinion in Psychology* 10: 6–11.

Townsend, Simon W., Allen, Colin and Manser, Marta B. 2012. 'A Simple Test of Vocal Individual Recognition in Wild Meerkats', *Biology Letters* 8: 179–82.

Trivers, Robert L. 1971. 'The Evolution of Reciprocal Altruism', *Quarterly Review of Biology*, 46.1: 35–7.

Trivers, Robert L. 1974. 'Parent-Offspring Conflict', *American Zoologist* 14: 249–64.

Tulving, Endel. 2005. 'Episodic Memory and Autonoesis: Uniquely Human?' In *The Missing Link in Cognition*, edited by H.S. Terrace and J. Metcalfe, 4–56. New York: Oxford University Press.

Tyack, Peter L. 1997. 'Development and Social Functions of Signature Whistles in Bottlenose Dolphins, *Tursiops Truncatus*', *Bioacoustics* 8: 21–46.

van Meijl, Toon. 2008. 'Culture and Identity in Anthropology: Reflections on "Unity" and "Uncertainty" in the Dialogical Self', *International Journal for Dialogical Science* 3.1: 165–90.

Vanutelli, Maria Elide, Nandrino, Jean-Louis and Balconi, Michela. 2016. 'The Boundaries of Cooperation: Sharing and Coupling from Ethology to Neuroscience', *Neuropsychological Trends* 19: 83–104.

van Vugt, Mark and Ahuja, Anjana. 2010. *Selected: Why Some People Lead, Why Others Follow, and Why It Matters*. London: Profile Books.

von Frisch, Karl. 1973. 'Decoding the Language of the Bee'. *Nobel Lecture, December 12, 1973*. https://www.nobelprize.org/uploads/2018/06/frisch-lecture.pdf

von Humboldt, Wilhelm. 1836 [1999]. *On Language: On the Diversity of Human Language Construction and Its Influence on the Mental Development of the Human Species*. Cambridge: Cambridge University Press.

Vygotsky, Lev S. 1934 [1986]. *Thought and Language*. Cambridge, MA: MIT Press.

Wacewicz, Sławomir. 2016. 'A Contemporary Look at Language Origins', *Avant* VI.2: 68–81.

Wacewicz, Sławomir and Żywiczyński, Przemysław. 2014. 'Language Evolution: Why Hockett's Design Features Are a Non-Starter', *Biosemiotics* 8: 29–46.

Walker, Stephen. 1983. *The Life of Vertebrates and the Survival Value of Intelligence in Animal Thought*. London: Routledge & Kegan Paul.

Watts, Ian. 2017. 'Rain Serpents in Northern Australia and Southern Africa: A Common Ancestry?' In *Human Origins: Contributions from Social Anthropology*, edited by C. Power, M. Finnegan and H. Callan. New York: Berghahn Books.

Webb, Christine E., Romero, Teresa, Franks, Becca and de Waal, Frans B.M. 2017. 'Long-Term Consistency in Chimpanzee Consolation Behaviour Reflects Empathetic Personalities', *Nature Communications* 8: 292.

Wegner, Daniel M. 2002. *The Illusion of Conscious Will*. Cambridge, MA: MIT Press.

White, Andrew A. 2013. 'Subsistence Economics, Family Size, and the Emergence of Social Complexity in Hunter-Gatherer Systems in Eastern North America', *Journal of Anthropological Archaeology* 32: 122–63.

Whitehead, Charles. 2001. 'Social Mirrors and Shared Experiential Worlds', *Journal of Consciousness Studies* 8.4: 3–36.

Whitehead, Hal, Rendell, Luke, Osborne, Richard W. and Würsig, Bernd. 2004. 'Culture and Conservation of Non-Humans with Reference to Whales and Dolphins: Review and New Directions', *Biological Conservation* 120.3: 427–37.

Whitehouse, Mary E.A. and Jaffe, Klaus. 1996. 'Ant Wars: Combat Strategies, Territory and Nest Defence in The Leaf-Cutting Ant *Atta Laevigata*', *Animal Behaviour* 51: 1207–17.

Whiten, Andrew and Byrne, Richard. 1988. 'The Machiavellian Intelligence Hypotheses'. In *Machiavellian Intelligence: Social Expertise and the Evolution of Intellect in Monkeys, Apes, and Humans*, edited by Andrew Whiten and Richard Byrne. Oxford: Oxford University Press.

Whiten, Andrew and van Schaik, Carel P. 2007. 'The Evolution of Animal "Cultures" and Social Intelligence', *Philosophical Transactions of the Royal Society B* 362: 603–20.

Wood, David, Bruner, Jerome S. and Ross, Gail. 1976. 'The Role of Tutoring in Problem Solving', *Journal of Child Psychology and Psychiatry* 17.2: 89–100.

Zahavi, Amotz and Zahavi, Avishag. 1997. *The Handicap Principle: A Missing Piece of Darwin's Puzzle*. Oxford: Oxford University Press.

Index

CPSIA information can be obtained
at www.ICGtesting.com
Printed in the USA
BVHW012321290920
589913BV00002B/10

9 781787 356313